HUMANI

HUGO SLIM

Humanitarian Ethics

A Guide to the Morality of Aid in War and Disaster

HURST & COMPANY, LONDON

First published in the United Kingdom in 2015 by
C. Hurst & Co. (Publishers) Ltd.,
41 Great Russell Street, London, WC1B 3PL

Printed in India

A Cataloguing-in-Publication data record for this book
is available from the British Library.

ISBN: 978-1-84904-340-3

This book is printed using paper from registered sustainable
and managed sources.

www.hurstpublishers.com

For Jessie and Solomon

CONTENTS

ACKNOWLEDGEMENTS

This book is the result of a truly cooperative effort. I just wrote it. Many other individuals and organizations helped to inform it, fund it and support it in a wide variety of ways. John Mitchell reminded me that many humanitarian workers are still unclear about humanitarian ethics and encouraged me to revisit the subject. Michael Dwyer at Hurst suggested that I write this book and has been extremely patient and encouraging throughout. Jennifer Welsh, David Rodin and Dapo Akande at the University of Oxford's Institute of Ethics, Law and Armed Conflict (ELAC) kindly hosted the Humanitarian Ethics Project here at Oxford. Several humanitarian organizations generously funded the project and engaged actively in roundtables that we held to discuss particular aspects of humanitarian ethics. The British Red Cross Society, Oxfam GB, Save the Children UK, World Vision, CAFOD, Islamic Relief and World Jewish Relief all co-financed the project while the International Committee of the Red Cross, Médecins Sans Frontières, Action Contre le Faim, ALNAP, Help Age International and Norwegian Refugee Council also joined in our roundtable discussions. In these organizations several people have been especially engaged and supportive, notably: Sorcha O'Callaghan, Ajay Madiwale, Amelia Kyazze, Jane Cocking, Nigel Timmins, Jasmine Whitbread, Gareth Owen, Juliano Fiori, Ian Gray, Jules Frost, Matthew Carter, Catherine Mahony, Atallah Fitzgibbon, Paul Anticoni, Richard Verber, Paul Bouvier, Mona Sadek, James Darcy, Pauline Chetcuti, Sara Tesorieri, Michael Neuman, Andrew Collodel, Paul Knox Clarke, Dan Hodgkinson helped early on with important research assistance. Jane Leek and Mark Vogt gave me invaluable support. A number of other people gave me important guidance: Greg

Johnson, Cheyney Ryan, Jim Astman, Judith Rosen-Berry, Sujata Godkar-Wilcox, Mark Philp, Kalypso Nicolaidis, Emilie Parry, Alex Leveringhaus, Ruben Reike, Janina Dill and Fernando Almansa. My many students at the Centre for Education and Research in Humanitarian Action (CERAH) in Geneva and at the University of Oregon have helped to bring some realism to my appreciation of the subject. Janice French, Rasangi Prematilaka, Julie Page and Liz Greenhalgh in the Department of Politics and International Relations at Oxford have been extremely patient with my inaptitude for administration. Stephen Whitefield and Elizabeth Frazer have been very supportive department heads. Writing up of this research also received funding from the European Research Council as part of the project on the Individualization of War.

My greatest thanks for her help with this book goes to my Research Assistant, Anais Resseguier, who has given me such expert support and led me to so many important texts and ideas. Anais' encouragement and good humour have been essential throughout, and she has been most tolerant of my unconventional academic approach and my inability to understand French postmodern ethics.

Many other people have helped me by their kindness. My children, Jessie and Solly, to whom this book is dedicated, have taught me much about humanitarian ethics over the years. Sarah Whyte very kindly gave me a beautiful place to write in Devon whenever I needed it. The Warden, Fellows and staff at Merton College, Oxford have given me a warm welcome into their Senior Common Room, their chapel and their beautiful college. Reneé, Richard, Linda, Mariana and Dickie in the café at Manor Road have been a vital source of coffee, smiles and encouragement. Others have been valuable friends to me during this time of writing. Timothy Radcliffe, Richard Finn, Richard Ounsworth and the community at Blackfriars; Nicholas King at Campion Hall; George Levvy, Michael Holyoke, Catherine Clarke, Anne Millais, Mari Pritchard, Lesley Burt, Serena Momberg, Adrian James, Alan Goodwin, David Alexander, Chris Cramer, Nabeel Hamdi, Janie Frazer, Colin Farrant, Mary Ann Slim and, most especially, Asma Awan.

Oxford, Advent 2014 H.S.

LIST OF ACRONYMS

ALNAP	Active Learning Network for Accountability and Performance
CERAH	Centre for Education and Research in Humanitarian Action
EPLF	Eritrean People's Liberation Front
ERD	Emergency Relief Desk
FPIC	Free, prior and informed consent
HAP	Humanitarian Accountability Project
ICC	International Criminal Court
ICRC	International Committee of the Red Cross
IDRL	International Disaster Relief Law
IDP	Internally Displaced Person
IHL	International Humanitarian Law
LGBT	Lesbian, gay, bisexual or transgender people
MSF	Médecins Sans Frontières (Doctors without borders)
NGHA	Non-Government Humanitarian Organizations
NGO	Non-Government Organization
OECD	Organization for Economic Co-operation and Development
SARC	Syrian Arab Red Crescent
SPLA	Sudan People's Liberation Army
TPLF	Tigrayan People's Liberation Front
UDHR	Universal Declaration of Human Rights
URD	Urgence Réhabilitation Développement

Agencies within the United Nations

UNDP	United Nations Development Programme

LIST OF ACRONYMS

UNFAO	United Nations Food and Agricultural Organization
UNHCR	United Nations High Commissioner for Refugees
UNICEF	United Nations Children's Fund
UNIFEM	United Nations Development Fund for Women
UNOCHA	United Nations Office for the Co-ordination of Humanitarian Affairs
UNWFP	United Nations World Food Programme

INTRODUCTION

This book is about the ethics of humanitarian action: the values that drive it; the moral problems that arise in doing it; and the various ways in which humanitarian organizations and their staff can think through these problems to become more professional and accountable in their ethical decisions.

Humanitarian action is a compassionate response to extreme and particular forms of suffering arising from organized human violence and natural disaster. At any moment, in any day, somewhere in the world a person is suffering from the violence of armed conflict or the devastation of disaster. As surely as this person is suffering, it is equally certain that someone will be trying to help them. First and foremost, this helper is usually a member of their family, a neighbour, or a friend. But, increasingly, this helper may be a professional humanitarian of some kind: a Red Cross or Red Crescent volunteer; a member of a religious organization; a local government official; a United Nations worker; somebody working for a national or international non-governmental organization (NGO); or someone in the military working as a peacekeeper or in a disaster response team. This book aims to help these various professional workers as they try to deliver humanitarian aid respectfully and fairly in difficult conditions.

In 2013, expenditure on international humanitarian aid rose to a record $22 billion and reached 78 million people around the world.[1] Alongside Red Cross and UN agencies, there are an estimated 4,400 NGOs carrying out humanitarian programmes of some kind and 274,000 humanitarian workers around the world.[2] This significant expansion in humanitarian action as a form of international relations and as an increasingly ordered part of nascent global governance requires that this growing sector and profession is ethically aware and ethically skilled.

Humanitarian action is about respecting, protecting and saving human life. At its best, it is a very practical affirmation of the value of human life and its unique character in each human person. Trying to help someone who is suffering is a fundamental gesture of care. It shows that we feel something very precious in our own lives and so recognize this preciousness in the lives of other people too. Wanting to help someone reveals that they mean something important to us. We want them to stay alive because they are valuable. We believe that the destruction of a person is a tragedy that must be prevented, and we also believe that people can live through and after suffering. Their life may be changed forever by damage, loss and pain, but we hold that renewal of life and some form of fulfilment are possible after war and disaster.

Trying to help other people is a very good thing to do, but it is not always an easy thing to do. Because it is difficult, helping can go wrong. Helping people requires some kind of access to them and a certain freedom of operation. More than this, helping people well takes knowledge, skill and resources. It also requires a counter-intuitive move towards cooperation rather than control. Good help enables a person or a community to remain the subject of their lives, not objects in the lives and purposes of others. Good humanitarian action makes people its goal but does not objectify them as "beneficiaries" or commodify them as "recipients" of aid. On the contrary, good humanitarian aid and protection increase people's autonomy and agency as human beings. The best humanitarian action is that which respects people and works with them to prevent suffering, repair harm, and enable them to come through their suffering and flourish.

The Expansion of Humanitarian Aid

The extraordinary worldwide rise in international humanitarian action is one of humanity's great moral achievements in the last sixty years. It means that everyone in the world stands a very real chance of receiving some form of aid or protection as they endure bombardment, displacement, natural disaster, impoverishment, personal attack, sexual violence, detention, family separation, hunger, thirst and disease. Humanitarian action can seldom stop these things from happening, but it can and does reduce the suffering and death that result from them. There is strong evidence that humanitarian aid can make the endurance of war somewhat safer for people, and make it easier for poor people to survive earthquakes, floods and hurricanes, and to recover from them.[3] In its best form, humanitarian action embodies a very human response of love and care to the cruelty and devastation of war and disaster, and is an ethical gesture that is universally understood. In a collection of oral testimony from people who have received aid, a survivor of the war in Kosovo said: "It saved our lives. I simply don't know where to start, to whom to say thank you." A Filipino health worker felt even more passionately: "With all the international aid that came, we are really thankful because even though we are here, far from them, we appreciate that they think of us. If we were to personally see them, we would hug them out of happiness."[4] The process of delivering and receiving humanitarian aid can bring significant problems but, at its best, the intentions and effects of aid are good.

The global increase in humanitarian action is one small part of a practical expansion in our ethics as a species. Most international humanitarian action involves individuals and governments in one country sending money and gifts to suffering individuals (whom they have never met and are never likely to meet) in another country. This gift-giving is mediated and administered through an increasing number of humanitarian organizations of various kinds. The long distances, profound anonymity and proliferation in contemporary humanitarian action are striking. They suggest a genuine resonance between human beings around the world and the increasing potential for social organization and international networks of help. In other words, expanding humanitarian action is one of many new innovative patterns of empathy and altruism in the contemporary process of globalization.[5]

The most obvious parts of the modern humanitarian movement have been manifest in high-profile United Nations and NGO with strong traces of a colonial past and a continuing hegemonic tendency. Most official funding for international aid still comes from a liberal "Western" core of OECD governments. The genuine humanitarian conviction of these governments does not operate alone to drive humanitarian funding, but combines with the national and geopolitical interests of these governments to shape and bias the main flow of aid.[6] It is likely that new international powers—like Turkey, China, India and Brazil—emerging to match the high levels of humanitarian financing and policy-making by

Western governments will also exhibit national and geopolitical interests of their own as they set their humanitarian priorities.

Beyond today's formal humanitarian organizations, new financial networks and transnational feelings of solidarity are gaining momentum. Diaspora aid is becoming much more significant, as people residing or working outside their country of origin send generous remittances back home to their families and communities suffering war and disaster.[7] Economies permitting, this form of direct humanitarian aid will probably lead to the continuing expansion of humanitarian funding and the emergence of many new forms of organizations. However, states affected by war and disaster rightly seek to take more direct control over humanitarian finances and operations in their countries, asserting their humanitarian sovereignty. Strong states like India, Sudan, Sri Lanka, Ethiopia, Pakistan, North Korea and Syria have always retained a tight control over humanitarian activity within their borders, through government or civil society organizations. This post-colonial pattern of assertive humanitarian nationalism or "localization" will probably increase to challenge the expeditionary humanitarian aid that has traditionally come from the West.[8]

This expanding, deepening and proliferating field of postmodern humanitarian actors and governments makes it all the more important to achieve a common ground of operational ethics in humanitarian action alongside the many international laws that affirm people's rights and govern the conduct of war and the protection of people in armed conflict and disaster.

International Humanitarian Standards

The international political community and the humanitarian profession have worked hard since the middle of the last century to elaborate humanitarian laws and principles. The Four Geneva Conventions of 1949 have been added to in three Additional Protocols (1977 and 2007) and a series of new UN laws on prohibited weaponry like chemical weapons and landmines. The Refugee Convention (1951) has been complemented by regional refugee conventions and by the UN's Guiding Principles on Internal Displacement (1998). Human rights law has increasingly been brought to the centre of armed conflicts as a legal framework of protection with its particular emphasis on the right to life, protection from torture, cruel and degrading treatment, and its special protection of women, children, indigenous people and disabled people. The UN's first ever law, the Convention on Genocide, now combines with international humanitarian law and human rights law to form the basis of the legal mandate of the International Criminal Court that prosecutes individuals for the four great crimes of aggression, genocide, crimes against humanity and war crimes.

Humanitarian agencies have also worked hard to develop values, principles and standards to guide the conduct of humanitarian operations. The Fundamental Principles of the Red Cross and Crescent Society were agreed in 1965 and have since infused the humanitarian practice of many of the world's inter-governmental organizations and NGOs engaging in humanitarian action (see Annex 1). The first four Red Cross/Crescent principles—humanity, impartiality, neutrality and independence—are now recognized in law as "humanitarian principles" regularly referred to by the UN Security Council, UN General Assembly, regional organizations, governments and international organizations.[9] These principles are an essential part of UN and international insistence on the necessity of humanitarian access and the protection of civilians in armed conflict.[10] The new field of international law on disaster response is a further sign of increasingly binding contracts between governments and peoples about disaster prevention, preparedness and response.[11]

In 1992, the Red Cross/Crescent movement combined with international NGOs to develop a more elaborate Code of Conduct for the International Red Cross and Red Crescent Movement and NGOs in Disaster Relief (see Annex 2). The principles and spirit of this code have been increasingly applied as the basis of ethical practice in disasters and, by informal extension, in armed conflicts. The humanitarian agency community has also developed and regularly updated the Sphere Standards since 1997. These standards are a major achievement and affirm a set of common protection principles and universal minimal standards in life-saving areas of humanitarian response.[12] Underwriting all these standards is a Humanitarian Charter that grounds humanitarian action in people's rights in international law (see Annex 3). This was drawn up by a number of leading agencies in 1998 and is the most complete articulation to date of the moral and legal principles that underwrite humanitarian action. Humanitarian action is, therefore, well founded in international law and in the important range of "soft law", like the IDP Guidelines, Humanitarian Charter, Code of Conduct and Sphere Standards, which have been developed from it.

Regardless of law and principle, the delivery of humanitarian aid and protection remains operationally challenging and problematic. Humanitarian action can face hard problems of access, fairness and collective action. Aid can be fiercely resisted and contested by parties in an armed conflict. It can be badly organized or inappropriate. It can be manipulated and abused by political powers within the humanitarian system, and it can be abused by people administering and receiving aid. Humanitarian action is less problematic in law than ever before, but it is still difficult in practice and many of its difficulties have an ethical dimension.

Ethical Tensions in Humanitarian Aid

Helping people should be the simplest thing in the world and is often presented to us as such in our early moral and religious learning as children. Acts of kindness are encouraged as things that we can easily do for others and that we appreciate greatly when they are done for us. Getting food and medicine to people who are starving and sick seems to be an obviously good thing to do, and so it is. But doing it at scale and often at speed within conflicted or degraded political systems and with insufficient knowledge about people's lives and culture is actually a very difficult and uncertain process as well. Trying to protect people when others want to kill and hurt them can also be a good thing to do, but usually brings aid workers into direct conflict with those intent on killing.

When I was a young humanitarian worker in the 1980s (we called ourselves relief workers then) several of us used to joke about the "wonderful work" we were doing. This was a phrase that people back home would repeatedly use when writing or talking to us about our humanitarian jobs. We jokingly queried the phrase because our work did not always feel wonderful but rather difficult, contested, confusing and prone to failure of various kinds. Indeed, I have never worked in or visited any humanitarian operation that people have described in purely positive terms. On the contrary, reading or listening to many critical academics, returning aid workers, journalists and politicians commenting on humanitarian operations, one might well think that the profession is actually an abomination. Humanitarian action is often portrayed as the inept self-interested work of ignorant neo-colonial devils, rather than as an efficient and effective caring profession.

Actually, I think there is much that is wonderful in humanitarian operations: lives saved; health restored; safety found; livelihoods recovered; families reunited; prisoners visited; communities re-made; skills learned; innovations made; humour rediscovered; improved gender relations; responsibility taken by young and old people who play key leadership roles in their communities' survival; unlikely and enriching cross-cultural human contact, and important instances of consolation, love, friendship and hope. Nevertheless, as a human endeavour now increasingly organized within large institutions and often carried out in a context of intense armed conflict or political contest, humanitarian operations inevitably have much about them that is also dysfunctional or seemingly paradoxical.

These dysfunctions can be over-emphasized. Discussion of humanitarian ethics is often far too biased towards the things that are thought to be wrong with humanitarian aid. Humanitarians and their critics tend to lament the paradoxes and difficulties of their work much more than they rejoice in its moral value and successes. This is a pity. The tone of humanitarian ethics should not only be precautionary and negative as a determination not to get things wrong. It should also be ambitious and positive about trying to do things well. The proper focus of humanitarian ethics should rest on how to be a good humanitarian worker, not on how to avoid being a bad one. The difference is subtle but significant. The call to do good is a much more positive professional motivation than the more censorious call to avoid doing harm. One is inspirational; the other is inhibiting. My aim in this book is to be encouraging. I want to remind humanitarian workers why their work is so important, and how it can be carried out with moral conviction and grounded optimism.

Yet, alongside a positive moral framing of humanitarian ethics we need to be aware of the risks and paradoxes that characterize the overall field and are key themes in several ethical critiques of humanitarian aid. This book cannot look at every problematic aspect of humanitarian action, so it is worth laying out at the outset some of the structural ethical tensions that affect the profession and which rightly pose profound moral questions of international humanitarian action as it is currently practised round the world. Much of what follows in this book will touch on different aspects of these core ethical tensions: here they are, to set the scene.

Boundary Problems

A fundamental issue in humanitarian ethics is the challenge of defining the field. Which ethical subjects are rightly of concern to humanitarian ethics? Are they acute suffering, the causes of suffering, entrenched poverty, the violations of all rights or some rights? Which forms of practice rightly and feasibly constitute humanitarian activity, and which fall outside the proper boundaries of humanitarian action? What state of affairs qualifies as a legitimate emergency? These questions about where humanitarian action begins and ends are recurring ones that never seem to be truly settled theoretically or in practice. The field is frankly fuzzy. A precise and unanimous definition of humanitarian scope and activity has eluded the profession to date.

Humanitarianism's boundary problem sets running a recurring pattern of moral quandary around humanitarian legitimacy that is voiced in every emergency, usually in key questions about limits. Is this activity truly humanitarian? Can that institution be humanitarian? Do I stop being a humanitarian if I do this? Is the crisis over? These questions arise because the boundaries of the field are pulled in various directions by three different forces: actors, methodology and context. Between them, these factors tend to stretch understandings of humanitarian action to give it an elasticity that covers a range of different things, and sometimes seems to go beyond its fundamental moral purpose.

Many different institutional actors have adopted the word "humanitarian" to describe particular aspects of what they do. The Red Cross and Red Crescent Movement and MSF use the word, as do multi-mandate UN agencies and NGOs who work as much for wider human development goals and global transformation. UN agencies like UNOCHA, UNHCR, UNICEF and UNWFP define themselves primarily as humanitarian. UNDP, UNFAO, UNIFEM and UN Habitat can refer to some of their work as humanitarian too. Governments have humanitarian departments. Peacekeeping forces, belligerent military forces and armed groups also refer to their humanitarian activities, as increasingly do commercial companies large and small. All these actors use humanitarian language broadly and with different interests attached. So, if one person's terrorist is another person's freedom fighter, then one person's humanitarian is another person's development worker, company employee or bomber pilot. When "speaking humanitarian", people can mean different things when they say the same thing.

Practical methodology blurs humanitarian definition too. If saving life from immediate threat can be readily understood as the main moral end of humanitarian work, the best means of doing this has naturally created mission creep towards a deeper ethics of social change. As the humanitarian Code of Conduct rightly affirms the need t men and women to empower them and create sustainable personal goods that significantly improve their lives in the long term. This moral pull towards a particular ideal of progress is more akin to the broad ideological aims of human development than simple life-saving. It means that in its actual practice and methodological concerns humanitarian action is often very developmental and progressive, usually along the explicitly liberal lines of universal human rights.

Thirdly, operational context stretches humanitarian definition too. Most wars last between five and ten years, and often longer. Many societies that are vulnerable to ecological disaster or armed conflict remain "on the edge" for decades, creating a permanent zone of uncertain emergency that has been so well described by Mark Bradbury as "chronic instability" and "protracted crisis" and by Peter Redfield as the "verge of crisis" and the "long durée" of humanitarian action.[13] In these long conflicts, protracted emergencies or situations of chronic vulnerability, agencies find it hard to leave off humanitarian activities completely, while they also understandably feel called more deeply into solutions to the more structural political and ecological dimensions of a crisis. As a result, and not unethically, they end up doing things that are not life-saving in the strict sense. This may be because they want to stay there "just in case" or are being paid to be there by powerful government donors, or because they feel morally bound to help people they have come to know and care about. These are all good and compelling reasons to stretch the humanitarian tent a little further.

Antonio Donini has encapsulated these and other aspects of humanitarianism's definitional problem with his usual panache:

> The concept of humanitarianism is fraught with ambiguities. It connotes three separate but overlapping realities: an ideology, a movement and a profession. Together, they also form a political economy. What unites the various facets of humanitarianism is a broad commitment to alleviating the suffering and protecting the lives of civilians caught up in conflict or crisis. Beneath this common goal, however, the ideology, the movement and the profession are themselves deeply fractured. Like other "isms" ... [there are] card carrying defenders of orthodoxy, heretics, fellow travellers, revisionists and extremist figures. It now even has for-profit and military wings.... Traditionally, there are two 'souls' in the humanitarian ethos, one focusing on

the universal values of compassion and charity and the other on the change and transformation of society.[14]

In this book, I suppose I am a defender of orthodoxy who can tolerate quite a lot of stretch. For me, humanitarian action must always be responding to extreme life-threatening conditions and operate an ethic of protecting and saving human life that is deployed apart from wider concerns of social transformation and specific political ambitions for the society concerned. This ethic must embody a struggle for the dignity, preservation and safety of all human life, rather than the struggle for a particular political dispensation. It is, after all, these particular political struggles that tend to create the need for humanitarian action and its reaffirmation of the value of human lives above human differences. However, I am not pedantically orthodox. I recognize that all sorts of different actors can be humanitarian in specific instances. I also believe that being effectively humanitarian requires methodologies of practice that are socially progressive in a way that respects people and gives them humanitarian autonomy instead of simply bossing them about and giving them things they do not particularly want in aid processes that are deeply frustrating for them. In short, for me, humanitarian action is an occasional practice for extreme circumstances. It puts the value of human life above the significance of human difference when this principle is in clear and fatal danger of being lost. Anyone can and should do humanitarian action so long as they do it well and are honest about what they are doing. It would be wrong to masquerade quite different moral or immoral goals and activities as humanitarian ones. In the same way, I don't suppose it would be right for a train driver to describe herself as a bus driver, or a person who eats chicken twice a week to say he is essentially a vegetarian.

Neo-Colonial Characteristics

Many of the world's large modern agencies that make up the formal humanitarian system emerged in a context of Western colonialism and are regularly and not unreasonably charged with maintaining neo-colonial interests, thought patterns and operational practices. The Red Cross tradition of war-related humanitarian action is rooted in European conflict, but there is no doubt that the major expansion of humanitarian action occurred along the geographic pathways of European colonialism, particularly in Africa and parts of Asia. Here, often in former colonies,

Western humanitarianism developed an expeditionary model of European- or American-led operations. These exogenous organizations raised funds and developed an operational paradigm of "going in" to war or disaster-affected countries, often "on missions" in which they then went "out into the field". This expeditionary pattern is still pervasive today, but is not the only model of humanitarian action. From the early 1960s more progressive agencies like Oxfam, which were conscious of neo-colonial risk, developed a model of partnership that was more deliberately supportive of local government and NGOs. Churches, above all, adopted a partnership approach, always working through their local diocese and congregations. As international organizations, UN agencies have always had to work closely with government.

Despite these more progressive models of operation, the power, resources and technical knowledge that construct the formal international humanitarian sector remain largely in Europe and North America. Humanitarian thought patterns still assume Western technical superiority and an obligation to act as tutors to poorer and badly organized countries. More than this, expatriates leading humanitarian operations have often developed a colonial lifestyle similar to their forebears. Many critical anthropologists and sociologists describe this post-colonial world of humanitarian power as "Aidland".[15] Personal lifestyles in Aidland are often privileged and can sometimes degrade into decadence. International humanitarian personnel rent big houses, drive big cars, have lavish parties and go to the best restaurants. UN employees frequently fly business class. The obviously rich are reaching out to help the obviously poor. That the rich are helping the poor is no bad thing in itself, and many international humanitarian workers are extremely good at what they do, work respectfully in a different society to their own and save many lives. But the colonial pattern of Aidland is real and feels uncomfortably resonant to many. It is also something of a block to developing radical new models of humanitarian action, because people who have the rich life quite like it. Naturally, they are reluctant to give it up. Instead they are widening their in-group to develop national humanitarian elites as well. One great post-colonial ethical challenge for humanitarian agencies is to distribute humanitarian power more fairly and localize humanitarian expertise and capability more effectively.

Professionalizing Voluntarism

Humanitarian action also has some natural confusion over entry requirements. Humanitarian ethics has long been torn between the passion of voluntarism and the importance of professional qualifications. Driven by the universal moral value of humanity, humanitarianism hopes for a world in which everyone is motivated by humanitarian impulses to care for and protect each other. Entry into humanitarian aid work is primarily vocational, impulsive and urgent. It is a voluntary response to a moral call that we feel and share, as immediate neighbours and global neighbours. In this sense, humanitarian help is the great domain of the amateur: literally, the lover of something, which in this case is our fellow human beings. We all can and must respond to become involved in humanitarian action. Because of this, many new humanitarian initiatives and organizations blossom in each new emergency. Humanitarian ecology is a lively and fecund ecosystem that springs to life whenever crisis hits.

G. K. Chesterton once said, "If something is worth doing then it is worth doing badly." In other words, where the pursuit of the good is concerned we should all try our hand at it and doing something is always better than doing nothing. The humanitarian sector acknowledges this truth. It cannot believe otherwise, because every humanitarian agency is started by a few determined people trying to do something for others, often as first-timers and amateurs. However, we would not want anyone having a go at brain surgery. So it is with many sophisticated fields of humanitarian action like health care, nutrition, shelter, family tracing and many more. Because of this, the sector naturally struggles ethically to find a responsible balance between voluntarism and professionalism. Agencies like MSF have done so very effectively by routinely mixing volunteer first-timers into experienced teams. The sector has worked hard to elaborate technical standards (like Sphere) and requires high-level professional qualifications in many of its staff. Agency umbrella groups are also now considering a system of accreditation and certification for agencies and humanitarian personnel so that they have proof of sufficient expertise and capability. The move to assure professional expertise must be right, but may come at the expense of amateur passion and entrepreneurial flair.

The tension between voluntarism and professionalism not only turns on expertise but on institutional culture. Like other human institutions evolving along the organizational life cycle from front room to boardroom, expanding humanitarian agencies are increasingly characterized by managerialism, bureaucracy and institutionalization. These organizational pressures may suffocate and diminish the powerful voluntary spirit of raw humanitarian energy. In humanitarian work, which requires speed, courage, judgement and leadership, big institutions can become slow, risk-averse, procedural, indecisive, and be ruled by managers not leaders. The Weberian struggle between charisma and bureaucracy is alive and well in humanitarian organizational culture today, and the dominance of bureaucracy is felt by many to have a negative effect on the type, tempo, daring and success of operations.[16]

Individual Mixed Motives

It would be inaccurate to overstate the motivational force of humanitarian conviction in the tens of thousands of people who work in humanitarian operations around the world. Not unnaturally, many humanitarian workers have mixed motives for doing what they do. Some do it in order to find themselves as well as to help others. Some do it for the money and the lifestyle. Some do it for a change and a challenge. Others do it because it provides well-paid and relatively safe employment in a vicious war. Many continue to do it because they do not know what else to do. Most people probably do it for a mixture of these reasons.

The particular psychological motivation of expatriate humanitarian workers from the West has long been recognized to have a broad range of drivers that reach back into heroic fantasies of medieval chivalry, foreign adventure, military daring and medical self-sacrifice. There is a rite of passage element to humanitarian voluntarism. Many expatriate aid workers set out to prove themselves just as much as they do to prove the principle of humanity. There is no doubt that narcissism plays a part in such a quest, alongside the attempt to understand who one is and who one could become in a testing trial of some kind. But not everyone is neurotic, and some of the best international workers are young people who seek adventure in a less complicated way and bring exceptional energy and interpersonal skills to very challenging settings. Many older people take to the profession at a different time of transition in mid-life as a rite of middle passage. At their best, the age and experience of mid-life humanitarians brings wisdom and stability as well as energy to a humanitarian programme. At their worst, mid-life expatriate humanitarians can bring cynicism, alcohol dependency and interpersonal chaos. This strong element of personal rites of passage in humanitarian work is no different from people testing themselves in business, medicine, policing, the army, sponsored runs or fast cars at critical junctures in their life. But it is a significant dynamic that shapes the field and can give agencies additional volatility.

The vast majority of humanitarian workers who are national rather than international staff have mixed motives too. Working for their own communities, they also combine humanitarian conviction and a sense of challenge with more self-centred goals of salary, job security, technical training and career advancement. In a damaged or deteriorating economy, humanitarian agencies are generally high payers and good employers, which can make recruitment into the sector a plum job. The frequent glass ceiling that can prevent national staff from taking the top jobs is a constant frustration, but can also be a relief in authoritarian societies in which taking responsibility and standing out from the crowd can be dangerous.

This variety of motivations across the humanitarian sector is significant because it means that while the profession presents itself as primarily an ethical pursuit it is also strongly influenced by other personal incentives that drive humanitarian individuals and create an accumulation of vested interests that are embedded within its institutions.

Political Funding and Political Pressure

If the culture of the sector is growing away from voluntarism, so too are the main sources of humanitarian funding which have become primarily governmental. The formal system of UN-centric humanitarian action is predominantly funded by a strong core of OECD states. Many of these states are conviction humanitarian donors who align their giving with humanitarian principles and try to meet humanitarian needs impartially around the world. Inevitably, however, some emergencies are especially geopolitically strategic to government humanitarian departments and their political masters. This means that the volume of funding is often skewed to priority conflicts like Afghanistan and Iraq in recent years, and agencies often find themselves bidding for money bundled into budgets for particular forms of programming that serve specific government agendas in these wars. Following the money in humanitarian work can often mean implementing wider Western government policies of liberal state building and winning hearts and minds (WHAM) in Western-led counter-insurgency campaigns.

National governments and armed groups in war and disaster-affected states are no different in their political manipulation of humanitarian aid. They too use their power and permission to steer the humanitarian sector into areas and activities that align best with their political interests. Frequent cries of agency outrage about the lack of "humanitarian access" are usually the result of governments or armed groups dictating what they want humanitarian agencies to do and not to do. Sometimes their choices are wise and humane. Often they are cynical and inhumane. Their decisions are often more aligned with their war aims or their election strategies after disaster. The influence of political funding and political pressure means that humanitarian action seldom, if ever, operates on an ethically level playing field that is refereed by humanitarian principles alone. Such is the operational realism that humanitarian idealists have to confront.

Collective Action and Competition

Humanitarian agencies also struggle ethically with a tension between going it alone and doing it together. This is yet another yin–yang challenge for humanitarian action. A tension between competition and collaboration, and between single-mindedness and unity of purpose exists across all human activities. When is it best to work as one or as many? Should humanitarian agencies work as a system or as a network? Is international humanitarian aid's resistance to a model of command and control a moral weakness? Is there a virtue in consensus and cooperation? Is it right to compete with other agencies for funds and programme territory?

To many observers and practitioners of humanitarian aid, the sector seems to be in a state of constant squabble over mandates, priorities, strategy, money and operational turf. If this is as true and routine as people suggest, then until a good system can be refined most NGOs will have to continue an in/out relationship with efforts to create an integrated system. Collective action is always ethically preferable if it enables more strategic and effective use of diverse resources. When collective action does not deliver these wider goods because of inefficiencies, obstruction or incompetence, then there is a clear moral case for trying something else. If the collective is failing, it can make good moral sense to go solo and do as much as you can on your own or with a smaller group that functions well together.

People often find something jarring about NGOs competing for attention in public advertisements and breathless media reports from their various operations. The ethics of humanitarian advertising are a significant issue that is examined later in the book, but the principle of competition seems sound to me even if it is potentially distasteful as a competition over vulnerable human lives. There is no doubt that the so-called humanitarian market place also delivers improvements (as well as inefficiencies) for people in war and disasters. Those of us who work in an NGO, donor agency or UN agency are constantly aware of the competition. This pressure makes us improve, innovate and define our comparative advantage more clearly on the ground. Markets can skew demand and supply, particularly when they are dominated by a few major investors or are concentrated too much on particularly appealing asks for help (like children), but they can also get people thinking and performing better. A market in different agencies also seems legitimate because it is reasonable that people should have a choice between different kinds of agency. This allows practising Muslims to support an agency that has Islamic humanitarian values, and enables Jewish, Christian, Buddhist, Hindu, secular and atheist supporters to do the same with an agency aligned to their values set. Diversity and competition in the humanitarian sector is generally positive. Ideas of a global super-agency are much more alarming than the current system; it risks being more cumbersome and getting captured politically by one set of powers and interests. The main ethical challenge for a diverse humanitarian system remains one of collective action, which as things stand may not always be possible or desirable.

Human Rights Workers or Humanitarian Workers?

The dramatic ascendancy of human rights as a global discourse for talking right and wrong in the last seventy years has posed a distinct ethical identity crisis for humanitarian workers. Are we humanitarian workers or human rights workers? Or are these two professions the same thing? Both fields certainly have many of the same ethical concerns about what is good and bad in war and disaster. The two fields have also come together to shape legal innovations like the ICC, the Humanitarian Charter, Sphere Standards and the Guidelines on IDPs, which aim to protect civilians and disaster victims around a common body of human rights law and international humanitarian law. In short, both professions care about the same international standards in war and disaster. Their moral and legal ends are very much aligned. The way they work, however, has traditionally been different.

This structural tension in current humanitarian work turns not just on theoretical and legal questions but also on significant questions about practice. Human rights work has developed a very specific practice that deploys investigation, exposure and confrontation to identify and rectify violations of people's human rights. This is the practice of the courtroom taken directly to the war zone. It is a form of practice that contrasts with humanitarian aid's tradition of a less adversarial focus on assessment, appeal and negotiation. The differences are important. Humanitarian practice has always deployed public appeal and advocacy, but has also always tempered these methods to guarantee an agency's operational needs for cooperation and access from governments and armed groups. Some form of territorial presence and continuing tolerance by authorities has always been essential to humanitarian action. These two factors will continue to be the *sine qua non* of humanitarian aid until the revolution in technology means that iron domes, three-dimensional printers and instant resource transfers can protect civilians and victims of disaster from a distance.

This need for access leaves many humanitarian workers feeling "rights-based" and convinced that the respect for human rights is their moral bottom line, while knowing that what they want to do on the ground means that they cannot "do human rights" as human rights are conventionally done. As we shall see, what troubles humanitarians most about their hybrid practice is that they often feel bound to stay silent in the face of human rights violations and cooperate closely with evident human rights abusers, both of which count as cardinal sins in human rights orthodoxy.

In my view, humanitarian workers are a certain type of human rights worker but not the full-blown adversarial type that currently dominates human rights practice. Nor would it be wise for them to be so, especially when many others are importantly fulfilling this louder hypercritical role. Instead, humanitarian agencies do best to work on the ground in people's daily lives to prevent and mitigate the suffering caused by human rights violations. They should be more concerned with working alongside communities rather than writing broadsides on their behalf. Their voice, when used, must have the advantage and kudos of the trusted operator who knows much but rarely speaks. Nevertheless, it is this discrete and properly grounded approach to humanitarian work that causes the next and most extreme ethical tension in the humanitarian project.

The Anxiety of the Grey Zone

The most iconic tension in humanitarian ethics is between help and complicity. The great fear that circles like a vulture around humanitarian aid is that its acts of kindness can enable or obscure concurrent acts of atrocity. Historically, it is the shadow of the Holocaust that makes humanitarian workers and their critics particularly sensitive to this perennial anxiety that there is the risk of complicity whenever humanitarian aid engages in situations of war and political violence. Intellectually, it is the work of Hannah Arendt, Primo Levi and Georgio Agamben that currently informs the critical theoretical discussion around humanitarian aid. Levi famously developed the idea of a "grey zone" in which Jewish inhabitants of Nazi concentration camps actively cooperated with camp authorities in the hope of finding ways to save others and themselves.[17] Arendt made a strong critique of the dangers of working for "a lesser evil" in certain situations, based on her analysis of the cooperation of the Jewish Councils in Nazi policies of deportation and genocide.[18] Agamben argues obscurely that a degrading spatial, social and political dynamic of "the camp" is being imposed as de-humanizing public policy in many parts of the world.[19] Many academic critics of humanitarian aid now use the work of these scholars to suggest that grey zone, camp and lesser evil strategies in humanitarian aid, which are intended to mitigate some of the worst effects of evil, could in fact simply enable them.

David Keen has made a lesser evil analysis of humanitarian action during and after the Sri Lankan government's final offensive against the Tamil Tigers in 2009.[20] He poses humanitarianism's fearful question directly in order to gauge the success of agency attempts to reduce civilian suffering by asking: "At what point does mitigation become complicity?" From his fieldwork, Keen concludes that the international political and humanitarian community judged terribly in Sri Lanka and their "working interpretation of a lesser evil proved deeply flawed". Instead of challenging and preventing widespread killing, displacement and detention, Keen reckons that humanitarian discourse and dynamics smoothed its path and obscured government war crimes as they happened. In his earlier analysis of lesser evil thinking in the Ethiopian famine and the Israeli–Palestinian conflict, Eyal Weizman draws similar conclusions in a gritty spoof of humanitarianism's Panglossian optimism.[21] The verdicts of these two distinguished scholars are what every humanitarian worker fears, but I am never wholly convinced by such academic arguments. Sometimes we academics can build cases that are more interested in proving theory than accurately describing a difficult situation. This temptation to generate theory-based evidence rather than evidence-based theory seems at play in many very intellectual critiques of humanitarian complicity. Much social theory that criticizes humanitarian action reads to me like a determined effort to show that the speculative concepts of theorists like Arendt and Agamben have a basis in current reality.[22] More often than not, as I argue later, it seems likely that even in the most extreme settings humanitarian aid is neither a materially significant factor nor profoundly ethically responsible in these grim situations. People of power will usually carry out their plans regardless of humanitarian dynamics. Nevertheless, the risk of humanitarian complicity is always present in some form and must be approached consciously with a strategy that mitigates the risks of mitigation itself. The primal humanitarian fear is not an imagined moral fear, but it is usually an exaggerated one.

Purpose of the Book

This book is written for humanitarian professionals and for those studying humanitarian action. The purpose of the book is to develop a better understanding of the ethical framework that guides humanitarian action and to help practitioners think through the ethical difficulties in running humanitarian operations on the ground in light of the moral tensions just described. In the pages that follow, I examine what the humanitarian profession espouses and believes. I then offer various ideas and models of practice to help humanitarian workers apply their ethics more consciously and effectively on the ground. I have tried throughout to illustrate the book's discussion of ethics with real world examples of the challenges that routinely confront people in humanitarian operations. Throughout the text, I use the words "ethical" and "moral" fairly interchangeably, the former coming from Greek and the latter from Latin.

Unlike many moral philosophers, I see no need to force a distinction between them.

This book is organized into three main parts. The first part examines the ethical origins of our humanitarian instincts as a species. To do this, Chapter 1 draws on various traditions of philosophy and ethics to understand how human beings have developed an intellectual understanding of our moral urge to help each other in distress. I trace various progressions in Western thought and their apparent confirmation in modern science with its neurological and psychological insight into empathy and compassion. This chapter is a little philosophical and so can easily be skipped over by readers who would rather start straight in at Chapter 2.

In the second part of the book I examine the modern elaboration of humanitarian ethics to understand how the humanitarian profession has formulated its core values and operational principles in the fast growing development of international humanitarian action since the end of the Second World War, including the Geneva Conventions of 1949, the steady flow of new human rights conventions, the Red Cross principles of 1965 and the Code of Conduct of 1994. In an analysis of particular humanitarian principles, Chapters 2 through 5 are intended to form a new commentary on humanitarian principles. Chapter 6 then looks at the overall system of humanitarian ethics that has emerged. I characterize humanitarian ethics on the ground as a particular kind of politically realistic ethics that publicly operates a strong idealist descant alongside the realism of its fieldcraft. I suggest that the principalist construction, politicized operating environment and pragmatic culture of humanitarian ethics imbue it with an intrinsically interpretive and realist ethical culture, despite its professed idealism.

The third part of the book then explores what it means to practise humanitarian ethics. Chapter 7 discusses the importance of combining emotion, reason and virtue in practical humanitarian ethics, and the significance of making choices and taking action on the ground. In Chapter 8 I offer simple frameworks for practising ethical deliberation. Chapter 9 analyses the typical range of ethical choices common to most humanitarian operations. Chapter 10 then gives a model for understanding moral responsibility in humanitarian action. In Chapter 11 I look in more detail at the structural ethical tensions in aid and discuss a range of persistent moral risks in humanitarian work that are likely to arise anew in every humanitarian operation. These include the risks of unintended harm, association, complicity, staff security, silence and the abuse of humanitarian power. Finally, Chapter 12 suggests how best to encourage and create ethical humanitarian workers and responsible ethical cultures in humanitarian organizations.

As always, I feel bound to explain my own position as author of this book so that you know something about the person you are reading. I studied theology at university and write as a European Christian with liberal political opinions. My intellectual tradition is confined to the canons of Western thought, with its classical and Judeo-Christian origins. I am largely ignorant of other traditions of human thought and feeling. As a result, there is very little in this book from Islamic, Hindu, Buddhist, Chinese, African and pre-Columbian worldviews and ethics. I am also no expert on modern science or on postmodern Western thought. I worked as a humanitarian worker for Save the Children and the UN for several years in the 1980s and early 1990s in Morocco, Sudan, Ethiopia, the Israeli–Palestinian conflict and Bangladesh. Since becoming an academic in 1994, I have tried to visit as many conflicts and humanitarian operations as I can and to remain aware of them from a distance. I have also tried to maintain some form of engagement with humanitarian agencies of all kinds, either by leading evaluations and training programmes for them, or by taking governance positions on the board of Oxfam and the Catholic Agency for Overseas Development (CAFOD) in the UK. I have always tried to listen hard to the experience of humanitarian workers whom I meet as students, colleagues or friends. All this means that this book is written from a very particular perspective and place; but I hope there is virtue in such a text. Humanitarian ethics make a universal claim about the profound value and radical equality of human life and the need to respect and protect it at all times. I support this claim and hope that this book's description of one particular view of this universalism will provide a clear text for people to challenge or confirm, both from within my own tradition and from other traditions.

To date, humanitarians have been good at writing their ethics in declamatory principles, but the profession remains strangely underdeveloped in exploring its applied ethics. It is my hope that this book will give us all a little more to go on and so enable a wider and more precise global conversation about the practical ethics of humanitarian action in the world's wars and disasters. In particular, it is my deepest hope that the following pages will help the world's many humanitarian workers and the communities with whom they work to think and feel their way through some of the difficult ethical situations they face.

PART ONE

ETHICAL FOUNDATIONS

I

THE ETHICAL ORIGINS OF HUMANITARIAN ACTION

To start our enquiry into humanitarian ethics, we need to step back a little to ask two fundamental questions: what is ethics, and how does it shape and inform humanitarian action?

The word "ethics" comes from the Greek word *ethos*, meaning character. The study of ethics, therefore, makes judgements about human character and the character of human actions. In essence, ethics is the field of human enquiry and endeavour that seeks to establish what is good and bad in human life and society, and so what is right or wrong to do in particular situations and to hold as particular attitudes. The English word "morality" comes from the Latin equivalent *moralis*, which means right behaviour, customs and manners. As we shall see, there are many different schools of ethics but all of them share a core concern to understand the meaning of value in this life, and so what it means to live well as an individual, a group, a polity and a global society. Most ethics, therefore, tend to discuss questions of value and fairness. They talk about moral goals and moral means, and praise policies, practices, attitudes, character and behaviour that are purposive, wise, just, reasonable, discerning, courageous and loving. In its own ethics, the humanitarian profession has decided that every human life is good and that it is right to protect and save people's lives whenever and wherever you can. So, why has humanitarian ethics reached this moral view and why does it suggest that we should all recognize this view as a universal truth?

The ground of ethics in humanitarian action is a profound feeling of compassion and responsibility towards others who are living and suffering *in extremis*. It is a feeling of identification and sympathy that demands some reasonable and effective action as a response to suffering. Humanitarian feeling can be born out of a warm glow or a cold shiver. It may burst from the chill horror at outrageous cruelty and a strong passion to stop it; or it may spring from the depths of love and a burning desire to care for someone. It may arise between the two in a sense of sadness at suffering, and a desire to encourage and build up.

Whatever the source and manifestation of this humanitarian feeling, it is a universal one. People can and do feel for others and seek to put these feelings into practice as help and protection. These positive feelings are evidently not the only universal feelings towards others that we exhibit as human beings. We also share a tendency to rage, hatred, greed, violence, power, selfishness and sadism. These destructive feelings are often the cause and context of humanitarian action, but they are not the main subject of this book.[1] It is also very clear that for much of the time and in certain particular political crises we can treat one another with what Norman Geras has called "a contract of mutual indifference".[2] We pass by beggars in the street. We look away from distant tragedies sometimes and ignore calls for help because of embarrassment or fear. Often we just get on with our lives so that, as Peter Ungar has observed, we live high while letting others die.[3]

However, this chapter and this book will focus on our desire as a species to repair suffering not to create it, and on our urge to do good rather than harm to other members of our species. It will explore the challenges to our morality when we choose not to ignore other people's suffering but to respond to it. So, at the outset, we need to understand how we account for our essential ethicity as human beings and for the positive feelings that drive humanitarian work.

The Australian philosopher Peter Singer takes an evolutionary view of our moral development as humans and traces our ethical history in three key phases of emerging altruism—three gradually expanding circles.[4] Singer argues that a fundamental concern for others in our pre-human and human ancestors was, and still is, primarily focused on our family and our biological desire for the survival of our DNA. This "kin altruism" means that an ethic of care and responsibility for others was laid down in ancient patterns of mammalian behaviour but was tightly limited in a way that suited the many thousands of years when we lived in small and isolated groups.

A second wider circle of ethics is also evident in our own and other species. There is an obvious "reciprocal ethic" that operates beyond families in our larger groups. Like other species, we do things for others that are difficult to do for ourselves, and they then do them for us in return. We delouse one another and scratch each other's backs. We care for one another when we are sick. Singer notes that this reciprocal ethic quickly introduced more subtle ethical notions that transcend an urgent survival goal to include principles like fairness, cheating, retribution, reputation, gratitude and praise. If I do not reciprocate, or only do so half-heartedly, then I am cheating and can expect some retribution. If I always reciprocate well, then I will get a good reputation and can be trusted. These moral ideas born of reciprocation began the more complex social process of intra-group ethics.

Singer's big ethical leap came with our increasing use of reason as a species. Our gradual ability to think objectively and to ask questions about existing customs meant that we could go beyond egoism and reciprocity to consider the interests of others from a disinterested position. We could think and feel ourselves in other people's shoes not just because we wanted to exchange some favour with them but because we could imagine what they were experiencing. Singer describes this as a major moral shift that enabled us to take "the objective point of view" and ask what is best for others regardless of kin and reciprocity. This objectivity allows us to imagine and understand the "point of view of the other" or POVO as it is called in conflict resolution theory. From this perspective, we could imagine what strangers and unmet people might want and need, and what might be good and fair to do to them. Most dramatically, according to Singer, we could then develop this into a "universal point of view" in which everybody's interests count and become a matter of ethical concern for us. The "universalization" of ethics is where we find ourselves today and is most easily seen (and contested) in international conventions of human rights that set out in international laws what is good and bad, and what is proper to a life with dignity.

There is always an element of myth-making in narrative accounts of the origin of human moral consciousness, whether we are in the hands of evolutionary ethicists like Singer or theologians and philosophers. Jewish and Christian theologians do not traditionally start with a slow build-up of ethics like Singer. Instead, they reverse the process. They imagine original moral perfection followed by a terrible ethical fracture, or Fall, in the distant past which we must now piece together again with an ethics of love and personal discipline. Political philosophers of the European Enlightenment, like Thomas Hobbes and Jean-Jacques Rousseau, also use retrospective ethical myths. They posit an original "state of nature" from which they elaborate and justify their political theories of governance. Rousseau imagined a primal state of nature into which we were all born free and instinctively moral with empathy for one another and an essential lack of cruelty. But our entry into society with its inevitable competition for power and domination means we become entrapped in immoral systems so that everywhere we are in chains, or somehow putting others in chains.[5] Society is our Fall and each one of us morally stumbles as we encounter it or is morally abused as society encounters us. In contrast to Rousseau, Hobbes' original state of nature is famously brutal and competitive from the start and is a state of permanent war. It requires strong sovereigns to govern firmly and introduce political and social ethics into society as best they can.[6]

Sympathy

David Hume, the great eighteenth-century Scottish philosopher, found the origin of ethics to be firmly in our feelings, and based his ethics on an empirical analysis of our nature as a species. Hume's simple analysis of compassion and sympathy is one of the high points of European ethics and anticipates contemporary scientific thinking about empathy. Hume imagined no great original catastrophe in human morality, but regarded our emotions and our imagination as the source of our ethics. Hume understood emotions as our inner agitations comparable to our immediate bodily senses like sight, taste, hearing and touch. If our "impressions of sensation" are stimulated by light, heat, flavour and sound, then our sympathy is shaped "by some particular turn of thought and imagination" that reflects upon our feelings. For Hume, the power and universality of our feelings and our ability to imagine what others are feeling are what makes us moral and concerned for others.

In his famous analysis of compassion in his 1739 *Treatise on Human Nature*, Hume describes sympathy as the universal emotion through which we identify ourselves with others in distress. Sympathy emerges because of our innate resemblance to others and is felt instantaneously as our imagination thinks about their situation:

> We have a lively idea of everything related to us. All human creatures are related to us by resemblance. Their persons, therefore, their passions, their interests, their pains and pleasures must strike upon us in a lively manner, and produce an emotion similar to the original one [that the other person experienced]... If this be true in general, it must be more so of affliction and sorrow.[7]

For Hume, this combination of shared feelings and imagination creates "the general rule of sympathy" across human society. He describes an almost neurological process in which thinking makes an "impression" on our passions, which then create an emotion proportionate to the idea we have had. It is by thinking and imagining that we feel with and for another person. To show how quick and visceral is the process of sympathy, Hume uses the example of a woman who faints at the mere sight of an unsheathed sword, even though it is in the hand of her friend, because she thinks about (and so feels) the pain and damage it could inflict.[8]

This insight into the immediate and visceral effect of the suffering of others upon our emotions is, of course, not new. The imitative power of drama and its ability to affect us instantly and deeply was well observed by Aristotle, writing in the fourth century BC. In his *Poetics*, discussing the best kind of tragedy in Greek theatre, Aristotle recognizes our ability to feel instinctively for others: "the plot should be constructed in such a way that, even without seeing it, anyone who hears the events which occur shudders and feels pity at what happens: this is how someone would react on hearing the plot of the Oedipus."[9]

Like Aristotle, Hume believed our feelings are contagious. The actual sight and sound of another's suffering, or the imagination of people's pain and predicament, are physically shared around. Like notes along the strings of a musical instrument, we humans can vibrate as one: "As in strings equally wound up, the motion of one communicates itself to the rest; so all the affections readily pass from one person to another, and beget correspondent movements in every human creature."[10]

Hume's friend and Scottish compatriot, Adam Smith, also placed sympathy at the centre of his great work on ethics, *The Theory of Moral Sentiments*. Writing twenty years after Hume's *Treatise*, Smith started with the famous lines:

> How selfish soever man may be supposed, there are evidently some principles of his nature, which interest him in the fortune of others, and render their happiness necessary to him, though he derives nothing from it except the pleasure of seeing it.[11]

Smith too called this phenomenon sympathy or "fellow feeling" and also saw imagination as its source: our ability to conceive of others' suffering and feel it as our own, albeit inevitably to a lesser degree than the person suffering.

In their attention to sentiment, Hume and Smith were following the great Italian medieval Christian theologian Thomas Aquinas, who had recognized compassion or *misericordia* as the instant heartfelt emotion in which we feel the suffering of others as if it were our own and which then prompts us with a desire to act in order to relieve their suffering.[12]

Hume and Smith were both convinced that the rule of sympathy or fellow feeling extends universally across the world but is inevitably reduced in power, but not in principle, by distance between people. Our actual ability to feel for people far away is not the same as our ability to feel for people who are near us or whom we know. The range of our sympathy varies but not the moral principle of care and concern that creates it. So passion varies, but principles do not:

> We sympathize more with persons contiguous to us, than with persons remote from us: more with our acquaintance, than with foreigners. But not withstanding this variation of our sympathy, we give the same approbation to the same moral qualities in China as in England.[13]

What is cruel and painful remains so, whether you know about it or not; but distance makes a difference to how we feel. Scale matters too. Modern psychological studies show clearly that there are quantitative limits to affect, and that larger numbers tend to move us less. Paul Slovic at the University of Oregon has coined the term "psychic numbing" to describe what happens to us when we are faced with the enormous numbers of dead and suffering in mass atrocities. He and his co-authors show how very large numbers far away "do not feel real", and suggest that our moral intuition seems to fail when faced with truly massive suffering. We cannot truly envisage it and our ethical response short-circuits to a certain kind of numbness. We care but cannot really imagine enough to trigger a proportionate sense of outrage and action. This numbing presents hard problems for mobilizing humanitarian and political action around mass atrocities. It is also the reason why "when it comes to eliciting compassion, the identified individual has no peer" in marketing and mobilizing humanitarian concern.[14] Our sympathy, although essentially universal, does have limits, it seems. If we cannot really imagine suffering, we cannot really feel it and so we fail or struggle to respond to it. Hume and Slovic are both realistic about the limits of compassion in global politics.

Responsibility

When sympathy is experienced, it encourages responsibility. Modern twentieth-century phenomenologist philosophers like Martin Buber, Emmanuel Levinas and Paul Ricoeur interrogate human language, especially (and relentlessly) pronouns, to uncover the origin of ethics in our individual consciousness. Their complex philosophical studies of subjective experience and our original sense of "being" uncover deep ontological epiphanies about our bond with "the other". In profound and often impenetrable prose, all three of these philosophers affirm that our deepest sense of being and meaning comes from our encounter with others and the sense of personal responsibility it creates.

In his book *I and Thou*, Buber observes that "the attitude of man [*sic*] is twofold, in accordance with the twofold nature of the primary words he speaks". Because of this, Buber states emphatically: "In the beginning is relation."[15] So we find meaning first in others. We see in them what we find precious in ourselves. We only discover that we are human when we meet someone else, as happens at birth. In others we are then able to identify and recognize ourselves. This recognition explains the value we sense in our own being and also instantly establishes the value of others. It moves us from a mistaken and egoistic Cartesian consciousness whose mantra is "I think, therefore I am" to a relational mantra that is more like "I meet, therefore I am". Ethics is born in knowing other bodies, not by knowing our own minds. As Buber puts it: "all real living is meeting".[16] From these interpersonal encounters, we develop a sense of co-humanity. Long before phenomenological philosophy, this insight was shared in the ancient moral rule of Judaism: "love thy neighbour as thyself".[17]

The human face has become the original site and central image of our ethical encounter in this philosophical tradition. At the end of the nineteenth century, the German philosopher Hans Lipps placed great importance on the human face as the essential and recurring origin of ethics.

He built his moral philosophy out of the idea of the unique look and face we have as human beings. Lipps noted that "the look" is how a human being is visible to others and how the soul reveals itself. In a very different way to other parts of our body, it is our face and its look that reveal us as unique individuals taking our place in the world and becoming someone. Lipps was particularly intrigued by the embarrassment that shows on our faces as blushing and awkwardness. In embarrassment, he saw a deeply primal awareness of the demands placed on us by others and the ethical awkwardness it creates in us. Our blushing proves our ethics. Lipps thought that our voices similarly distinguish us as unique beings. Altogether, he argued that face, look and voice affirm the unique reality of others, and that just by seeing and hearing them our encounter with others is instantly "born" as ethical.[18]

Emmanuel Levinas, the twentieth-century French philosopher, also puts the face of the other at the centre of his philosophy, as does Paul Ricoeur after him. For Levinas, coming "face to face with the other" is a call to a profound responsibility. This is responsibility in its fullest sense, combining a spontaneous emotional response with a moral sense of duty and obligation. For Levinas, seeing the look or face of another is the moment of conscience, and indeed bad conscience, because the very presence of another reminds us that in the struggle of life we might want to compete against them and do them harm. But this conscience also reminds us that we could equally reach out to them and do them good. Because of the primal existential shock of the other, Levinas is adamant that "ethics is the first philosophy" and that the presence of another person instantly reframes the main problem of human life from an ontological problem about death to an ethical problem about living fairly. Referring to Shakespeare's famous soliloquy, Levinas corrects Hamlet to reframe the deepest question of human life. The question, says Levinas, is not "to be or not to be" but to be fair or not to be fair. The look from the face of the other means that:

> Being and life are awakened to the human dimension. This is the question of the meaning of being: not the ontology of the understanding of that extraordinary verb, but the ethics of its justice. The question *par excellence* or the question of philosophy is not "Why being rather than nothing?" but how being justifies itself?[19]

For Levinas, questions of being and time rightly take second place to questions of ethics and responsibility.

This primal sense of responsibility to the other person, found so decisively in Buber, Levinas and then Ricoeur, continues a deeply original part of Jewish thought in which existence itself is a kind of permanent dialogue between me, my neighbour and my God. The great topic of this conversation is what is good and what is right. All three philosophers return again and again to the phrase in the Torah with which humans like Adam, Abraham, Sarah, Hannah, Isaiah and many others respond instinctively and immediately to God in three simple words: "Here I am." This is how we answer when truly called by the other. We identify ourselves and make ourselves available. We take responsibility. These three words are the answer we must try to give to every ethical call, and they are implicit in humanitarian action. Responding is the first move in ethics whereby we recognize our responsibility to others.

Ricoeur goes further than Levinas in his interpretation of the original ethical moment in our face-to-face encounter with the other. Like Levinas, he sees the moment of our recognition of and by another person as "a summons to responsibility" and an "epiphany of justice". But he does not see this summons simply as a duty born of bad conscience and fear, as it is in Levinas' rather gloomy interpretation. Instead, Ricoeur sees our response to the suffering other as compassionate and life-affirming. He spots in the sudden reflex of our ethical response the "springing forth of goodness" and the "very moment of the golden rule".[20] He sees in it a "benevolent spontaneity" which he understands as a genuine "solicitude".[21] In his emphasis on intuitive goodness, benevolent spontaneity and solicitude, Ricoeur comes closer to Hume and his idea of sympathy being a contagious emotional manifestation of a strong and compassionate moral sense.

In all these philosophical traditions, we see the recognition that compassion (or sympathy) is a political emotion. It makes demands of us in relationship with others and influences the way we organize our lives together in society. If Aristotle rightly defines politics as "the science of the good for man",[22] then sympathy and compassion are strong drivers of politics, and humanitarian action is political action in the most profound sense of reordering human relationships around goodness.

Empathy and Intersubjectivity

Modern science is now catching up with these philosophical and theological insights with its new neurological understanding of empathy. In the 1990s, philosophical ideas of sympathy and compassion were scientifically confirmed in a laboratory at the University of Parma in Italy where the neurophysiologists Vittorio Gallese and Giacomo Rizzolati discovered what they called "mirror neurons". These were first discovered in monkeys and then confirmed in humans too. They showed that our brain automatically imitates what we are watching, even though we are not physically doing the thing we are watching:

> Whenever we are looking at someone performing an action, beside the activation of various visual areas, there is a concurrent activation of the motors circuits that are recruited when we ourselves perform that action. Although we do not overtly reproduce the observed action, nevertheless our motor system becomes active *as if* we were executing that very same action.[23]

This characteristic of our brain doing and feeling things as if we were actually undergoing what we are only observing gives a neurological account of an important part of classical and modern ethics. It explains the whole area of our consciousness that philosophers and scientists label as intersubjectivity—our ability to move between our own and others' experience. Intersubjectivity had been observed by another Lipps, Theodore Lipps, in early-twentieth century Germany. Lipps wrote about empathy as the "inner imitation of the perceived movements of others" and noted how, when watching an acrobat walking perilously along a high wire in a circus, "I feel myself so inside of him" as he does it.[24] This was Lipps' motor neurons running at full tilt. Our tendency to intersubjectivity, or empathy, means that when we are faced with the suffering of others our brain produces an embodied simulation of what they are experiencing. This physical identification with people suffering seems to be neurologically and emotionally hard-wired, as Hume described, and is, as he argued, a fundamental source of our ethics.

Universal Ethics

Whichever account one chooses about the origin of ethics, and there are many more, they all agree that human beings have emerged with common ethical features: a profound sense of responsibility to one another; rich emotions of empathy for the suffering of others; a strong feel for good and bad; an often urgent need to choose between right and wrong, and a desire to act on this choice. The ethical intent that drives humanitarian action shares all these key features of ethics. Humanitarian action manifests an emotional concern for other people, and acts from an intuitive sense of responsibility.

Humanitarian ethics recognizes these ethical calls as universal. It builds its legitimacy around the world on the claim that this feeling and responsibility for the other is universal, and is evidence that human life is profoundly social, precious and is rightly protected. This universalism sits at the foundation of humanitarian ethics. We now turn to the main ethical principles of humanitarian action to see how the humanitarian profession makes the case for such universalism.

PART TWO

THE MODERN ELABORATION OF HUMANITARIAN PRINCIPLES

2

THE HUMANITARIAN GOAL

HUMANITY AND IMPARTIALITY

International humanitarian action has become a significant field of international relations in the last 150 years, most notably since the founding of the International Committee of the Red Cross in 1863. This was followed by a wave of national and international NGOs during the First World War and the Russian Civil War and the development of the League of Nations. After the founding of the United Nations in 1945, humanitarian ethics established itself even more in the laws and institutions of international society. The creation of specific UN agencies like UNICEF, UNHCR and the World Food Programme set in train the modern inter-state practice of humanitarian action. The Geneva Conventions in 1949 and the new weapons conventions at the UN saw a rapid development in modern international humanitarian law.[1]

In this modern history of humanitarian action, the essential ethical goal of helping and protecting others in wars and disasters has been elaborated around the key concepts of humanity and impartiality. From these core values, new standards of international humanitarian law (IHL) and a set of operational humanitarian principles have been derived. Together, these laws and principles now delineate the ethical field of humanitarian action and seek to guide its practice.

This chapter examines the two ethical principles that have evolved as central to humanitarian action. But first, it is important to look at the notion of principle itself that so dominates current understandings of humanitarian ethics. What is a moral principle and what purpose does it serve in a system of ethics?

Principle-Based Ethics

Humanitarian ethics has developed as principle-based ethics. International humanitarian law (IHL) is built on a range of key principles—humanity, distinction, proportionality, protection, precaution and military necessity—that should guide the conduct of hostilities in armed conflict. Humanitarian action is grounded in the principles of humanity, impartiality, neutrality and independence that have been developed to guide the provision of humanitarian assistance and protection. Subsequent codes and standards have introduced a range of new principles to guide specific areas of humanitarian action as the profession has matured. There are now thirty-three principles that are routinely used in the pursuit of humanitarian action. These are set out in Figure 1. They range from the foundational principle of humanity, which is the essential moral insight of humanitarian law and action, to everyday ethical principles of operating efficiently and effectively.

33 Principles in Humanitarian Action

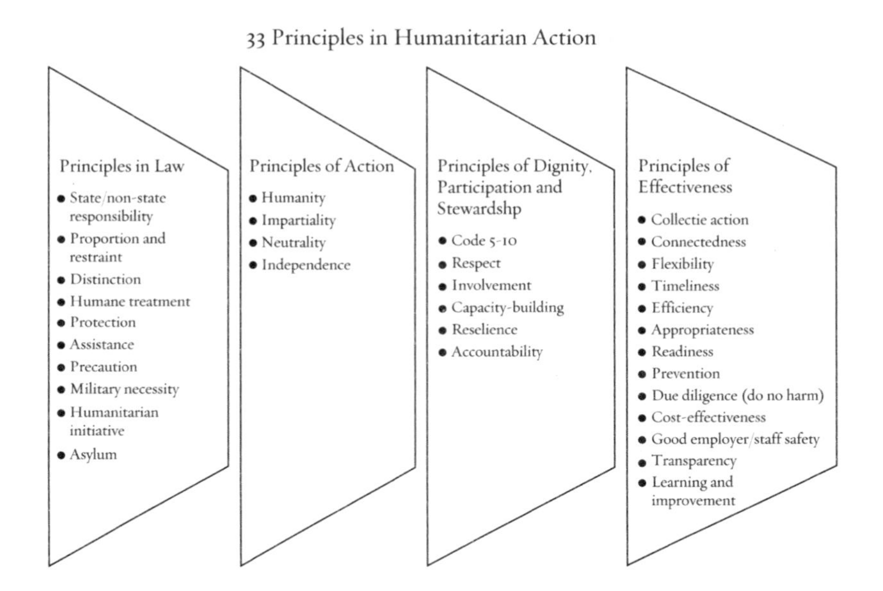

Because of the strong emphasis on principles in humanitarian action, it is important to understand the purpose and limits of principles in ethics.

A principle is a fundamental proposition that governs a system of belief or behaviour. It expresses a basic truth or moral norm that should be routinely applied as a universal standard of practice. From this truth a number of specific rules can be derived. These rules then prescribe how we should live and act in accordance with the principle. So, for example, from the principle of honesty are derived specific rules that we should not lie, deceive, forge, exaggerate or cheat. In applied ethics, principles are used for three main purposes:

- To affirm moral norms
- To act as constant operational guides to ethical decision-making
- To generate specific rules

Principles, and the rules that flow from them, are typically presented in codes of conduct and laws that set out a framework to govern professional practice.

Humanitarian action is not alone in having developed a principle-based system of ethics. The modern elaboration of medical ethics has built on its original guiding principle of nonmaleficence (do no harm) to develop numerous codes of practice that set ethical guidelines to different areas of practice. In the USA, the simplest and best known principle-based framework in medical ethics is the Four Principles Approach that identifies autonomy, nonmaleficence, beneficence and justice as the fundamental principles of medicine, and the main obligations on all health staff.[2] These four principles are core to most medical codes of practice, often with fidelity and competence separately identified. In the UK, social work ethics has been elaborated in thirty-two major principles.[3] These range from "upholding and promoting human dignity and wellbeing" to "empowering people" and "maintaining clear and accurate records". A large part of business ethics is also principle-based and formulated in company codes of conduct, or larger international principle-based frameworks for business ethics like the ten principles of the Global Compact.[4]

Principles set out to influence character and actions. They are "guides to being and doing" and are of three main types: absolute; obligatory and aspirational.[5]

- Absolute principles—these are "exceptionless norms" which always apply in any situation. The prohibition of murder is an absolute principle, in contrast to killing for a moral reason. Murder in its strict sense is an act that is always absolutely bad in itself, or *malum in se* as it is known in the Latin of traditional jurisprudence.
- Obligatory principles—most principles are strong obligations and apply to all but exceptional circumstances. The principle that one should care for one's children is a clear example of a constant moral obligation that ensures the life and health of others and delivers important personal and social benefits. But obligatory principles are not always absolute because they can imagine and tolerate exceptions arising from the impact of other moral considerations that must always be weighed in a situation. John Finnis gruesomely illustrates the point: "There are many moral norms which are true, but not absolute: 'Feed your children', for example. This moral norm is true, forceful, but not absolute. When the only food available is the body of your neighbour's living child, one (morally) cannot apply the norm in one's action; nor does one violate it by not applying it."[6] Sometimes, breaching an obligatory principle is the right thing to do.
- Aspirational principles—these represent an ideal of perfection to which we ought to aspire. These are principles of excellence in which the very process of aiming at them has moral value for drawing us towards them, even if we are never likely to reach them fully. Aspirational principles are hortatory and encouraging rather than obligatory and binding. In religious traditions, love and self-sacrifice are examples of principles of perfection to which we must turn and strive but to which we will seldom conform in full. In recent years, the Millennium Development Goals (MDGs) have acted internationally as aspirational principles for the global political community.[7]

Humanitarian principles include a mixture of all three types of these action-guiding principles. The way in which the principle of humanity has been developed in international humanitarian law means that there are absolute prohibitions on certain acts like murder, rape, torture, cruel and degrading treatment and indiscriminate attacks in armed conflict. The wider principles of humanitarian law, like proportionality, precaution and military necessity, are less easy to judge. In the principles of humanitarian action, humanity and impartiality seem close to being absolute principles; while neutrality, independence and the dignity principles are obligatory. Many of the principles relating to effectiveness inevitably appear more aspirational.

Interpreting and Balancing Principles

Because most principles are not absolute in the strict sense, they are what Ronald Dworkin calls "interpretive concepts".[8] They require interpretation in any given context: either because they are relative principles like fairness and proportionality that need specification in a particular situation; or because principles can compete with one another to create moral conflicts, or even a moral paradox whereby when I do one thing right and according to principle, I do something else wrong. Any ethical system that involves more than one principle is bound to experience tensions between competing principles in certain situations. This is certainly true in the practice of humanitarian action.

The first form of interpretation involves understanding the best meaning of a principle in a particular situation. Intrinsically relative principles like fairness require judgement and calculation based on the number of people concerned and the resources available in a given situation. Deciding what is fair in a food distribution for 30,000 people in a refugee camp in a forgotten emergency where food supply levels are lower than Sphere Standards needs to be interpreted there and then on the ground. This requires a judgement on how best the principle of fairness can be met in a bad situation. This involves deciding the particular meaning of fairness in this situation. What does fair mean when you have a lot of people and not enough food?

The second scenario in which it is necessary to interpret principles occurs when moral common sense requires us to prioritize one principle over another. This means we have to weigh the relative importance of two particular principles when they seem to compete with one another in a given situation, in order to find the right balance between them at a particular moment.[9] In such situations, one cannot easily rely on the precise rules derived from principles. Instead, you need to find a good balance between different principles. For example, in a Red Crescent hospital that strictly prohibits weapons within its grounds, a member of a local militia rushes to his wife's bedside in order to comfort her as she lies mortally wounded from a bomb blast forty minutes earlier. As he sits down beside her, weeping, he hurriedly takes off his coat to hold her hand, and the nurse sees a pistol strapped to his waist. The nurse then challenges him and insists he go back to the gate to hand in his gun, even though he might then not be with his wife when she dies. Such a literal application of a rule makes little ethical sense within this particular context. It is an instance of the long-observed problem of following the letter not the spirit of the law. Much better just to ask him gently to give over his weapon or defer the discussion to a better moment. This conflict between humanity and neutrality requires a particular judgement to be made about the relative weight of these two principles in a given situation, and to balance one's actions accordingly.

Principles can help with many moral predicaments by guiding us in specific situations, but they do not instantly solve every problem. As we have just seen, they can create moral problems because they tend to clash or conflict in certain situations. Because of this, principles are seldom simply prescriptive but have to be interpreted. Principles always tell us what is good to do but they do not easily tell us what is best to do in difficult situations. We have to work this out. This means that principle-based systems of ethics are necessary but not sufficient to the ethical challenges in humanitarian action. All sophisticated principle-based systems are aware of the weakness of simplistic "principalism" and so value and include other ethical practices of deliberation, good judgement and the cultivation of practical virtues in their ethics. The inclusion and integration of these wider ethical traditions is currently the main challenge for humanitarian ethics and will be explored in Part Two of this book. But first, we need to understand the main principles that currently structure humanitarian ethics.

The Ethical Goal of Humanitarian Action

The Greek word for "goal" is *telos*, from which we get the longer word "teleology". The teleology of any particular project is its eventual goal, its ultimate purpose or final objective. It is the target at which the arrow is aimed or the fulfilment of a personal or political desire. The moral purpose of humanitarian action (and of a humanitarian agency) can be understood in the light of Aristotle's conviction that everything has an inherent goal at which it aims. This goal is an end that it is constantly becoming, or a call to which it is always responding. So what is the goal of humanitarian action? Just as the goal of a boat is to be a boat, so the

goal of humanitarian action is to be humanitarian. But how do
stand being humanitarian? What is its aim? What makes a
humanitarian act rather than any other kind of act?

A humanitarian act is one that aims to respect and protect the humanity in everyone. This overall goal of humanitarian action has come to be expressed in two key terms: humanity and impartiality. The first encapsulates the purpose of the action, the second its universal and non-discriminatory application. In international relations and international law, the term "humanitarian" has become particularly linked to organized assistance and protection for people who are suffering, or who are likely to suffer, from armed conflicts or disasters. Like other words in political discourse such as state or party, the word humanitarian can be used in other non-political ways, but increasingly it has come to have a particular political and legal meaning as a legitimate form of organized action in the extreme settings of armed conflict and disaster.[10] The ethical goal of this politically and legally recognized action is the preservation of humanity itself, regardless of the more specific and detailed identities developed around each human being. This requires us to understand the most fundamental part of humanitarian ethics, the idea of humanity itself.

The Principle of Humanity

The notion of humanity is the ethical and linguistic root of humanitarian action. It expresses a fundamental value that is the goal of all humanitarian action—why such action exists and the end it seeks to achieve. Humanity is traditionally described in Jean Pictet's famous 1965 formulation of the goal of the International Red Cross and Red Crescent Movement:

> To prevent and alleviate human suffering wherever it may be found. Its purpose is to protect life and health and to ensure respect for the human being.[11]

Pictet's powerful twentieth-century elaboration produced this core phrasing which continues to define the principle of humanity in humanitarian ethics today. But Pictet's formulation is largely one of objective not value. It states what humanitarian action wants to do, but does not explain why it is good to do it. Pictet's principle of action is obviously deduced from some more fundamental value that precedes it. He assumes this value but never fully spells it out in his commentary. Why would we want to prevent and alleviate people's suffering in war or disaster, especially when some of those suffering are our enemies? Here, on the question of its most profound moral goal, humanitarian ethics has remained strangely quiet and undeveloped.

In his commentary on the principles, Pictet describes humanity as "the sentiment or attitude of someone who shows himself to be human" and so expresses "active goodwill towards mankind".[12] For Pictet, humanity is a kindness and fellow feeling in the helper that relates naturally and universally to any other human in need. It is Hume's sympathy or Aquinas' compassion. Humanity is someone being humane. This affective aspect of humanity is certainly a vital part of the importance of humanity: something we all share and which we can all express. Pictet rightly finds this moral feeling to be close to love—a word that he does not use himself directly but quotes in others—or as the Latin word for love, *caritas*, and its modern version charity. This loving and affectionate aspect of humanity in the helper might best be called the caring virtue arising from the principle of humanity, and we shall return to it as the second aspect of humanity. But there is something deeper than this responsive sentiment. The sentiment itself is prompted by recognition of a deep good in the suffering other. Humane sentiment arises because we feel that life itself is intrinsically valuable. I do not want to ease your suffering and save your life because I am kind. I am kind because I know that human life is beautiful and precious. It is a good in itself. We might call this the essential value of humanity rather than its accompanying virtue. It is the enormous value of a human life and a human person that makes us humanitarian. So, the most fundamental of humanitarian principles, humanity itself, has two aspects to it: a value and a virtue. We value human life and we can be humane.

Humanity as Value

The goal of humanitarian ethics springs from this appreciation of the preciousness of every human person, an appreciation that each of us shares because we ourselves are human and know that our life is valuable. It is this value of life itself that then naturally becomes the humanitarian *telos*. Each person is an end in herself or himself.[13] It is good that she is. And it is good that she becomes herself as fully and uniquely as possible in life. A person's life is a natural good that he should desire and that others should desire for him.

The goal of humanitarian ethics is, therefore, very immediate and intimate. It is pressing rather than prospective. When human life is threatened amidst violence and disaster, the person is the humanitarian goal rather than some grand vision of political society. Humanitarian action is a teleology of person, not politics. There is no greater goal beyond the person in humanitarian action: not peace; not democracy; not religious conversion; not socialism; not political Islam; and not military victory. Humanitarian action is an urgent and limited ethics of protection and assistance *in extremis*. It may have interests in peace and the wider political, economic and social flourishing of human beings, but these interests function more like hopes than goals. In the same way that a boat, if it could hope, might hope for good weather rather than bad; so humanitarians hope for peace and good government, but the actual goal of their work is to protect the human person. The defining goal of humanitarian action is to save and protect individual lives so that they have the opportunity to flourish. It is not to determine how they should flourish and organize this flourishing. The goal is not the good society and some specifically elaborated political project. The goal is life. The humanitarian *telos* is the breath of human life and the dignity of being alive and well, by being imbued with self-esteem and surrounded by other people's love and respect for your humanity.

It is this basic good of a human life that the principle of humanity, as it is currently formulated, suggests but does not articulate in depth.[14] In many ways, the modern UN tradition of human rights expresses humanity more fully than the clipped and urgent humanitarian formulation. The Preamble to the UN Charter is very explicit in its recognition of the essential value of human life, and the human person that this life creates. On its first page, the UN Charter of 1945 affirms "the dignity and worth of the human person" as the ground of its ethics and the primary goal of politics.[15] Like humanitarian ethics, the political ethics of the UN finds its first good in life itself, in humanity as essence. The Humanitarian Charter, more than the Red Cross principles, digs down into the UN tradition of dignity and rights to understand humanity. It makes clear that the humanitarian goal is "the fundamental moral principle of humanity: that all human beings are born free in dignity and rights".[16] This affirms the moral foundations and the ethical goal of humanitarian action: that human life is a fundamental good that must be protected and respected.

But what is a human life? And why is it good? How should we understand this basic good that commands our most fundamental morality and requires humanitarian action?

Life is all we have as human beings. It is because of life—its pulsing, breathing consciousness—that we know joy and pain, others and ourselves. With life we exist and face outwards to create meaning, relationships and love. Most importantly, human life is a unity of body and mind. There is no dualism between the life of the body and the life of the mind. Instead, human life is to be understood biographically as personhood and individuality, as well as biologically as flesh and blood. Our person is nothing without our body and our body is nothing without our person. We live embodied. Our life is body, mind and feeling lived in a single experience as a human person. As human beings we meet each other as a unity, not in parts. Our face, our voice, our movements, our aura, our scent, our bodily warmth and the touch of bone and muscle through our skin express who we are as a person. The combination of body and person are precious together and impossible apart. Together, they are who we are. Because we live in our bodies we can feel others living, even when they are only barely living. This is why a corpse seems empty, incomplete; a precious reminder but no longer the person we knew. A human life is always a person, not just a body. Living is being somebody and uniquely someone.

The term humanity rather than human life is the first principle of humanitarian action, precisely because humanitarians have always wanted to capture this personal depth to a human life and to talk of persons not bodies. The idea of humanity linguistically captures this unity of breath and personality in an individual life and the knowledge that we all share this life collectively as a species. Our humanity is more than just a body and more than just a mind. It is created by the unity of both and by our association with others. Our life is lived; it does not just exist. A book exists; a human being lives.[17] And living involves this richness as a unique individual full of a personal life of her own: a me and an I. Each human life has what Ricoeur calls its own "singularity".

In humanitarian ethics, the notion of "dignity" tries to supply this particular sense of the me and the I of every single person. This strange word, with its roots in European feudalism and the dignity and social status of Lords and Ladies, is the word that humanitarian and human rights discourse deploys to try to encapsulate the depth of personhood in human life. The moment we say I or me, each one of us affirms our human life in its uniquely personified fullness with identity, loves, social ties, memories, cares, traits, failures and achievements. Our dignity, therefore, is our beauty as persons living a conscious life experienced in the first person, rather than as a simple organic existence. Dignity is the grace that comes from an honest self-knowledge of our delicate and temporary place in the world. It is our sense of I, and our conviction that this I can be lived well before it dies. If I suffer torture, hunger or carelessness, it is not my body that hurts but me. It is my own personal pain. My humanity, therefore, is my consciousness of life lived as me in struggles and affection with others, with my own personal goals, flaws and hopes in a future. This is the personal richness of human life conveyed in the moral idea of humanity. All of this richness is then of ethical concern to humanitarian action which must seek to assist and protect people's health, relationships, dignity and individual futures as integral to a personalized human life—their humanity.[18] Humanity as value asks that humanitarian action take account of the human person, all of her or him.

Humanity as Virtue

As value, humanity captures our moral sense of the great importance of a human life as a richly personal treasure that extends beyond physical existence in a lived sense of identity, affections, relations, achievements, memories and hope. But our humanity is not just a value. It also functions as a virtue to preserve life. Because we know our life is valuable, we want to reach out to other lives and protect them too. Having humanity ourselves makes us humane. Being humane is the virtue of human kindness realized in attitudes, actions and rules.

We know that all human life is valuable because we ourselves are such a life and we can experience and imagine this richness of life in others, especially in their faces. So we know from where we stand that this beauty in human life is universal and we hear others speak of this beauty all over the world in stories, politics, religion and art. We also know that some of the texture in our experience of humanity is painful and tragic. Life is a basic good but it does not always feel good and does not turn out all good. We find it hard to get on with others and we can hate and fight in conflicts of many kinds. Bad things happen to us like accidents, disease and the death of people close to us. Bad things are also done to us by acts of cruelty and greed and by the way society is unfairly organized. And we can do bad things and become those cruel, greedy and unfair people. In short, suffering is part of the fabric of humanity and of our own humanity. Knowing and imagining what this suffering is like makes us reach out to people who are suffering, and to consider it right to preserve and assist human lives whenever we can.

This reaching out, which is so clearly described as sympathy and compassion by Hume, Aquinas, Ricoeur and many others, is the second aspect of the principle of humanity. It is the affective aspect, the one emphasized by Pictet in the humanitarian tradition. In the thirteenth century, Thomas Aquinas developed the idea of this affective aspect of humanity in the Latin word *misericordia* or compassion, which he understood as simultaneously an emotion and a virtue which, at its best, works in three phases.[19] A feeling of compassion arises when, being affected by other people's suffering, one moves to alleviate the distress of another. This feeling is the first move in the virtue of humanity. The second move is gathering the will to act, the moment of volition for Aquinas when we will ourselves into action. The third move then requires a more considered contextual engagement with the particularity of the suffering involved to decide the right action to take in the circumstances.[20]

Humane engagement is first a question of attitude and look. It concerns how we turn and face a person who is suffering in front of us or in our imagination. As Timothy Radcliffe, a Dominican priest, has said: "we live or die through the faces that other people turn to us".[21] Therefore the virtue of practising humanity starts with how we look upon each other and the attention we give them, how we behave in front of someone who suffers. Simone Weil, the French philosopher activist, placed great emphasis on the importance of attention in our engagement with our own and others' affliction. She believed that "truth, beauty and goodness in the activity of a human being are the result of one and the same act, a certain application of the full attention to the object".[22] As the first move in humanitarian action, this kind of humane attention is the reciprocal expression of our humanity to the humanity of others in trouble. Genuine attention is given with a sense of equality and respect. Humanitarian attention is not a looking down at people but a looking straight at them to connect on equal terms as two people who share the condition of humanity. Proper attention is a meeting not an inspection by one side. In the focused attention of this meeting, a spirit of caring, curiosity and response needs to be present to ask important questions. What has happened? How do you feel? What do you need? How can I help?

This process of humanitarian attention requires people to come close to one another. This closeness combines physical closeness with mutual understanding and practical cooperation. This is the doctrine of proximity that has long been important to the humanitarian practice of the ICRC and MSF: the importance of being close to the victim. This closeness is the same attitude that is found in the more political notion of solidarity that has infused leftist traditions of humanitarian action, and the commitment to accompaniment in religious manifestations of humanitarian action.

This attention to the truth of another's condition is difficult and hard to sustain. At its best, humanitarian attention is not an attachment that seeks to control but a looking and desire that seeks to connect, understand and respond appropriately. Not surprisingly, for Simone Weil "the name of this intense, pure, disinterested, gratuitous, generous attention is love".[23]

Humanity as Love and Solicitude

Where Pictet was perhaps a little reticent to speak directly of love as the fundamental virtue in humanitarian action, we might be able to do so more freely these days when love is increasingly given back a wider meaning than romantic love. In his seminal work on love in the modern world, the psychologist Erich Fromm recovered a broad understanding of love. Critiquing the predominant model of romantic love as a bias towards the "fusion" of two individuals, he re-emphasized the power and responsibility of love as a social and political force.[24] Fromm defined love as "the active concern for the life and the growth of that which we love".[25] He described "the active character" of love as always embodying the four elements of responsibility, care, respect and knowledge. Love responds to others, cares about them, respects them and seeks to know more about them so as to understand them better. After all, "care and responsibility would be blind if they were not guided by knowledge".[26] The principle of humanity seems to involve love in this deepest sense. Humanitarian action is an attention born of love for one another and, at its best, is a manifestation of love that respects, cares, understands and responds.

In his philosophy and medical ethics, Paul Ricoeur develops the idea of "solicitude" to capture the original ethical impulse we have to "live together".[27] Like love, this solicitude is the mark of friendship that is conscious of "the life, needs and lack of another person". Ricoeur sees solicitude as a spontaneous part of being human and one that precedes what he calls "dreary duty".[28] Our solicitude for one another "reveals our similitude" and is the "like me" and "you too" moment when we recognize our common and vulnerable humanity with someone else who suffers. It is this solicitude, this humanity, which good quality humanitarian action tries to show when getting close to people and attending to them in moments of crisis. Like Aquinas and Hume before him, Ricoeur distinguishes between a spontaneous "naïve solicitude" and a more "critical solicitude" which needs to be developed between people as they make complex decisions together about caring and the distribution of resources. Both kinds of solicitude are important to the affective aspect of humanity: one moves us; the other then takes over to inform and guide us with reason. The practical business of being humane becomes more complicated as it is scaled up in major relief programmes for large populations in difficult political conditions. In such contexts and at such scale, humanitarian professionals will need a judicious and critical solicitude—a wise love and reasoned compassion—as they work with people to find the best possible humanitarian strategies.

As Pictet pointed out in his initial commentary on humanitarian principles, the principle of humanity is the goal and inspiration of humanitarian action but is not really a guiding principle at all. Instead, it serves as an absolute moral value that affirms the individual richness and basic good of human life, from which flows a universal imperative that we should be humane by preventing, or responding lovingly, to human suffering.

Humane Principles in Law

Humanitarian ethics has, over time, derived a number of specific principles of humane treatment in armed conflict from the more general moral value of humanity. In the development of international law, these humane principles have been shaped as particular duties, rights and rules or constructed into specific moral identities like non-combatant, civilian and refugee. These moral and legal norms have been derived as specific secondary principles to regulate the humane conduct of armed conflict. As precisions of the principle of humanity in action, they represent the second important elaboration of humanitarian ethics in armed conflict.

These legal precisions have ancient moral roots that run far back in human history in the religious and customary ethics of war.[29] Humane ideas of protecting certain types of people from armed conflict have always existed in varying degrees throughout history (especially women, children, unarmed men, the elderly and professional religious) but these norms have been respected very inconsistently. As François Bugnion observes of the principle of civilian protection in his magisterial legal history of ICRC's protection of war victims: "it has taken centuries for this principle to be accepted".[30] Nevertheless, in modern times this and other principles of humane conduct are now agreed in international law to an unprecedented extent. The Humanitarian Charter of humanitarian agencies summarizes and affirms these legal principles as the basic moral parameters of any humanitarian action by warring parties and humanitarian agencies.[31] They can be divided into humane principles that guide three main aspects of armed conflict: the identification of protected persons; the military conduct of hostilities; and appropriate types of humanitarian aid.

Humane Identification

The first precision of the principle of humanity reflects a legal effort to protect certain groups of people in armed conflict and to ensure they receive humane treatment. The laws of war have gradually but consistently defined a range of moral identities in armed conflict that confer distinct legal status and protection on people covered by these terms. These categories include the notions of non-combatant, civilian, refugee and internally displaced people (IDPs).[32]

- Non-combatant and civilian status—this group is legally defined by "taking no direct participation" in the hostilities of an armed conflict and confers a right to humanitarian protection and assistance.[33]
- Refugees—these are a particular civilian sub-group and are legally entitled to asylum if they have fled across an international border in fear of their lives. The principle of non-refoulement means they cannot be forced out of asylum against their will.[34]
- Internally displaced people (IDPs)—these are another civilian subgroup. They are people forced by armed conflict to flee within their own state. This category of person is increasingly recognized in the soft law of international relations. They are regarded as especially vulnerable because of displacement. They are often of particular humani-

tarian concern, and specific forms of humanitarian support to them are recommended by states and international organizations.[35]

Humane Conduct

International humanitarian law has also deduced a specific range of humane principles to be adopted by warring parties in order to respect the principle of humanity in the conduct of armed conflict. These principles are designed to encourage a range of protective actions that specify the general principle of humanity in operational principles for the harsh context of conflict. They are the principles of distinction, precaution, proportionality and unnecessary suffering.[36]

- Distinction—military forces are required always to distinguish between combatants and non-combatants in their military strategy and operations. This is the principle of distinction.[37]
- Precaution—civilians and non-combatants must be protected from harm as much as possible and significant precautions must be taken to warn them of impending military action, protect them from hostilities and avoid them during combat. This is the principle of precautionary measures.[38]
- Proportion—humanitarian law also makes clear that the "means and methods of war are not unlimited" and that force deployed by a military unit should only ever be used in appropriate proportion to the threat posed against it. This is the principle of proportionality in the use of force.[39] It is closely linked to another humane principle developed in IHL, that military force should always avoid "unnecessary suffering and superfluous injury".[40]

Together, these humane principles of military conduct must always guide combatants in armed conflict. However, at the same time, they are balanced by (and contend with) the equally significant principle of "military necessity" in international humanitarian law. This principle entitles combatants to use whatever force they deem necessary in pursuit of military advantage but without breaking the laws of war. It does not entitle combatants to do "whatever it takes".[41] As such, as Professor Marco Sassoli realistically observes, it does mean that current international humanitarian law is always "a compromise between humanity and military necessity: a compromise which cannot always satisfy humanitarian agendas, but which has the immense advantage that it has been accepted by states as law that can be respected, even in war".[42]

Humane Assistance

As part of the humane conduct of war, certain kinds of humanitarian activity have also been elaborated as legal and legitimate expressions of humanitarian concern. This distinguishes the kind of help that marks out humanitarian aid as morally distinct from other kinds of aid in armed conflict, like the supply of weapons, propaganda equipment or military salaries. These principles of aid specify appropriate humanitarian action as help of three main kinds: assistance, protection and advocacy.

- Humanitarian Assistance—recognizes the necessarily material nature of humanitarian help as food, shelter, water, health and livelihood support that sustain a dignified human life.
- Humanitarian Protection—recognizes types of aid that help to keep people safe from violence and degrading treatment and connected with their families, like communications technology, protective buildings, identity cards and prison visiting.
- Humanitarian Advocacy—specifically humanitarian advocacy is an increasingly recognized humanitarian activity that impartially and neutrally draws attention to the needs of vulnerable populations and violations of international law.[43]

These humane principles of assistance, protection and advocacy are given legal force in the specific injunctions and prohibitions of international humanitarian law, most notably the Geneva Conventions and their Additional Protocols and in Refugee Law. These laws set out the kind of humanitarian aid and protection that is the legal responsibility of warring parties and humanitarian agencies.[44] The appropriate types of aid in humanitarian action are also given very practical substance in the specific soft law standards of humanitarian assistance and protection elaborated by the humanitarian agency community in their Minimum Standards in Humanitarian Response. These standards run to 330 pages of detailed description of good practice in the provision of aid materials and the management of aid processes in the four key areas of humanitarian action: water, sanitation and hygiene promotion (WASH); food security and nutrition; shelter, settlement and non-food items; and health.[45]

The Principle of Impartiality

Impartiality, the second main principle of humanitarian action, finesses the rough edges of the absolute value of humanity in two important ways. First, it explicitly universalizes the value of human life to ensure we are not biased in the inevitable choices we face in preserving human life. Secondly, it guides the emotional virtue of humanity (compassion) with some rational objectivity based on the criterion of need.

In Pictet's Red Cross formulation, the principle of impartiality reads that humanitarian action:

> makes no discrimination as to nationality, race, religious beliefs, class or political opinion. It endeavours only to relieve suffering, giving priority to the most urgent cases of distress.[46]

So, the doctrine of impartiality is a principle to affirm the universal application of humanitarian action, but also offers practical guidance on how best to prioritize this application in extreme situations. Impartiality embodies a value (universality and non-discrimination) and an operational principle (objectivity and needs-based prioritization). Humanitarian impartiality, therefore, bundles together important ethical concerns of universalism, non-discrimination, equality, objectivity and fairness in the actual practice of humanitarian action.

The Radical Equality and Universalism of Non-Discrimination

If human life is a basic and universal good, then every single human life is good. There can be no discrimination between human lives which values one life as better than another because of superficial and morally irrelevant distinctions in the ethnicity, wealth, gender, beliefs or political opinion of a life. Taking humanity as the mark of value trumps all other identities in a human life and leads to a radical equality in humanitarian action. Humanitarian action must try to save anyone who is suffering in armed conflict or disaster. The poor garment worker is as valuable as the rich factory owner. The life of the fanatical ideologue inciting indiscriminate violence is as valuable as the gentle primary school teacher encouraging peace. The life of the wounded enemy soldier is as important as our own starving civilians. The principle of humanity dictates that this equality is true because a human life is good in itself, not only as a means to wider political or social ends. Human value is based on life not utility.

This radical equality in the application of humanitarian values creates a potentially enormous range of responsibility in humanitarian practice. It suggests a moral demand that humanitarian agencies should help everyone suffering from armed conflict or disaster. This introduces immediate problems of feasibility for humanitarian agencies on the ground. To deal with the pressing operational problem of scale and feasibility in humanitarian response, the principle of impartiality introduces a necessary moral qualifier to target help in an ethically legitimate way. This is the principle of needs-based objectivity.

The Rationale of Needs-Based Objectivity

Because social and political distinctions are morally superficial when compared to life itself, the doctrine of humanitarian impartiality dictates that the only thing that can legitimately distinguish the necessity of attending to one person over another in humanitarian action is their relative need. In other words, the measure of prioritizing between different people's lives is based only on who is more likely to lose their life. Objective levels of suffering, not subjective ties of attachment and identity, determine the proper criterion for the prioritization of humanitarian acts. Humanitarian response is prioritized in proportion to people's need, not their identities.

This needs-based objectivity is a morally reasonable way to apply the value of humanity in situations where it is impossible to help everybody in need equally because of limited resources. It introduces a sense of fairness that respects people's essential equality but acts reasonably to be as humanitarian as possible when not everyone can be helped. In extreme situations when food or medical services are overwhelmed by need, the medical objectivity of triage is used to narrow down humanitarian focus even more. Triage is not based on the criterion of need but survival. A person is judged on how likely it is they can recover. Importantly, this kind of survival-based objectivity seems to make painful but genuine moral sense to those involved—carers and patients alike. In his important ethical ethnography of Médicins Sans Frontières (MSF), Peter Redfield recounts the experience of James Orbinski and his MSF colleagues who provided humanitarian health care during the Rwandan genocide, in which hundreds of thousands of people were murdered by machetes. With so many terribly wounded people arriving at their clinic, the MSF team triaged people by writing a 1, 2 or 3 on tapes stuck onto their foreheads. As Orbinsky recalled: "1 meant treat now, 2 meant treat within twenty-four hours and 3 meant irretrievable. The 3s were moved to the small hill by the roadside opposite the emergency room and left to die in as much comfort as could be mustered for them." The MSF team found this process extremely upsetting, but Orbinsky remembered the words of a terribly disfigured woman in the 3 queue who, seeing his distress, whispered to him to take courage and attend to the others.[47]

This episode reflects an extreme and very intimate problem of impartiality, but humanitarian agencies have to make much more strategic decisions about impartiality as well. They have to look at whole national populations and decide in which locality it is best to work, and with which groups (men, women, young or old) and which range of needs. Agencies also have to look between countries to see, for example, if it is more reasonable and feasible for them to work in Syria or the Central African Republic (CAR). Whether impartiality decisions are intimate choices made in clinics or strategic choices made at headquarters, the reasonable objectivity of these decisions requires evidence. What is the precise nature of a person's wounds? How do levels of hunger compare across a country? What differential impact could we have on human lives between Syria and CAR? Needs-based impartiality depends on evidence about needs. This makes evidence a very important part of ethical practice.

Problems of Fairness

The radical equality of humanitarian impartiality and its idea of discriminating objectively between people on the basis of their need is morally shocking in many situations. It is an ethic based on people as people rather than on people as actors. Most normative ethical frameworks are rightly concerned with individual actions, behaviour, wrongdoing and personal responsibility. A large part of ethics, therefore, is interested in justice and fairness. Humanitarian ethics seems to have moral blind spots in these areas that have given rise to a consistent criticism of humanitarian action as being politically naïve and irresponsible.

The needs-based objectivity of humanitarian impartiality seems fair in most situations where people share an overarching identity as victims. As we have seen, people intuitively understand the idea of a hierarchy of care that is based on urgency, need and medical feasibility. This makes moral sense and people can consent to it, all things being equal. But many people feel that the idea of equal treatment between perpetrator and victim is deeply unfair. It seems only right that people's ethical behaviour in war and disaster should count in how and when they are treated humanely. Non-discrimination and the strict doctrine of objective needs-based help is a very hard thing to stomach in armed conflicts when enmity and injustice are felt so fiercely and often with good reason. From the point of view of fairness, it is deeply problematic to say that the life of someone who has deliberately chosen to kill, hurt and rape people is equal to the lives of those who have endured that viciousness.

Here, in the morally important ideas of deserved and undeserved suffering, humanitarian ideology meets a serious ethical objection to its fundamental principles. Surely, what people have done must affect their place in the queue? A person's liability for the suffering of others should reduce their right to be treated humanely. Perhaps MSF should have created a fourth category in their Rwandan triage—"not deserving of treatment"—for anyone from the genocidal Hutu army and militias who had presented themselves wounded at the clinic. Ethical asymmetry and differences in liability are genuine between people who fight unjust wars and those who wrongly suffer from them. In disasters, people who shape people's vulnerability to disaster by evading safe building regulations or stealing public funds are also ethically culpable for the disaster which follows. People's conduct means that they are not moral equals. Yet, on principle, humanitarian action still helps fighters who are *hors de combat* and anyone who is a non-combatant or civilian regardless of what they have done, said or brought about. It does so because people who fight and behave immorally in armed conflicts or disasters are still human beings and so intrinsically valuable. But how does humanitarian ethics account for this rigorous conviction in equal and universal humane treatment, no matter what people have done?[48]

Humanitarian ethics has two answers to this problem of unfairness in humanitarian action. The first is legal and turns on the principle of due process and humanitarian law. The legal answer to this objection is reasonable and clear. An important part of humanitarian ethics has always been its determination to develop international and national laws that apply and enforce the humanitarian values of respect and protection of human life in armed conflict. Because of this, the ethical behaviour of people in war is rightly a matter for legitimate processes of law and justice during and after armed conflict. Quite simply, it would be wrong for humanitarian agencies to regard people as war criminals and refuse to help them before they have been afforded due process of law. To do so would be to prejudge them and refuse to recognize the basic good of their lives on the assumption that they are guilty and are likely to be found guilty in a court of law. It would be a breach of the absolute value of humanity. Humanitarian action will not do this, but as mitigation and in reasonable coherence with its values it will actively encourage states to enforce humanitarian law.

The second answer of humanitarian ethics to this problem of unfairness in armed conflicts is almost theological and certainly psychological. It hinges on notions of mercy, forgiveness and providence. Humanitarian ethics respects the value of mercy as a part of the virtue of being humane. Deep down, humanitarian ethics seems to believe in a potentially redeeming aspect in human kindness. Traditionally, mercy and forgiveness is shown to people because it gives them space in which to turn away from what they have been doing wrong. It allows them to renew themselves and think again. Showing mercy is a way to recognize a profound equality between human beings in our universal ability to do bad things. The honest self-knowledge of merciful people recognizes that they are also capable of similar wrongdoing because they too are human.

In humanitarian impartiality's non-discriminating universalism there is, perhaps, a humanitarian hope that the mercy and kindness of humanitarian action may inspire reflection and a turn away from inhumane acts. In the Christian tradition, which infuses so much of the European and North American practice of humanitarian action, there is always greater celebration over one bad person who repents than over the moral consistency of the ninety-nine who are routinely good.[49] Theologically, mercy can embody forgiveness which then leaves space for acts of grace and divine providence to change people. In most armed conflicts, there comes a point when humanitarian agencies find themselves helping people who have been exceedingly violent and inhumane, or people who volubly support such inhumanity in pursuit of their political goals. In humanitarian ethics, showing mercy to inhumane people by feeding, healing and protecting them regardless of what they believe and support involves a very deep commitment to the principle of humanity. It affirms that even the most unethical human lives are valuable because they always have the freedom and possibility to become better.

This kind of religious description may horrify many secular humanitarians, but it does seem to give one account of how humanitarian ethics is able to be so absolute about non-discrimination, refusing any ideas of discrimination based on deserved suffering. But this hope in a process that turns people away from inhumane actions does not have to be framed in religious language. It is equally recognized in secular psychology and social science. Criminologists and therapists alike agree that the best way to recover people from violent gangs, criminal activity and anti-social behaviour is to approach them in their humanity as responsible persons, to treat them with respect and affection and not to judge them outright but let them find a place where they can judge themselves. The idea goes that showing people humanity can awaken in them a desire to show it back. This is by no means a guaranteed process, but it does seem to play a part in the humanitarian conviction.

Another potential problem of fairness in the ethics of humanitarian impartiality arises when some people seem to be better or more strategic than others and so more deserving of humanitarian help. Insisting on equal treatment may feel unwise when certain wounded or suffering people, like gifted politicians, women, humane soldiers or NGO health staff, may have more power to have a positive influence on the crisis in question than ordinary suffering civilians. Perhaps people with exceptional power to do good should jump the queue at the clinic? Maybe humanitarian help should be given partially on the basis of a person's potential beneficence and not impartially on the basis of his or her need? If inhumane people are potentially undeserving of humanitarian equality, then particularly good people might be especially deserving of humanitarian preference. These questions of fairness are certainly not confined to humanitarian agencies. British scholar Zoe Marriage quotes a former member of the Sudan People's Liberation Army (SPLA) describing their policy in the 1990s: "The SPLA thought that if people were not contributing to liberation, why should they benefit from relief?"[50] In war, many arguments for preferential treatment come from within the logic of the conflict.

This problem of fairness in positive discrimination arises because of prudential and utilitarian concerns, rather than matters of justice. If someone seems to have exceptional utility that could save many more lives or deliver freedom and peace, then maybe they are not morally equal. It may make sense to try to ensure these good consequences by prioritizing their life and giving them favoured humanitarian provision.

Many arguments for prioritizing women in emergencies are made in these terms, because of evidence that women have a wider impact on the health, care and education of their children than men, and because women are thought to have a tendency to be more pro-peace than men. Former combatants have also been prioritized in early recovery programmes on the assumption that diverting their energies into positive livelihoods will reduce the risks of their returning to violence and hurting people once again. But is either kind of preference fair?

The political philosopher John Rawls addresses the problem of "permissible inequalities" by recognizing the legitimate existence of what he called the "difference principle".[51] This principle permits differences in status and reward on the two conditions that "first they are attached to offices and positions open to all under conditions of fair equality of opportunity; and second, they are to be to the greatest benefit of the least-advantaged members of society".[52] As usual with Rawls, it is not easy to find a complete fit between his smooth ideal theory and the rugged reality of daily politics. However, a strong consequentialist case for permissible inequalities could be made for the preferential humanitarian treatment of some individuals and groups, even though the first of Rawls' ideal conditions cannot be met; because, of course, in most armed conflicts most senior positions in society are not open to all and, in matters of gender preference, not all men are free to become women and vice versa.

The preference for women and children in many humanitarian programmes seems to require clear ethical justification. Such preference can be seen as a breach of impartiality by favouring certain groups of others. There are two ways to justify positive discrimination in favour of these two groups: first on the basis of excess need, and secondly on legitimate preference for women's wider utility in the process of communal recovery. In making distributive decisions around gender and age, agencies may well find that children's vulnerability genuinely sees them have greater needs. Children cannot explore so many coping strategies as adults and certainly not without great risk of exploitation. The fact that children are growing and developing means that any health damage and social loss they suffer in childhood will have a lasting impact on their life chances, and so their immediate needs may be more strategic than adults. Women's greater needs may also be fairly argued on the basis of their role working a double or triple shift. These are the terms used to describe women's extra reproductive roles in birthing, caring and home-making alongside their productive roles in farming, marketing and other forms of commerce. The extra roles that women play may well justify an extra range of assistance that enables them to play these excess burden-sharing roles. The notion that women tend to care more about family welfare and are more strategic and less self-interested stewards of communal resources may also justify preferential and extra assistance to women, but only if this thesis is true. In making this more utilitarian argument for extra aid to women as wiser stewards, agencies will need to prove this logic and ensure it is not based on some reverse sexism that sees all men as feckless individualists who prefer to spend what they have on beer rather than on their families.

Humanitarian agencies also seem to apply the difference principle routinely when it comes to their own staff, especially international staff. It is often noted, and keenly felt, by national staff that humanitarian agencies are extremely partial when it comes to different treatment in medical evacuation, security measures and pay between national and international staff. This apparent unfairness is often justified by a combination of the difference principle, the particular duty of care that an organization has towards its international members with regard to their home base, and the relative costs of living. Increasingly, as Rawls would insist, agencies are opening up all senior jobs to national staff and working on better staff development to make such applications feasible. Repatriation can be justified because an organization has a duty to fund people's return home to their family in emergency, even if this means an expensive trip between Africa and Brazil. Pay differentials can also be justified because of relative differences in purchasing power parity between home bases. But differential medical treatment in an emergency is very difficult to justify. In the event of a car crash in which an international and national staff member are both equally critically injured, it would be wrong to send one to an ill-equipped local hospital and the other to the top hospital back in the capital city. This should also apply when the best treatment is abroad. However, visa restrictions often put genuine obstacles in the way of such equal treatment. In this case, an agency needs to do everything it can to secure a visa or try to import the requisite medical care in mitigation of the worst effects of such an obstacle.

A final problem of fairness arises in the tension between impartiality and coverage. Can an agency's relief programme or a comprehensive inter-agency relief programme ever really be impartial if it is not achieving complete coverage? This is particularly the case in conflicts where aid is easier to deliver on one side of a conflict rather than another. In such situations, which are typically the norm, needs-based objectivity is obviously not functioning across the whole conflict. There is profound unfairness, but the reasons for this unfairness may not be of the agency's making. Most individual agencies do not have the capacity to achieve critical mass across a whole emergency. WFP, UNHCR and ICRC may be exceptions to this rule. As a result, comprehensive coverage and strategic impartiality is really a challenge to the collective action of all agencies combined, rather than a genuine moral problem for individual agencies. Most agencies are too small to worry about strategic impartiality. Instead they need worry only about local impartiality in the areas where they work or could reasonably work. Here, within their reach, they are obliged to operate on the basis of need alone. Nevertheless, some agencies adopt a policy of "balance" as if to mitigate the risk of being partial by working only on one side. So, they will do a bit on the government side and a bit on the rebel side, "to make sure they are impartial". This is often a tactical strategy to manage perceptions and emphasize neutrality. Sometimes it is more to do with ensuring their agency's security than paying detailed attention to impartiality. Such balancing strategies may be ethically legitimate as a security measure, but are not necessarily the best use of an agency's limited resources in accordance with the impartiality principle.

3

POLITICAL PRINCIPLES

NEUTRALITY AND INDEPENDENCE

The second fundamental elaboration of humanitarian ethics involves humanitarian action's reasonable accommodation with political power in order to achieve humanitarian goals within the inevitable politics of a given situation. Humanity and impartiality set out the universal ethical goal of humanitarian ethics as the preservation of every human person as a good in itself. The next two principles of humanitarian action serve as practical ethical measures to achieve this goal in the actual political conditions of armed conflict and disaster. In this pragmatism, they continue to build on the needs-based objectivity of impartiality that has already begun to rationalize the application of humanity with a notion of reasonable prioritization. Neutrality and independence aim to increase this objectivity still further by building trust and access within highly politicized environments.

Neutrality and Independence as Prudential Principles

With neutrality and independence, we begin to move clearly from moral ends to moral means in humanitarian ethics: from what is good to do, to how it is best done. The ethical emphasis in humanitarian principles now changes from why we should have a humanitarian goal to how we should achieve it in the real conditions of intense political rivalry and competing interests that characterize war and disaster. Our discussion now moves from ethical ideas of moral value to consideration of ethical practices of moral wisdom, in particular the virtue of prudence or practical wisdom. In English, "prudence" has become overly associated with ideas of caution; but in its original ethical usage it referred to the skill of being able to get things done in imperfect and difficult circumstances. Aquinas used the Latin word *prudentia* as a translation of Aristotle's idea of *phronesis*, which is the practical wisdom of choosing the right means to a good end, and so the operational ability to achieve good things and avoid bad things. As John Finnis suggests, prudence is perhaps best translated as "practical reasonableness".[1] For Aquinas, it reflects the idea of "right reason in doing" as distinct from an artistic reasoning that makes things or an intellectual reasoning that thinks theoretically and speculatively.[2] Essentially, practical wisdom is the virtue of being able to put good things into practice and so is the foremost operational virtue in politics, business, humanitarian action or any kind of practical project. In armed conflict and disaster, humanitarian ethics has consistently argued that putting humanity and impartiality into practice is most wisely and prudently done by working neutrally and independently. This operational posture is deemed to be the best way of being inside a conflict without being problematically invested in it.

The Principle of Neutrality

In Pictet's analysis of humanitarian principles, he defines neutrality as follows:

> In order to enjoy the confidence of all, the Red Cross may not takes sides in hostilities or engage at any time in controversies of a political, racial, religious or ideological nature.[3]

Neutrality is here expressly defined as an instrumental principle rather than an absolute value. In Pictet's words, neutrality like independence is "derivative [and] relates not to objectives but means".[4]

Pictet and the wider humanitarian tradition are not saying that neutrality is a good thing in itself and a principle for life; rather, it is a wise thing in humanitarian action, in which it serves a particular purpose. This purpose is essentially to generate trust and fairness in dealings with all sides. For this purpose, neutrality is practically reasonable in humanitarian action, but is never recommended as a general moral rule. Nobody would reasonably argue that neutrality is an ordinary virtue to be cultivated in everyday life. On the contrary, it is an extraordinary and exceptional kind of prudence for specific roles and situations. While neutrality makes sense in the role morality of humanitarian action, it is generally regarded as a moral failing in personal ethics. In his description of hell, Dante Alighieri, the great Italian Renaissance poet, reserves a special place of torment for those who have been neutral in this life. Their punishment is to stay stuck in the outer part of hell, excluded even from hell itself. Their particular sin was moral indecision, vacillation and evasion of responsibility. They stood for nothing and as such they are punished by forever running behind a banner that "whirls with aimless speed as though it would never take a stand", while at the same time they are chased and stung by swarms of hornets.[5]

The claim of humanitarian ethics, therefore, is that it makes particular moral sense to be neutral in humanitarian action but not in all areas of life. Indeed, it becomes a particular role responsibility to be neutral in humanitarian action.[6] Like a sports referee, for a peace mediator or a marital therapist it is best not to take sides in a conflict when you are offering humanitarian assistance and protection to its victims. This neutral posture is morally coherent with humanitarian action's claim of equal, fair and universal treatment. As Pictet suggests, it is also prudential in order to achieve the trust of all sides in a conflict in which the main purpose of humanitarian neutrality is not to stand aside from the conflict but to get right into the middle of it. In his most abiding image, Pictet observes the ICRC's challenge of neutrality as follows: "Like the swimmer, who advances in the water but who drowns if he swallows it, the ICRC must reckon with politics without becoming a part of it."[7] Pierre Krehenbuhl, a former Operations Director of ICRC, has similarly said: "no one in ICRC is born neutral but we become so in a given situation to enable our humanitarian work".[8]

In humanitarian ethics, therefore, neutrality is unusually a form of action rather than inaction. Counterintuitively, therefore, humanitarian neutrality is activism not passivism. Being neutral is something humanitarians really have to work at and achieve. For Pictet, this distinctly engaged form of humanitarian neutrality is built upon the idea of reserve.[9] To be neutral means to withhold and reserve one's opinion and limit one's effect in two key areas of a conflict: the operational military struggle and the ideological political struggle that surrounds the fight. Humanitarian reserve involves both military neutrality and ideological neutrality.

Military Neutrality—No Unfair Advantage

Military neutrality means that a humanitarian agency cannot takes sides in the fight by contributing an unfair advantage to one side or another by the provision of aid. This principle is clearly marked in Article 23 of the Fourth Geneva Convention. This article makes clear that humanitarian aid can be stopped if "a definite military advantage may accrue to the military efforts or economy of the enemy".[10]

People who do want to take sides in a war can and do pursue strategies of political solidarity in which they explicitly join forces with one party in the conflict and support its struggle politically, militarily, emotionally and with one-sided health and welfare programmes. Such partisan strategies can be highly ethical and morally commendable when seen in the light of political ethics. They can involve gifts in kind that mix food, medical support, cash, information, weapons and recruits. But they are not to be confused with neutral humanitarian aid, nor pretend to be humanitarian action. To make this point, Antonio Donini helpfully distinguishes between "partisan politics" and "a politics of humanity".[11] Partisan politics makes contributions towards a specific political outcome; the politics of humanity engages with political power only for a humanitarian goal.

The history of partisan support in wars is a long one with notable examples of non-state solidarity movements joining wars, like the International Brigades in the Spanish Civil War and more recently the many thousands of Jihadist fighters who have volunteered to play a partisan role in armed conflicts in Bosnia, Afghanistan, Iraq and Syria. States also take sides in such partisan struggles. During the Cold War, the USA and Soviet Union engaged in many so-called proxy wars in which they took sides and provided all kinds of material and personnel in solidarity with one side or another. In recent years, NATO and the UN have similarly taken sides in wars in Kosovo, Iraq, Afghanistan, Somalia and Mali to become parties rather than third parties in these conflicts.

Few people see a major ethical problem with the intention behind military neutrality and reasonably accept that humanitarian action should avoid military effects in order to be trusted by all sides. The main problem of military neutrality in humanitarian ethics, therefore, does not seem to lie in the moral principle of adopting a neutral third-party role but in the technical difficulties of sustaining this role and restricting the effects of aid. What seems like a simple and reasonable prohibition of "unfair advantage" can be difficult to gauge in practice. Humanitarian aid does have effects. Just as importantly, aid is very often perceived to have strategic effects within the dynamics of a conflict, even if it does not. Achieving humanitarian neutrality in military terms thus requires ongoing impact analysis to take account of potential military and economic changes on the one hand, and some form of tracking that can attribute any changes and unfair advantages directly to aid itself. In most conflicts, such military advantages from aid are usually more dramatically claimed than empirically proved. Most analysts of the "aid prolongs conflict" and "give war a chance" schools are long on generalization and anecdote but short on empirical evidence. In a recent overview of what actually drives conflict, Francis Stewart makes no mention of humanitarian aid as in any way causative or contributory at any significant structural level.[12] However, a moral obligation always lies with agencies to check constantly for any unfair advantage produced by their actions, and to prove and safeguard their neutrality.

Ideological Neutrality—No Opinions

Ideological reserve requires that humanitarian agencies "do not engage in controversies of a political, racial, religious or ideological nature". In other words, humanitarians must hold in reserve their opinions on the causes of the conflict and any political views they may have on which side is right and which is wrong. In legal jargon, humanitarians should withhold their view on the *ad bellum* issues of a conflict (the rights and wrongs of going to war) but they can discuss the *in bello* aspects of the conduct of the war in strictly humanitarian terms.[13]

There has sometimes been confusion between neutrality and silence. Being neutral does not mean being silent in a conflict or disaster. Humanitarians can and must speak out, but only to draw attention to humanitarian facts about the respect or violations of international humanitarian law, or evaluative details of needs, priorities and practices. Humanitarian advocacy is above all an advocacy of restraint in the conduct of armed conflict, not an advocacy of political strategy and social change.

Ideological reserve is, therefore, another simple and logical condition of being neutral. However, it has not proved an acceptable condition to all agencies because of the limits it imposes on the subject matter of their advocacy and their wider organizational values. When NGOs were negotiating the Code of Conduct in the 1990s, the principle of neutrality generated much controversy and still does. For many NGOs who campaign on poverty and injustice, the ideological reserve of neutrality seemed to compromise their ethics of "speaking truth to power" by pointing out political wrongs and advocating for positive and transformative change.[14] Because of this, Article 3 of the Code of Conduct avoids the principle of full neutrality. It holds to military neutrality and makes clear that agencies will not tie or bias aid to any particular constituency but it retains "the right of NGHAs (non-governmental humanitarian agencies) to espouse particular political or religious opinions".[15] In other words, NGOs continue to be essentially political and religious organizations, able to play a humanitarian role but also likely to make specifically political comments and advocate for various forms of political intervention. This combination of humanitarian ethics and the wider ethics of social justice introduces ethical tensions in many so-called multi-mandate agencies.[16] Not surprisingly, these agencies can sometimes be regarded more as campaigning political organizations than humanitarian agencies by warring parties.[17]

Neutrality and Disasters

Reluctance to adopt full ideological reserve makes more sense in natural disasters, where access and trust are not so problematic. Disasters are now widely understood and accepted as being politically and socially constructed and they are not usually such dangerous violent settings as conflicts. The vulnerability that causes disaster is internationally recognized as contingent on political policies around land rights, poverty, building regulations, urbanization and preparedness capacity. This means it is often much more feasible for agencies to criticize political actions and government policies after disasters, while simultaneously continuing to operate humanitarian and development programmes. Agencies do not usually need to be as neutral in natural disasters as they do in armed conflict. In disasters, therefore, as an instrumental principle of humanitarian ethics, neutrality can become less relevant. Indeed, in relatively open societies it might become ethically irresponsible for a humanitarian agency not to speak out against certain vested interests and horizontal inequalities (discrimination of minorities, for example) if they are free to do so, and their access and programmes would not suffer as a result. Neutrality may not always be as mission-critical a role responsibility in disaster work as it is in armed conflict.

The Principle of Independence

Pictet's formulation of the principle of independence for the Red Cross movement states that National Societies of the Red Cross must:

> always maintain their autonomy so that they may be able at all times to act in accordance with the Red Cross Principles.[18]

Independence is a very particular challenge for national Red Cross and Red Crescent societies, because they are also established as official auxiliaries of government. There are difficult histories of national Red Cross societies being totally co-opted into the war aims of governments. This was particularly true in twentieth-century Europe during the First World War, and then even more acutely under Fascism.[19] Independence has remained a real challenge for many Red Cross and Red Crescent societies in more recent conflicts in South America, Africa and the Middle East. It has also been a real challenge for international NGOs in the Western-led counter-insurgencies in Afghanistan, Iraq and Somalia. Pictet notes that independence is primarily about resisting undue influence and "intrusion" from "outside forces" and that "it is naturally in connection with politics, both national and international, that this independence must be asserted".[20]

Independence as Humanitarian Autonomy

With his usual precision, Pictet puts his finger on autonomy as the key ethical ingredient in independence. Autonomy is essentially the power to choose and act for oneself, the right of self-government. Pictet emphasizes the importance of maintaining humanitarian autonomy from government, in particular to avoid becoming "mere tools of officialdom, only in the service of government policy". His concern about humanitarian autonomy in the 1960s is similar in urgency to current early-twenty-first-century concerns from Mark Duffield, Antonio Donini and others about the "instrumentalization" of humanitarian action by warring parties, Western counter-insurgency and Western liberalism in recent humanitarian policy and practice.[21]

Humanitarian autonomy and its resulting freedom to act in line with a purely humanitarian goal and methodology are essential if humanitarian action is to have operational integrity. In armed conflicts and disasters, there are a range of outside forces who may be willing and able to compromise humanitarian autonomy from a local, national and international level. These may be: local leaders of vulnerable communities; political, military and welfare representatives of warring parties; politicians seeking re-election after a disaster; or donor governments funding humanitarian aid. Any of these parties may deliberately or unconsciously attempt to influence, infiltrate, co-opt, restrict or coerce a humanitarian agency in such a way that humanitarian autonomy is lost, and with it impartiality and neutrality.

Article 4 of the Code of Conduct is the independence article in the Code. It is explicit about resisting undue influence from any government and is particularly concerned to ensure that humanitarian agencies avoid becoming "instruments" of the foreign policy of their donor governments. However, Article 4 says nothing about local parties and power structures that may unduly influence humanitarian action. This silence may well represent the ambiguities that many agencies face when working in partnership with local organizations and groups. The common NGO strategy of working through partners may mean that NGOs realistically feel unable to adopt full independence as well as full neutrality.

Humanitarian Interdependence

Like neutrality, humanitarian independence is a role responsibility designed to enable impartial humanitarian action in a deeply contested political and military atmosphere of mistrust in which many people's desire to win is stronger than their desire to be humanitarian. Once again, independence is not being put forward as a universal human virtue. Independence—as freedom of will and action—is a good in itself, but it is never considered as an absolute good. None of us sees a life of total independence from others as a good life or even a possible life. We all depend on other people for various things, to varying degrees and at different times in our lives, and we all compromise with power. In truth, we are all interdependent and enjoy others being important to us and being valuable to them in return. Significant autonomy is important to us but we know that our independence is never total and that total independence would in fact be isolation.

Humanitarian independence shares this mix of autonomy and mutuality in practice. Humanitarian agencies need significant independence in humanitarian action—a genuine operational autonomy that allows them to move around, make humanitarian choices and act upon them. This is the sort of operational autonomy and independence from political interference that enables an agency to visit a community, weigh and measure malnourished children, assess economic needs and listen to people describing the conduct of the war and what they need to be safer. With this knowledge, agencies can then make informed, impartial and neutral choices about how best to assist and protect people. But in doing all this, agencies are of course heavily dependent on others: the goodwill of the warring parties to give them safe access; people's consent to discuss their situation and have their children examined; and then the generosity of donors to finance the necessary humanitarian activities. Realistically, high levels of interdependence are inevitable and desirable in humanitarian action, and much "balancing" of principle on the ground involves difficult judgements about optimal levels of independence and interdependence.

So, while independence refers most usefully to freedom from outside interference, humanitarian autonomy must not be understood as going it alone and acting autocratically. Humanitarian action is always co-generated by a variety of different actors, and a humanitarian agency is always dependent on their goodwill or, at least, their tolerance or acceptance. Organized humanitarian action on a large scale is a joint enterprise born of negotiation and cooperation. It is seldom the single-minded dash of the all-powerful, self-sufficient and heroic rescuer. When it is, it is likely to be a disastrous act of humanitarian hubris because, as we shall now see, humanitarian action morally requires the inclusion and cooperation of others.

4

DIGNITY PRINCIPLES

RESPECT, PARTICIPATION AND EMPOWERMENT

The next part of the modern elaboration of humanitarian ethics rightly attempts to give moral detail to the quality of attention and solicitude that we identified as central to the virtue of humanity. How should we best help others? These are questions of humanitarian process and approach. This is not bureaucratic process but concerns the ethics of relationship, attitude, behaviour and power-sharing in humanitarian action.

In 1991, the Code of Conduct added six new principles to Pictet's "core four" principles of humanity, impartiality, neutrality and independence. These six principles, Articles 5–10 of the Code, are about the ethics of working with affected communities and their various organizations and authorities. They draw upon political ethics, community development ethics and human rights principles to define the proper working relationship between humanitarian agencies and the people they aim to help. In particular, the new principles affirmed the importance of respect for people's dignity and their rights to participate in the process of delivering humanitarian action. The Code also confirmed the moral importance of lasting investments that sustainably improve people's ability to manage their own survival. This was reckoned as more ethical than top-down short-term fixes—the kind of aid that tends to be delivered paternalistically and soon sees people back in their original state of powerlessness, vulnerability and risk.

These process principles are best summarized as principles of dignity. Their concern for dignity is shown in their determination to respect people's individuality, agency and authority in the management of their own lives and communities. In the discussion that follows, I take the articles of the Code slightly out of their current numerical order and treat Article 10 before Article 9 because Article 10 is so specifically concerned with dignity. I then treat Articles 8 and 9 in a separate discussion of the ethics of sustainability and accountability. Articles 5, 6, 7 and 10 of the Code of Conduct focus on affected people's dignity in armed conflicts and disasters, specifically by emphasizing their agency as human beings and their right to participation in matters that affect them. These principles are important and well judged, but they are not as simple as they sound—as any humanitarian worker will tell you.

Respect Culture and Custom

Article 5 states that "We shall respect culture and custom". It is the shortest article of the Code and its explanation only runs to another two lines: "We will endeavour to respect the culture, structures and customs of the communities and countries we are working in."

Although short on text, this principle is long on implication. At first glance, it reads like sound moral common sense hedged carefully within an aspirational principle by the conditional word "endeavour". This tentative element to the principle—that we will try but not always succeed in respecting culture and custom—reflects an operational pragmatism in emergency work. This pragmatism retains the moral right to sometimes prioritize humanitarian speed over cultural respect. It rightly suggests that it may occasionally be necessary just to get on and do things very directly in moments of extreme emergency, when there is no time for village meetings or when the sudden arrival of large groups of humanitarian workers in a slum or rural area may leave little time for the proper courtesies of introductions, permissions and agreements on local norms. Such initial expediency is sometimes legitimate, but any initial deficit of respect or violations of local custom must always be made good as soon as possible by apology, reparation and new commitments.

The fundamental concern of this principle is certainly correct. It is morally right to respect people's diversity and their freedom to organize their culture and society in a particular way.[1] A secondary moral concern here is the desire not to cause offence. In order to prevent hurting people by offending them, it is right that humanitarian agency staff should be ready to wear trousers, long skirts, sleeves and scarves if this is the culture of dress in a particular society. Likewise, humanitarian workers should have meetings sitting under trees and not around tables where this is the norm, so that people may be granted the dignity of their own space and speaking conventions. Humanitarian workers should be ready to show deference to local people on important community issues. For example, humanitarian workers should give up alcohol in a place where it is forbidden and abide by the sexual customs of the society in which they are living and working if love affairs or pre-marital sex are firmly restricted or pursued only in private with discretion. Such respect makes good sense in order to recognize people's rights to be different and their freedom to choose the particular nature of their own society. The basic moral norm in such decisions is the rightful concern not to cause harm by giving offence, and to show respect for freedom, diversity and autonomy in human society.

But, of course, there is an ethical minefield below the simple moral principle of not giving offence to people who behave differently to you. Cultural differences are of various kinds. Some are just aesthetic differences in clothing, music and cuisine. But other aspects of cultural difference may embody deep moral differences that are serious and ethically challenging. Respecting a taboo on alcohol is not morally problematic, because it does not pose a grave restriction on a fundamental freedom or a basic human right. Indeed, it might be beneficial. Most different clothing rules would be similarly morally benign. Indeed, adopting local dress may become a moral duty if it helps to increase acceptance and humanitarian access. However, a culture that is sexist or misogynistic and only involves men in humanitarian decision-making, or which gives preference to male children in emergency food distributions, would conflict with fundamental rights and freedoms and become ethically problematic. To respect this culture and its structures would be to become complicit in wrongful acts and would breach absolute principles of humanity and impartiality as well as important human rights. Cooperation with such structures and customs would require significant justification on grounds of a greater good if it were to be pursued by any agency. Normally, these customs would need to be challenged.

Cultural differences regularly pose questions of appropriate sexual morality and business ethics in humanitarian operations. For example, in many societies cultures of prostitution are commonly accepted and widely practised. Some humanitarian workers may pay for adult sex workers in their free time and justify their choice because it is "normal here". In some cultures, girls in their teens are customarily encouraged to seek older sexual partners as an acceptable rite of passage in their sexual education before marriage, or as "sugar daddies" for the benefit of their social and educational advancement.[2] Aid workers may decide to play these roles. In many countries, conditions are also more extreme and girls are recruited into prostitution before they are eighteen years old and have reached the internationally agreed age of adulthood. Many are forcefully recruited against their will. Bribery and corruption are other areas of political and commercial morality that can also be seen as cultural or customary. In many societies that lack effective governance, proper salaries and a strong tax base, people are required to pay bribes for public services, political access and business opportunities. Humanitarian agencies are regularly challenged by corrupt practices which would be culturally taboo in other parts of the world but which operate as norms in many societies. Humanitarian workers rightly find ethical problems in respecting these kinds of customary sexual and commercial customs. They may seriously conflict with their own personal morality and often involve exploitation, abuse of power or an outright violation of a person's freedom and rights. In addition to the wrongs humanitarian workers bring about by engaging in such practices, there are also strong prudential reasons to avoid them because they can bring an agency into disrepute. This can damage an agency's wider humanitarian capability, which undermines the main moral purpose of a humanitarian worker's presence and role in any community.

It is also important to recognize that not every custom that happens in a society is generally acceptable within that society, even if it is widespread. Because something is customary does not mean that it is right. If it were, then slavery, infanticide and female genital mutilation would be considered moral goods, which they are not. Not every social, sexual, political or commercial practice is properly understood as an agreed and acceptable custom or culture in a society where they are prevalent. Bribery or child prostitution may be common practice, but most people in that society might not choose them to be so and might recognize that they involve great harm. Ethically, such things are better recognized as harmful practices not customs, and humanitarian workers should be careful not to seek dubious cultural justifications for wrongdoing.

Another ethical clash emerges in sexual ethics when local custom places a moral taboo on something which global norms and rights agree to be a moral norm. Homosexuality is currently the most obvious case in point. Some groups and governments within certain societies regard homosexuality as morally wrong. Yet most humanitarian agencies with liberal roots will agree with the conviction of modern human rights that sexual orientation is a matter of personal freedom and that any negative treatment of lesbian, gay, bisexual or transgender people (LGBT) is discrimination and a violation of their rights. Liberal humanitarian agencies want to welcome and recruit LGBT people equally and would not consider it immoral if their employees are in same-sex relationships or have a transgender identity.

In such situations, it seems clear that a humanitarian agency should pursue its non-discriminatory policy with conviction, but also with reasonable discretion and practical wisdom. It would not be wise or right for an agency to put LGBT employees in harm's way in an operational context that is hostile to homosexuality and transgender identities. Agencies would be bound to protect LGBT staff as much as possible from such risks by careful and consensual deployment choices or by policies of discretion agreed in advance and monitored on the ground, especially where homosexuality is illegal and punishable by prison or death. In an explicitly humanitarian context where LGBT people are being deliberately discriminated against and targeted in an armed conflict or disaster, then humanitarian agencies would need to confront this strategy explicitly as inhumane and a violation of humanitarian and human rights law. Agencies also have an obligation to protect LGBT employees, as they do so.

These deeper problems of custom and cultural difference are glossed over in the minimal formulation of humanitarian ethics as it currently stands. Its emphasis on respect for individual difference and social diversity is well made when it poses no risk of a serious moral breach. But the Code of Conduct remains vague about how to determine a genuine clash of values and how to identify something as a benign or positive custom rather than a morally regrettable practice. In short, humanitarian ethics needs to be clear when a cultural difference is in fact a significant moral difference. In such situations, humanitarian agencies and their staff should avoid or confront what they deem to be wrongful practices.

Building Local Capacities

Article 6 of the Code of Conduct affirms the principle that "we shall attempt to build disaster response on local capacities" and specifies that this means "employing local staff, purchasing local materials and trading with local companies". It also means "working through" local humanitarian NGOs and "cooperating with local government structures where appropriate".

The main moral thrust of this principle concerns affected people's capability and their right to take charge of their own survival and recovery. As a dignity principle, it is about people's right to retain the dignity of their own agency and autonomy as actors in their own lives and the lives of others dear to them. The principle affirms people's dignity as human subjects and not the humanitarian objects of others. Rightly, this theme continues strongly in Articles 7, 8 and 10.

The local capacity principle combines the autonomy and self-determination of political ethics with the principle of grassroots effectiveness and sustainability in community development ethics. Politically, this aspect of humanitarian ethics is particularly intended to avoid the wrongful interference, paternalism and authoritarian practices of colonialism that rightly haunts the conscience and traditions of many Western agencies. Politically, Article 6 properly seeks to pass humanitarian power to affected populations and to their own governing structures. Developmentally, the principle recognizes the technical wisdom that local knowledge often knows best and is also best placed to respond if it has sufficient resources and skills. Local capacity is thus the best value for money and the most likely humanitarian structure to succeed and last. Much of the development ethics implicit in the Code draws on the ideas of developmental relief or the relief-development continuum that were converted from philanthropic common sense into formal disaster theory in the 1980s and 1990s.[3] These ideas were then actively taken up into humanitarian policy and programming by the Red Cross Movement, UN agencies and humanitarian NGOs.

Like Article 5, the local capacity article is also hedged with a conditional phrase—"where possible"—which again marks out the principle as obligatory but open to exceptions. As with Article 5, expediency might be one legitimate exception to this principle too: the need for speed, high levels of capacity and large volumes of relief commodities which local structures cannot manage and absorb during a period of extreme crisis.

This urgency exception would mean balancing humanity above the local capacity principle for a certain period. But any initial exception to the capacity-building principle would need to be mitigated by subsequent efforts to integrate local capacities into wider humanitarian programmes by carefully handing over roles, resources and responsibilities for the remainder of the crisis and in preparation for new ones.

Another exception to the local capacity norm is likely to arise from more principled concerns around neutrality and independence rather than logistical concerns of capacity. This political exception to the local capacity principle will arise from a conflict between neutrality, independence and capacity-building where humanitarian action's political principles of neutrality and independence balance out above the local capacity principle. This rightly happens when local agencies and/or local government and local communities cannot be politically relied upon to operate in line with humanitarian ethics but are likely to use aid resources to pursue partisan or inhumane military or political objectives. A government may manipulate aid to discriminate against enemy civilians or rival groups, or it may take control of aid only to withhold it. A local elite within an affected community may capture aid processes and exclude important parts of that community. In such situations, and if it is feasible to do so, it is right for international agencies to retain more control and capacity in humanitarian programmes than usual.

Collective Action

Interestingly, the local capacity principle in Article 6 of the Code of Conduct also contains the ethical principle of collective action: "we will place a high priority on the proper coordination of our emergency responses". This should really be extracted as a separate principle in humanitarian ethics.

Collective action is an important principle in ethics because it places a moral requirement on people in any common activity to optimize their various resources in search of the common goods they seek. They should do this by coordinating activities, pooling resources, avoiding duplication, maximizing coverage and presenting a stronger counter-force to opponents. Sometimes this means reducing an agency's own individual ambitions and empire-building in the service of better collective action.[4] In protection work, the benefits of collective action have been encouraged in the somewhat clunky principle of "complementarity". This recognizes the importance of agencies with different mandates playing to their vertical strengths in different sectors (like health, water, advocacy, settlement design) but working together horizontally to achieve complementary results that bring wider protection benefits to civilians than if they each worked separately.[5]

Achieving effective collective action or complementarity is one of the greatest difficulties in humanitarian action. Discussed mainly as the problem of coordination, it has rightly been an object of obsession, reform and despair among humanitarian professionals and policy-makers. The most recent structural reforms have involved the development of inter-agency sectoral clusters that have been supposedly enhanced by the so-called "transformative agenda" led by UNOCHA and the Inter-agency Standing Committee.[6] More widely, it is a major problem in international relations and all forms of emergency management and welfare programmes. But its difficulty and occasional complexity does not detract from its ethical importance. The importance of acting cooperatively and organizing a "moral division of labour"[7] remains a major moral obligation, because it is often only when we combine resources that we achieve critical mass. A series of unrelated acts by individual agencies may only ever make a marginal contribution, but if they are joined up and strategized more widely, these same resources could have a much greater aggregate effect. In his thinking on the ethics of collective action, Christopher Kutz recognizes a two-tiered structure of obligations in any collective action of rescue and mutual aid: a vertical obligation between the claimant who is in need and the potential donor; and a horizontal obligation between the wider group of potential donors who must pool and prioritize their aid in the best way to ensure its fair and effective redistribution.[8] Agencies must work to and be accountable to both obligations.

People's Participation

Article 7 of the Code of Conduct affirms the principle that: "Ways shall be found to involve programme beneficiaries in the management of relief aid." The article specifies that "disaster response should never be imposed" on people and that it is done best when people "are involved in the design, management and implementation of assistance programmes".

It goes on to say that "we will strive to achieve full community participation in our relief and rehabilitation programmes". This principle logically precedes Articles 5 and 6 because it sets out the basic good of human agency and participation, which is the prerequisite of local capacity and sustainability.

Participation is a fundamental ingredient in the principle of humanity itself. Being human means being actively oneself and engaged with others. Our ability to participate—to become, to build, to share, to join in and to contribute—is a dynamic of humanity itself. It is the conscious agency of our personal being that distinguishes our humanity from mere existence. True being is participation in individual and communal activities that create our own goods and enable us to share in the common goods around us. So we must count participation as a basic good in human life. The ability to join in and become personally involved in society is a fundamental value in modern Western philosophies. We find it in the sociability or friendship that John Finnis identifies as one of his seven basic goods, and in the practical reasonableness that enables us to engage actively and wisely in the world.[9] In less individualistic and non-Western societies, participation and collective identities often make much more sense to people than the West's emphasis on the individual. Being part of a community is often people's primary experience of life. For people in many communities, the pronoun "we" can be more instinctive than the singular "I", but their individual agency and involvement is still central to this more collective sense of identity.

Participation is also a good that brings about other goods. Participation is enabling of wider benefits as well as a pleasurable good in itself. Participation is at the heart of Amartya Sen's idea of freedom as the mainspring of human development. By being able to participate in the world around us, we are free to "convert" the goods we hold within us and between us and to make the most of the opportunities we have before us.[10] Participation is essential in two of Martha Nussbaum's ten "central capabilities" that "enable people to pursue a dignified and minimally flourishing life". Participation is central to "affiliation", which is the capability "to live with and toward others, to recognize and show concern for human beings, to engage in various forms of social interaction". Participation is also the core of Nussbaum's tenth capability: "having control over one's environment", which means "being able to participate effectively in political choices that govern one's life ... having property rights on an equal basis with others ... and being able to work as a human being".[11] Legally, the basic good of participation is encapsulated in human rights law, which regards participation as a fundamental human right in the Universal Declaration of Human Rights. This right also makes clear that everybody has a responding duty to contribute to their community, without which their full development will not be possible.[12]

When we participate justly in shaping our own lives or in building the common good, we find our personal dignity by building and realizing our capabilities. This participation can take the form of work, governance or simple enjoyment in a friendship, a birth, a wedding or a meal.[13] When we are prevented from participating in the making of our lives, we soon feel this lack as an indignity and impoverishment. We lose our subjectivity and inter-subjectivity and are relegated to exist as the object of others. They decide things for us, give things to us, parade above us and tell us what to do. People still achieve great personal dignity waiting in a queue, being illiterate, being fed by another or being pushed in a wheelchair. This is usually because they have a deep sense of self and are still in active and equal contact with people in other parts of their lives where they are respected as themselves. But there can be significant indignity in a humanitarian operation when people from outside rush in to solve your problems without consulting and involving you, drive big cars that spew dust in your face and then make all sorts of decisions over your head.

The ethical and political justifications of participation inherent in this principle are again complemented by a more practical moral insight from development ethics. Participation is also good because it works. But it is seldom simple. Community development practice has long focused on participation and has noted gradations of participation in the relationships between aid agency and community. These gradations make clear that not all participation is qualitatively the same. The most popular model of participation is the "ladder of participation" whose rungs climb from activities that are essentially non-participation (like manipulation, tokenism and decoration) through mid-states of participation (like consultation and placation) to full participation at the top (like partnership and control).[14]

Consent

There is a significant social science to participation that analyses who you include and how you include them. Article 7 sets out the aspirational principle of striving for "full community participation". This is rightly ambitious and puts an obligation on humanitarian staff and affected people to work closely together in a wise and effective way that reaps the benefits of people's dignified inclusion and involvement without becoming bogged down in bureaucratic process or creating isolated humanitarian structures that sideline people from proper and inclusive state governance. This is the careful approach taken in the ALNAP/URD Participation Handbook for Humanitarian Fieldworkers.[15]

There is a persistent criticism that NGO participation schemes depoliticize people's real traction on hard mainstream politics by creating soft parallel participation structures that are time-consuming and stand apart from real politics.[16] This critique is significant, and the ideal of "full participation" in humanitarian programmes would best involve working towards a model of "active citizenship" of the kind recommended by John Gaventa.[17] A citizenship approach keeps people's participation politically engaged and connected with the duties and obligation of the state and local authorities wherever possible. This is rightly the trend in armed conflicts and disasters where international humanitarian law (IHL) and the development of national and international disaster law makes people's suffering and recovery a serious political responsibility for governments. There are, of course, important exceptions to the wisdom of mainstreaming humanitarian participation within national politics. When governance is dangerous, genocidal or kleptocratic, it may well be best to set up parallel humanitarian structures that buffer and protect people from their government. In certain situations, the most dangerous thing you can do to a community is to connect it with its government.

In medical and business ethics, the principle of consent has become increasingly important as a means and measure of people's active involvement in medical and business decisions that affect their lives. The principle of free, prior and informed consent (FPIC) is one that could usefully contribute to the principle of participation in humanitarian ethics.[18] The key ingredients of the FPIC process would suit humanitarian operations especially at a stage when full participation is not feasible. In an FPIC process, first an individual or group's consent must be free and not forced. In line with Article 7, therefore, people could not have aid programmes or strategies "imposed" upon them.[19] Secondly, the process of consent cannot be retroactive but must precede humanitarian action as much as possible so that people can be involved prior to and before things happen. Thirdly, people need to be properly informed of the purpose and process of humanitarian programmes if they are to consent meaningfully. Many agencies constantly pursue active FPIC strategies (whether consciously or unconsciously) in vaccination programmes, family tracing programmes, food and cash transfers and protection work. It may be useful to formalize consent (and its free, prior and informed conditions) as a firm part of humanitarian ethics. Consent is obviously not full participation but it is an important part of it and may be an essential ethical principle in periods of humanitarian activity that cannot reasonably achieve full participation.

Dignified Human Imagery

Article 10, the last article in the Code of Conduct referring to humanitarian agencies, reads: "In our information, publicity and advertising activity, we shall recognize disaster victims as dignified humans, not hopeless objects." This article requires that agencies use ethical imagery and discourse in representations of people's suffering and experience in armed conflicts and disasters. This article also concerns people's dignity. It prioritizes "respect for the disaster victim" and rightly commits agencies to provide "an objective image of the disaster situation where the capacities and aspirations of disaster victims are highlighted, and not just their vulnerabilities and fears". It also makes clear that it will not let media priorities, inter-agency competition or internal agency demands trump this commitment to a dignified and balanced representation of people's experience of disaster.

Article 10 determines to put an end to a tradition of selective, manipulative, infantilizing and even sadistic and racist imagery in aid agency advertising. Urgent humanitarian advertising is designed with an essentially commercial purpose: to elicit maximum donations from the public. Raising people's consciousness about the causes of poverty and crisis is a significant but usually a secondary objective in such appeals. Aid agencies have consistently used explicit bodily representations (often semi-naked, female and infant) of individuals suffering from hunger, destitution and injury. Combined with the commercial goal involved, this has repeatedly created a strong sense of moral revulsion in people within suffering communities, as well as in agencies and across the general public. Many people associate these forms of images with the exploitative sex industry.

Humanitarian advertising has, therefore, been regularly and critically described as "disaster pornography".[20] In contrast, balancing dignified images of suffering with "positive imaging" of people as survivors has been rightly regarded as more truthful and respectful.

These ethical instincts on certain degrading forms of humanitarian advertising are sound. In the classic *pieta*-like[21] humanitarian image of the rag-wearing desperate mother cradling her starved and dying child, there is undoubtedly the dynamic of a commercial enterprise selling anonymous bodies for money without the knowledge and full consent of the people concerned. More sinister still, with its racist and supremacist overtones, are similar pictures in which the victims are passive and mute as they are being "saved" by a medic who sits or stands above them, complete with visual cues of Western medical technology and higher powers. This imaging and its attendant us-and-them discourse of agency and victim is morally problematic for two main reasons. First, it is incomplete as a version of events and is therefore deceptive. It tends to tell half-truths. For example, imagery of a suffering mother and child sitting in a camp may fail to show the great lengths to which these two people and those close to them (but not in the picture) may already have gone in order to survive. Their courage and survival may be truly heroic for the many days' journey they have made to this clinic. Hidden behind the image of the white aid worker may be the fact that the great majority of humanitarian workers helping these particular people (but not in the picture) are from their own society. Secondly, by perpetrating this incomplete and potentially racist myth of emergency, agencies also do moral damage to the viewers by misinforming them and skewing their perceptions.[22]

These images and their discourse serve as propaganda or pornography that might encourage viewers to look down upon certain fellow human beings in distant parts of the world. By constructing such a distorted gaze upon people struggling to survive, these images run the risk of encouraging an essential disregard for distant others rather than an equal and compassionate regard. This disregard may still produce money (even from feelings of superiority) but it is unlikely to encourage care, respect and human solidarity. It is more likely to foster the dangerous pity inherent in paternalism that is discussed later in Chapter 9. Instead of increasing understanding, it may simply raise unfair and despairing remarks like: "What's wrong with these people? Why is it always the same and why are they always in trouble?"

These negative images highlight the moral problems of humanitarian advertising and agency mis-selling of suffering and aid. Humanitarian advertising will always be inhumane and wrong when it degrades people, misinforms people and encourages disdain alongside charity. But the ethical problems of humanitarian advertising are not confined to the subject matter of suffering alone. Advertising is by nature morally problematic. It is a profession that deliberately deceives, eroticizes, sublimates and lures: this detergent is much better than all the others; this beer will make you friends; you could have a mid-life love affair with this new car instead of a mistress. Although the implication is often that the former will helpfully lead to the latter: this flashy red credit card will solve your problems and win you respect; this face cream will keep you young. Advertising naturally defaults to illusion unless it is given very firm instructions otherwise. In advertising agencies, therefore, humanitarian ethics has another encounter with a type of organization with which it must cooperate to succeed but which does not necessarily or naturally share all its principles and goals. To raise money ethically for humanitarian action, humanitarian agencies must work very deliberately with advertising agencies to represent suffering, survival and recovery in a way that raises money and simultaneously preserves the humanity of both givers and receivers.

This process need not involve some sort of positive whitewash. Endless images of cheerful survivors would be equally unethical. People's suffering in armed conflicts and disasters is real and excruciating. It does indeed involve destitution, the loss of clothing, the wasting of limbs and the emotional agony of looking on the death of those you love. We need this suffering to be felt and imagined by others if Hume's general law of sympathy is to be leveraged into the funds needed to respond. In this moral mobilization, after the insight of Levinas and others, we also need people's faces to be obvious to us as the main site of their humanity and the clearest revelation of their individual lives. By seeing a person's face, we can most easily recognize them as people like us.

Marketing and finance directors of humanitarian agencies know that showing individual suffering works and increases donations. Paul Slovic's work on the psychic numbing that takes place when we are faced with large numbers in trouble reinforces their instincts.[23] If the individual representation of suffering can be done ethically and lucratively, it serves the double purpose of dignity and donation. Suffering must not be avoided in humanitarian advertising, but it must be represented with respect, without any hint of racism or superiority, and with more consent than has often been the case in agency appeals to date.

Labelling People in Humanitarian Discourse

The word "beneficiary" is used throughout the Code of Conduct and in humanitarian discourse generally as a label to describe people who receive humanitarian assistance or protection. Beneficiary comes from the Latin words *bene* and *facere* meaning to do good. People who are beneficiaries are therefore people who have benefited from something or someone. In English, the word became a key contractual term in the English law of charity and trusts. Every charity was established to benefit certain groups of needy people. These beneficiaries subsequently had certain claims on money earmarked for their good. Legally, therefore, the idea of a beneficiary comes with certain rights and entitlements. However, in charitable discourse it has also tended to embody the power differential between giver and receiver in a way that puts the beneficiaries of a charity in an inferior position: lucky to have been chosen, and required to show some gratitude for the gifts they have received.

The need for a single, simple label to work as a catch-all term in humanitarian action and reporting is understandable. Businesses and public services have customers and clients. The medical profession has patients, derived from *patiens*, the Latin word for one who suffers. Airlines and railway companies have passengers. Humanitarian professionals have beneficiaries. But I have never been comfortable with this word and always avoid it, as I have done throughout this book. My doubts stem from observing the word being degraded into a term of disrespect in the mouths of some humanitarian workers, and being rejected as a passive label by disaster-affected communities themselves. Often frustrated and exhausted in difficult situations, humanitarian workers can be heard almost spitting out the word sometimes. Like bad shopkeepers and harassed bus drivers who start seeing their customers and passengers as the problem in their business, some humanitarian workers come to see "the beneficiaries" as the problem in a project which would run much more smoothly without them. I have also noticed that when I used the word myself, I quickly lost sight of the fact that I was thinking and talking about people, most of whom were having a terrible time.

Like all labels we use to categorize things, the word beneficiary can evolve to encompass the category alone, no longer conjuring up the individuality of those within. The same thing happens with terms like the rich, the poor, peasants, landlords, Protestants, Catholics, Sunni, Shia, criminals and saints. Each of these labels can take on a pernicious meaning over time that reflects the power differences and bias of their users. At worst, these categories become terms of abuse. Using the abstract and essentially bureaucratic word "beneficiary" to refer to people in humanitarian operations runs three particular moral risks:

- Firstly, the very word assumes that people are benefiting, and only benefiting. It continuously and subconsciously reinforces the idea that people are passive and not active in their own survival. They benefit but do not contribute. Beyond these implications about personal agency, the label also assumes that what beneficiaries receive does actually benefit them and is indeed good (beneficent). So, if I talk all the time of beneficiaries in my project I will inevitably and unconsciously lose a sense of objectivity about the quality of the project. I will be less likely to think about the potential maleficence of the project or the difficulty of people's experience.
- Secondly, labelling is lumping. By calling everybody beneficiaries we tend towards generalized thinking that assumes that people in communities are all the same, have experienced the same things, need the same things and should get the same things. Lumping inhibits nuanced thinking about people's diversity, which we know to be so important in humanitarian programming.
- Thirdly, when we talk about people in categories we can begin to de-humanize them. Refusing to talk about people as people is the first step in the numbing and negative reframing that is so critical to the construction of enmity.[24] This is obviously a long way from how humanitarian workers view people they are trying to help, but the risks of numbing and de-humanizing are possible in humanitarian work if we constantly talk about people as an abstract category rather than as men, women, children, young or old people. As a general moral rule, the more personal we are in the language with which we talk and think about people, the more humane we are likely to be.

Humanitarian action has other labels for people, notably: civilians, non-combatants, refugees and IDPs. The first three of these labels have very specific status in international law, and the fourth is increasingly gaining such a status. Like any labels, these terms carry the negative risks of lumping and de-humanizing, but this risk is significantly reduced by the very idea of dignity and rights they carry with them from the law. Because of this inherent status, it is wiser and more respectful of people to use these labels when it is necessary or unavoidable to talk about general categories of person in humanitarian discourse.

The other conventional humanitarian term is "victim". This label is an important one because of its emphasis on criminally imposed suffering or tragic accident, and is more widely used in the continental European tradition of humanitarian action than in Britain and North America. However, while the victim label is legally powerful and demands a certain reciprocal duty to punish the perpetrator and repair the damage, the word can smother people with an overwhelming and incomplete identity they do not want or are seeking to overcome. There is also a danger that humanitarian action has political interests in creating and sustaining victim identities as an unconscious part of its global expansion around the world.[25] So-called "victim consciousness" is a mixed emotion that comes with strengths and weaknesses in different phases of survival. Victim is not usually an identity that serves people well in the long term. This is clearly shown in Holocaust studies, where people prefer to be called "Holocaust survivors"; or in the field of health, where people prefer to be known as "people living with HIV" rather than "AIDS victims". Once again, the moral rule is to focus on people's humanity: on who they are and not on what has happened to them.

The dignity principles in humanitarian ethics emphasize that enabling people to restore and achieve their dignity in the practical method of humanitarian programmes is a moral obligation with deep roots in the principle of humanity itself. The next concern of humanitarian ethics is to make such improvements last and to show humanitarian effect to those who have invested in it or are entitled to it. These are the questions of sustainability and accountability.

5

STEWARDSHIP PRINCIPLES

SUSTAINABILITY AND ACCOUNTABILITY

The current elaboration of humanitarian ethics has rightly focused on sustainability and accountability as central to its sense of moral obligation. These two concerns are really about good stewardship: how humanitarians can wisely care for their resources and the future.

Sustainability of effect is an ancient humanitarian concern that runs deep in all philanthropic manifestations of responsible giving. There is a long-held idea dating back to ancient times that the best charity changes a person's abilities and opportunities and does not only meet their immediate needs. Environmental sustainability is a more modern incorporation into humanitarian ethics, but one that is now pressing. Accountability is also a traditional moral principle in most forms of mediated distributions of aid in which many individuals give through a single organization. It is widely agreed that they have "a right to know where their money has gone". Increasingly, however, humanitarian agencies have recognized that they also need to account for their actions to the people they are trying to help, and not only to the people who finance their operations.

The Sustainability Principle

Article 8 of the Code declares: "Relief aid must strive to reduce future vulnerabilities to disaster as well as meeting basic needs." This is the ethical concern for the sustainability of human goods. The Code shows a proper awareness that all humanitarian aid will have wider and longer effects than immediate humanitarian effects alone. Responsibility for these wider and longer effects requires agencies to think how their programmes can function positively and negatively now and in the future. Article 8 identifies positive effects as especially related to creating "sustainable lifestyles", respecting "environmental concerns", "reducing future vulnerabilities" and avoiding long-term "dependence upon external aid".

Because it is thinking long term, this principle is the one most concerned with the consequences of aid. It makes a firm commitment to account for the intended and unintended effects of humanitarian action, recognizing that aid inevitably has a wider impact even when its primary intention is to meet immediate needs. It also makes clear that many of the consequences of aid should be deliberately positive by ensuring that people's lives are better than they were before the crisis and by helping to prevent future suffering. This ethic is well encapsulated in Bill Clinton's strapline for tsunami aid: "Build Back Better". With this vision of lasting improvement and positive consequences in mind, Article 8 requires humanitarians to operate with several horizons in view: now, soon and later. This very consequentialist principle raises two important points in humanitarian ethics: the moral significance of sustainability in humanitarian work, and the limits of humanitarian responsibility for negative outcomes.

If humanitarian ethics is about balancing principles to ensure basic goods in emergencies, then how far can we reasonably expect humanitarian agencies to set goals around multiple and complex goods like the various dimensions of sustainability? Sustainability typically concerns environmental protection, livelihoods and lifestyle, often summarized as the three pillars of sustainability: ecological, economic and social.[1] At first glance, this is a much bigger moral project than the principle of humanity's goal of preserving and protecting the human person in armed conflict and disaster. In view of the scale of long-term problems, does sustainability fall fairly within the scope of humanitarian ethics? The answer must be yes and no. No because humanitarian agencies are not ethically focused on environmental, economic or lifestyle change. This is not their primary intention or their main ethical concern. They cannot be expected to be environmental agencies. Yes because ethics evolve and develop.

New problems arise or a new moral consciousness emerges around things that were once regarded as acceptable (like slavery, racism and misogyny) but are now better understood as unacceptable. Our constant ethical development means that new attitudes and new forms of behaviour become morally significant, creating new duties and new rights. Environmental sustainability is an issue that has rightly achieved new moral significance and now imposes obligations on us all.

This means that humanitarian agencies do have environmental duties without being environmental agencies. These duties are not primary or equal to their humanitarian goal, but they are important subsidiary ethical obligations that should guide the way they work to achieve humanitarian goals. When humanitarian agencies have any contact with the environment, they must take into account reasonable considerations of sustainability. This is particularly true in the way they use energy, consume natural resources and exploit land, or encourage affected populations to do so.

Environmental concerns first impinged upon humanitarian ethics when massive volumes of firewood were consumed in refugee and IDP camps. This dramatically deforested large areas which local people living around these emergency settlements relied upon for their present and future needs. Relief packaging, medical waste and general waste from humanitarian camps were also soon recognized as causing serious problems of pollution. Increasingly, therefore, humanitarian agencies need to think about their energy footprint in their distribution models, particularly around food aid. As cash-based transfers prove equal to or better than direct food deliveries, agencies need to think about how best to reduce intercontinental shipments and increase local purchase, with its shorter supply lines and locally sustainable livelihoods. NGOs should also be helping to pioneer new low-energy vehicles, just as they have already adopted solar power for offices, computers and mobile phones. Greening the humanitarian profession is now rightly a significant part of humanitarian ethics.

The Code is right to point up the ethical significance of economic sustainability too. One of the great insights of humanitarian action in the last twenty years, led by Sue Lautze and others, has been that good humanitarian action should be focused on "saving lives and livelihoods" or "saving lives through livelihoods".[2] This is because one of the best ways to keep people alive with dignity is by preserving the livelihood that sustains them physically, socially and economically. This means that humanitarian responsibilities for "creating sustainable lifestyles" are similar but not identical to their environmental responsibilities. Article 8's concern for "sustainable lifestyles" seems to refer mainly to economic and social sustainability: how a family's livelihood earns them a living, and how the investment and consumption patterns of this livelihood are able to last over time for one generation without destroying the livelihood of the next generation.

Here, in economic realities, many humanitarian agencies have a very direct moral responsibility for sustainability, because agencies are often deliberately and significantly intervening in people's economic lives with programmes which aim to recover old livelihoods or invent new ones. In this process, Article 8 asserts that agencies must focus on sustainability by "reducing [people's] future vulnerabilities" and boosting their capacities to withstand future crises and shocks.[3] In areas of earthquake risk, this might mean building stronger housing, advocating for improved land rights, building regulations and safer urban zoning so that when an earthquake strikes next, people are safer than they were before. In a war-induced famine, it may mean supporting pastoralists with improved water points and pre-arranged strategies of livestock de-stocking and marketing to prevent animal deaths, asset depletion and destitution.[4] Either way, it means thinking about the future and doing more than saving lives. Inside this emphasis on reducing future vulnerabilities, the moral idea of prevention is nested carefully but silently within the current Code. Article 8 allows for humanitarian action to think both short and longer term, and to focus on sustainability and prevention as well as life-saving.

Obviously, humanitarian agencies can offer the bare essentials. They can just "give a man a fish" if he is hungry, or give someone "a bed for the night" if they are homeless.[5] This is often a good thing to do, especially if an agency cannot do more and the people concerned do not need more. But if people need more and an agency can do more, then ethical demands change. Livelihoods rightly enter into the question, the moral horizon is extended and sustainability and prevention become significant moral principles in humanitarian action. Peter Redfield quotes an MSF field coordinator summing up this proper moral shift in Northern Uganda in 2004: "At first the focus is not to die. Then come other questions of living."[6]

The future is morally important. Human relationships are such that if I help you now, I retain some residue of responsibility for helping you in the future too. You carry my responsibility with you somehow as a moral asset and it sits with me as a moral liability. In friendship this is routine, as friends call upon each other's help even if they have not been especially close for several years. In modern commerce, this sustained responsibility often takes contractual form in a five-year guarantee for the car you bought, or a one-month guarantee for the computer you got repaired. Responsibilities have futures and last; obligations thicken with the deepening relationships we have with one another. If aid agencies have been alongside communities for several long years of war, they begin to share a common horizon and try to do things together in the present that will last into the future, like resilience planning and programming.[7] Ethics stretch across past, present and future. What we have done and what we are doing with people creates legitimate expectations of what we will do for their future, and what we will do in the future if we are called upon again. People have sustainable claims and obligations. This sense of sustained humanitarian responsibility that stretches into the future seems morally right but cannot be limitless. An agency's responsibility for people's futures must always be dependent on an agency's current capacity and on the relative importance of competing calls on its services in the present. The quintessential example of these limits is the ubiquitous "seeds and tools" rehabilitation package in rural humanitarian programmes. Helping people return to their farming livelihoods after encampment and asset depletion from drought or armed conflict is often as much as an agency can do to engage in a family's future. Seeds and tools are a very practical moral send-off that takes limited responsibility for the future and plays a minimal role in people's livelihood sustainability. Often, this is all an agency can reasonably manage. But when it can do more, it should.

The risk of "dependency" so clearly flagged in Article 8 requires special attention because it represents the iconic fear of all helping professions. Actors dread "drying up" on stage and forgetting their words; business people dread running out of money; soldiers dread being found to be a coward in battle; humanitarians dread making people dependent, sapped of initiative and poorer than before. Good helping is about re-empowering people, so if people are disempowered in the humanitarian process and rendered totally dependent on aid, something has gone badly wrong.

Dysfunctional aid dependency is certainly not desirable in humanitarian aid and should be counted as a failure in most instances. But not all dependency is wrong in itself and not every dysfunctional dependency is the fault of humanitarian agencies. Humanitarian scholars distinguish between positive dependency and negative dependency in aid.[8] Positive dependency is "when an individual, household or community cannot meet its immediate basic needs without external assistance".[9] This dependency is a good thing if it serves to be "welfare enhancing" and protects people from destitution. It shows aid serving a valuable moral purpose. In countries with no effective health and social services, people are often genuinely and importantly dependent on external aid. For example, children fighting for their lives in an NGO therapeutic feeding centre during a famine or adults being treated for HIV by US-funded retroviral programmes in IDP camps in Northern Uganda are certainly dependent on aid. These situations are a highly functional and morally valuable dependence.

Negative dependency is when "meeting current needs comes at the cost of reducing people's capacities to meet their own needs now and in the future".[10] This kind of dysfunctional dependence happens when aid creates disincentives for food and labour markets to function effectively, or creates disincentives in individual behaviour that stop people pursuing previous livelihoods because they are not compatible with staying close to aid distributions. Some negative dependency arises because humanitarian practice is just bad. It creates aid magnets that pull people away from their socio-economic networks to isolate them in a recipient-only zone that creates disincentives for more active coping strategies. Without reasonable justification, such practice would be a moral failing.

The risk and fear of dysfunctional and unethical "aid dependency" is probably overblown by anti-aid media pundits and anxious NGOs. The great majority of vulnerable people suffering from armed conflict or disaster do not want to be dependent on a humanitarian organization. Instead, like most of us, they prize financial independence and personal autonomy. People in crisis typically set out to invest actively in a range of survival strategies that function as a sort of coping portfolio for an extended family. This usually involves a division of labour and risk-spreading of some kind. Some members of a family will take a stake in the benefits of a relief camp or regular relief distributions. Others will stay near the family livelihood (the farm, herd, shop or former employer) to try to preserve and leverage opportunities as they arise. Others will travel far to seek migrant work or refugee status. Some people may deviously play the aid system with multiple registrations in a way that is immoral but more entrepreneurial than hopelessly dependent. Most people who have suffered want to get on and recover, and aid is very seldom estimated to make up the major part of an average family's overall survival strategy.

The Principle of Accountability

Article 9 of the Code states that: "We hold ourselves accountable to both those we seek to assist and those from whom we accept resources." This principle is concerned to meet the rightful expectations of the two key "constituencies" to whom humanitarian agencies are morally and financially accountable: the individuals and institutions who give money or aid, and the people who receive it. This principle understands humanitarian agencies as the "link" between the two groups, so playing a practical mediating role between the intentions of one and the needs of the other for which it must be accountable in an "attitude of openness and transparency". It recognizes accountability as relating to finances as well as "effectiveness", "impact", "limiting factors" and minimizing "the wasting of valuable resources". It also makes clear that "our programmes will be based upon high standards of professionalism and expertise". This last point is important because it makes plain that humanitarian agencies expect to be judged as expert professionals rather than well-intentioned amateurs. This implies that the only mitigating factors they will claim in any failures of effectiveness and financial reporting will be external ones of context and circumstance beyond their professional control. They guarantee their essential skill and expertise.

The Ethical Importance of Evidence

Accountability in ethics is very important. It is about taking responsibility for one's intentions and actions. As such, it is a vital ethical principle in humanitarian action, just as it is in any individual or collective enterprise. Accountability requires evidence. Agencies need to be able to "know and show" what they have intended, decided, done, and the results that have flowed from their actions.[11] The importance of evidence in determining moral responsibility makes the process of gathering evidence a very significant ethical activity, which should be more clearly spelt out in humanitarian ethics. Ideally, humanitarian professionals need to gather evidence before they act, while they are acting and after they have stopped. Without it, they will struggle to be held accountable in any meaningful way.[12]

But what is a feasible assessment of humanitarian action? Armed conflicts and disasters can be extremely confused events in societies which have very limited means to gather effective information. More than this, knowing everything has always been impossible for human beings. Humanitarian accountability should, therefore, be looking for some kind of optimal rather than absolute knowledge of results in a given situation. The reasons for this are twofold:

- Firstly, it is necessary to gauge the effects of humanitarian action in order to improve the targeting and programming for those who are suffering from war and disaster. This aspect of accountability is about an agency taking responsibility for what it has done already, and learning to improve its competence for the future.
- Secondly, Agencies need to be able to report back to the communities involved, and to the individuals and institutions that have provided financial support on the condition it be used for humanitarian purposes. Payments to humanitarian agencies are wrongly described as donations and gifts. They may be gifts in accounting terms, but in their ethical intent they are much more than gifts. They are specific investments in humanitarian operations that carry a high expectation of a very particular return.[13] This humanitarian return must be accounted for and discussed as part of the moral contract between investor and agency.

In short, if a humanitarian agency does not know the useful and significant facts about what it is doing, then it runs the moral risk of doing things badly and deceiving people who trust the organization and are investing in it.

Operational effects are complicated to assess. Rightly, there is a deep discussion across the humanitarian sector about how best to measure and report results. This discussion moves between simple quantitative measures of humanitarian input and output, that count food tonnage delivered or lives saved, to more subtle assessments of humanitarian outcome and impact. First-order responsibilities of accounting for quantitative measures are very important and must be collected and reported. They are immediate results that refer directly to humanitarian action's fundamental goal of preserving human life. Agencies need to know as well as possible the details of their activities and distributions, and the immediate results in terms of human life and health. More complicated is the second-order responsibility to gauge the more comprehensive impact of humanitarian action. The wider effects of humanitarian action—both intended and unintended—are morally important. They are spelled out positively and negatively in the Code, which makes clear that simply saving lives is not sufficient in humanitarian action. For example, dignity, capacity-building and resilience are positive wider impacts, which are properly intended in humanitarian action; negative impacts, like indignity, increasing the risk of violence or environmental damage, are equally significant as wider impact.

Impact is often difficult to gauge precisely. Oxfam's Chris Roche and others have long pointed out that there are significant evidential problems with assessing impact, turning on problems of measurement, attribution, aggregation and ownership.[14] What are the best things to measure in a particular operation, and how easy is it to measure these things well? How can an agency compare its interventions to measure them against a "without scenario" in which it had not intervened, or had opted for another kind of intervention instead? How much are certain outcomes (like better health, safety or greater danger) directly attributable to an agency's action or to the actions of other actors? How can an agency add up and aggregate the many different things it does (therapeutic feeding, international advocacy and capacity-building) to assess its overall impact? Who is prepared to own impact failure when careers and agency reputations depend on success? All this means that assessing impact is technically and politically difficult, but agencies must try to do what is reasonable, and point out what remains uncertain. It is not enough just to report input and output numbers; outcomes and impact must be assessed as much as possible, and people have a right to be alerted to intended and unintended consequences in advance and retrospectively. As we shall see in Chapter 8, good ethical deliberation can be the first step in flagging wider impacts of various kinds.

Value for Money

Value for money is a very important aspect of humanitarian ethics and relates to the Code's concern of not wasting valuable resources. Again, this is a correct moral instinct and an essential principle in humanitarian accountability, just as it is in all areas of life. Writing about medical practice, Aristotle famously noted that there are only two kinds of mistake: "we either fail in working things out, or fail in attention when we are putting things into effect".[15] Similarly, there seem to be two potential types of wastage in humanitarian action: one born of miscalculation, and the other of carelessness. Mistakes born of carelessness are not as complicated as calculations of relative value. For example, if a UN agency has a large stock of vaccines in a hot and humid part of Eastern Congo and it fails to keep these humanitarian resources in optimal cool storage conditions so that they are ruined, then the agency has wasted these valuable resources because of negligence and incompetence. If an NGO in Somalia loses $50,000 to thieves during a cash relief programme because its security measures were unnecessarily lax, then this too is a careless waste. Calculations of value for money, however, can be complicated. They tend to involve more consequentialist thinking about the best use of resources. For example, will an agency achieve better humanitarian value by investing in a high-cost therapeutic feeding programme that reaches 2,000 malnourished children in an IDP camp, or a rapid market intervention that gives a similar amount of cash to local merchants to import food into the district and drive down prices in an area? The first project may save 2,000 children; the second project may reach 10,000 families with malnourished children, addressing both adult and infant malnutrition, and preventing further displacement.

In an article on cost-effectiveness in global health care, Oxford philosopher Toby Ord starts with an even more striking example of value for money decision-making:

> Suppose we have a $40,000 budget that we can spend as we wish to fight blindness. One thing we could do is to provide a guide dog to a blind person in the United States to help them overcome their disability. This costs about $40,000 because of the training required for the dog and its recipient. Another option is to pay for surgeries that reverse the effects of trachoma in Africa. This costs less than $20 per patient cured [and would] cure more than 2000 people of blindness.[16]

Ord suggests that if we think that people are of equal moral value, then the second option is more than 2,000 times better than the first, which would waste about 99.95 per cent of the potential value of the original £40,000. This is an extreme example because it can rightly be argued that US health budgets have a first moral call on US citizens. But Ord's kind of utilitarian thinking must play a part in humanitarian programming and accountability. It is clear that some humanitarian interventions offer much better value than others and they must be prioritized wherever possible, or included as part of a spectrum of interventions when higher cost interventions for certain individuals may also be justified. Value for money is essentially a matter of fairness and equity in the allocation of resources between people. Cost-effectiveness demands that we examine what is the most reasonable course of action when we are faced with many similar needs and limited resources. If we are careless in seeking value for money, we may well breach the principle of impartiality by discriminating in favour of a small group who are receiving high-cost and inefficient interventions while others remain poorly served or ignored.

The UK government's thinking on value for money in aid is perhaps the simplest to follow. The UK's Department for International Development (DFID) emphasizes "the three Es: economy, efficiency and effectiveness" as a guide to making value for money decisions.[17] Cheapest is certainly not necessarily best value, but the relative cost and effectiveness of different programmes must be weighed. In the 2011 famine in south central Somalia, access to food was the essential priority for hundreds of thousands of people. Large food delivery programmes were costly and inefficient because of serious access problems. Instead of waiting for improved access, UNICEF's Hannan Sulieman led an innovative NGO consortium that delivered $92 million of cash transfers into the area via the Hawala network of Somali banking. Both food and cash transfers were too late to save the 257,000 people who died in the famine, but the cash transfers were a more cost-effective way of responding. They were more economical, and more efficient, and more widely effective than simple food rations, because of the greater autonomy and participation they encouraged in Somali women. Even though a small percentage of funds were misdirected and abused, the level of corruption was also less than with in-kind aid like food.[18] Designing and reporting on programmes with value for money or cost-effectiveness in mind is, therefore, a significant imperative in humanitarian ethics and must be recognized as integral to Article 9 of the Code.

Humanitarian Stakeholders

The Code's emphasis on two-way accountability focuses on two major types of stakeholder: sometimes known as upward accountability (to donors) and downward accountability (to people who receive aid).[19] This vertical imagery is unfortunate because it implies a hierarchy; it is therefore best avoided. It might be better to talk simply about investor and recipient accountability.

The binary bias of current thinking on accountability in the Code is not entirely realistic. Humanitarian organizations certainly have to be accountable to investors and recipients of aid, but not only to these groups. They also have to account to local and national authorities that are responsible for governing the areas in which they work. They have to account to people they have decided not to help. In practice, explaining why some individuals and groups are not getting aid takes up quite a lot of the day job of many frontline humanitarian workers. Agencies also need to be accountable to one another as they plan complementary programmes and develop collective action. In reality, humanitarian accountability is a more 360-degree responsibility than is currently presented in Article 9.

Nevertheless, there is a particular moral and operational intimacy in the relationship between an agency and its investors, and between an agency and the people it helps. It is right that both relationships receive particular attention in matters of accountability. Ideally, investors, agencies and recipients will all share deep humanitarian goals, as they are described in humanitarian principles, and they should be able to speak openly and transparently with one another in verbal and written monitoring and evaluation reports. To do so requires honesty and cooperation on all sides; but frankly, this is hard to achieve.

Institutional donors, humanitarian agencies and people in need of aid are often defensive and struggling with hard problems of self-interest alongside wider concerns for how the overall programme is performing. In my experience, donor government officials are seldom content to be as transparent as they ask others to be. UN agencies are also notoriously selective about what they report, because they are seeking to protect turf, careers and reputations. NGOs are wary of a bad report that may dramatically affect their income and organizational survival. People affected by conflict or disaster find it hard to treat any assessment or evaluation interview at face value, naturally concerned that it may have an influence on what they receive now or in the future. The humanitarian sector is not alone in these problems of honesty. But this big dose of political realism makes humanitarian accountability difficult, and explains why its significance is still token rather than transformative within the international system of humanitarian action. Accountability and evaluation are usually hived off to social scientists and smooth-talking accountability bureaucrats in UN agencies and NGOs. They tend to obscure the ethical importance of taking responsibility by reframing accountability as technically complex, so obscuring the simplicity of its greater political problem of truth-telling.

Even within such entrenched truth-telling problems, there are important things that can be achieved in humanitarian accountability. Because these are feasible, they must be achieved. Finances can and should be tracked and audited to high standards. Certain key humanitarian outcomes can be agreed in every programme along the chain of stakeholders, starting with recipients and agencies (who, together, can best define positive outcomes) and including local authorities, national government, other cooperating agencies and donors. These may be as simple as clear food security measures, health status targets, levels of safety, dignity indicators and numbers of people reached. From a clear identification of targeted outcomes, judgements about the efficiency of inputs and outputs can be made, and an overall view of effectiveness becomes possible.

Accountability to Humanitarian Principles

Essential to any humanitarian accountability is a sense of a programme's alignment with humanitarian principles. The conduct of humanitarian ethics in any operation must itself be an essential measure of effectiveness to gauge how far the programme was humane, impartial, neutral, independent, dignifying, capacity-building, participative and sustainable. It is amazing how seldom specific ethical accountability is demanded in humanitarian evaluations; more often they tend to be obsessed with agreeing a narrative of events, estimating timeliness, connectedness and efficiency, but ignore ethics.[20]

Another unacceptable bias in humanitarian accountability is its predominant focus on donor accountability. This is not surprising because, at the moment, donor demands come with more political pressure, more financial risk and much more bureaucracy than accountability to recipients. So far in humanitarian history, the risk of losing a major donor is much more likely to keep a humanitarian chief executive awake at night than the likelihood of an uprising by dissatisfied recipients or a community boycott of agency aid. This is not the case for the chief executives of mining companies, and it may soon change for humanitarian executives too. However, this paper bias may also suggest that many humanitarian agencies are already good at recipient accountability and are doing it all the time, if not actually writing about it. It may be in their DNA and come more naturally than donor accountability.

Good humanitarian professionals spend a lot of time explaining what they are doing and why. Most frontline workers have to give a constant running commentary on their project's rationale to individuals and community leaders to justify decisions and explain aid objectives and criteria. Humanitarians are getting better at formalizing this information-sharing as they now develop appropriate reporting methods for local communities and set up routine grievance procedures. Much of this more formal accountability practice has emerged from the Sphere Standards, which explicitly and openly set humanitarian outcomes and accountability procedures on the ground. Two of Sphere's Core Standards (1 and 5) insist on people-centred programming that involves aid recipients in managing programmes and monitoring performance and evaluation.[21] The seven accountability principles of the Humanitarian Accountability Project (HAP) demand recipient accountability from its member agencies by similarly focusing on explicit standards, strong communications, participation and complaints procedures.[22]

The accountability principles in the Code, Sphere and HAP are sound. Yet, all this leaves humanitarian professionals and commentators still thinking that there is an unethical "accountability deficit" in humanitarian action, in the words of journalist Michael Jennings; or a profound "cognitive dissonance" between what aid says and what aid does, according to academic Zoe Marriage.[23] If this is so, then there are two structural weaknesses in the current architecture of humanitarian accountability that render it ethically vulnerable.

The first weakness, as Alice Obrecht points out, is that humanitarian evaluation and accountability are dominated by the principal–agent model, whereby the principal (usually government donors) evaluates the agent (humanitarian agencies). Much better and more ethical would be a system of reporting and evaluation that made a "moral appraisal" of humanitarian operations as a whole and of particular interventions too.[24] This idea of "mission accountability" stressed by Obrecht and by Nicole Bieske should be the main emphasis of humanitarian accountability, with its focus being the experience of the people who need humanitarian help.[25] At the end of the day, mission accountability is essential to the humanitarian legitimacy of agencies. Humanitarian operations will only be legitimate if they are actively and effectively pursuing the ethical goal that they claim for themselves. This kind of mission-centred moral appraisal has only really been done well once, in the system-wide evaluation of the response to the Rwandan genocide.[26] It needs to be done much more. Humanitarian action can then be rightly appraised on how well it has met its humanitarian goals, how well it has lived its values in the process and how it has decided on and reacted to particular ethical challenges like indirect harm, complicity, moral entrapment and others identified in Chapter 9. In short, humanitarian accountability should be more focused on principles than principals.

The second structural weakness in humanitarian accountability is regulation. Humanitarian action is essentially voluntary and self-regulating. No party, whether donor, agency, local authority or recipient community, is under real external scrutiny to see if and how they are making the most of aid and are abiding by humanitarian law and principles in its application.[27] This situation is increasingly untenable for a sector that continues to expand, that is now vital in many countries and is an important component of international relations and global governance. There is evidence from other areas of human rights, and in commercial sectors that run public utilities, that an independent rapporteur, ombudsperson or official regulator can bring higher levels of accountability and improvement to a sector. Some such mechanism should be adopted for humanitarian action. People need some form of official public mediator to oversee the political contract around aid that is emerging between people, governments and agencies.

•

Effectiveness and Everyday Ethics

The fundamental humanitarian principles described above define the particular role responsibility of humanitarian professionals. But there are also several generic principles of professionalism that apply to any human activity carried out in the public interest. These general principles of good management are about being effective as well as moral. Results matter in ethics as it is not enough just to be caring and humanitarian. You must be caring and humanitarian to the best of your ability. Managerial principles include personal integrity and a strong professional ethic of doing things to the highest possible standard in the best interests of the people you serve. This is, above all, a question of professional competence.

If people's lives depend on a profession, it is important that the people in this profession take both the efficiency and effectiveness of their operations very seriously. In humanitarian action, as in many other professions, it is unethical to manage operations badly. Failures of efficiency and effectiveness that are the fault of an organization itself (rather than circumstances beyond its control) can have predictable and harmful consequences for people. These failures need to be investigated when they happen and then corrected with a combination of good leadership and management. The whole of the Sphere Standards—its core standards and specific technical standards—make clear what high-quality humanitarian action looks like in practice. In addition to Sphere, most agencies have set their own internal standards of technical response for their own specialism and specific standards of good management. This process of good management is all part of the everyday ethics of a humanitarian agency and the business of doing things well that preoccupies most humanitarian workers throughout their working day.

Several initiatives have begun to work on professional competencies in humanitarian action. While these are still debated, it seems possible to identify ten key operational principles that are particularly important in everyday management if humanitarian action is to be efficient and effective.[28] Some of these, like collective action and value for money, have already been highlighted in the discussion on fundamental principles, because they are either implicitly nested or explicitly mentioned in the Code of Conduct.

1. Humanitarian integrity—every humanitarian professional should be true to humanitarian goals and principles in the operational decisions they make and the way they represent themselves and their organization to others.
2. Collective action—the willingness and ability to join up with other organizations that are delivering or facilitating humanitarian action to

seek economies of scale, streamlining, greater reach, complementarity and improved performance to create the maximum humanitarian effect possible in a given situation.

3. Appropriateness—the choice and application of humanitarian commodities and strategies that are fit for purpose in a given context and precisely meet the needs of all different types of affected people.
4. Agility and flexibility—the operational desire, readiness and ability to adapt and innovate in changing situations in order to meet needs better as they develop.
5. Timeliness—the determination and ability to understand the timings of people's various needs and so deploy commodities or programmes to people before they need them or just in time as they need them.
6. Efficiency—the desire, resources and ability to run an organization or a project using the minimum of time, expense, resources and personnel to achieve optimal effectiveness.
7. Value for money—comparing the cost-effectiveness of different humanitarian interventions that target the same or sufficiently similar outcomes, and choosing the intervention that delivers the most value to the most people at the least cost.
8. Due diligence—making sufficient enquiries about the ethics, interests, risks and professional reliability of individuals and organizations in your agency's political, commercial and humanitarian supply chain and delivery network; and acting upon information received.
9. Being a good employer—recruiting and retaining the best staff available, and taking due care to train, equip, protect, reward and refresh your staff fairly and to the best of your ability so that they can carry out their roles to optimal effect.
10. Learning and improving—being ready and able to learn lessons from your current and previous operations and the operations of other agencies, so that you can improve your organization significantly and regularly to the benefit of those people who need your organization's services now and in the future.

The real effectiveness of humanitarian operations is achieved by successfully applying the combined values of the fundamental principles, managerial principles and the Sphere Standards as much as possible in a particular situation. Only then can humanitarian action live up to all its ethical obligations. Designing and implementing a humanitarian programme that is principled, effective and high quality must be the mark of operational and ethical success. In contrast, an aid operation that very effectively reduces malnutrition in only one group of women and children by using expensive imported food, and without involving them or the men in their family in the design and management of the programme, is deeply problematic. It may produce a reduction of malnutrition in one group, but it is not a humanitarian success. It would be unethical and incomplete.

The stewardship principles of sustainability and accountability, with their emphasis on effectiveness, are critical to any understanding of humanitarian success. Having now reviewed all the main principles of humanitarian ethics, the next chapter will explore its overall character to see how it compares with other systems of applied ethics.

6

WHAT KIND OF ETHICS IS HUMANITARIAN ETHICS?

As we have seen in the previous chapters, the modern elaboration of humanitarian ethics has emerged as a principle-based system of ethics. In these principles, the humanitarian profession describes itself to the world in ideal terms. This chapter now stakes out the field of humanitarian ethics more widely than its principles alone, in order to understand the actual shape and character of humanitarian ethics when they are applied in practice. A wider look at humanitarian ethics shows that the ethical concerns of humanitarian action operate at different levels in any conflict or disaster and across several disciplines. It is also clear that, in practice, humanitarian ethics is not a simple matter of application but is an ethics of struggle that is essentially realist rather than idealist, adopts a role morality and is increasingly turning to an ideology of rights in addition to its earlier principles and rules.

The Different Levels of Humanitarian Ethics

Humanitarian ethics engages at three very different levels of practice: the intimate, the operational and the strategic.

- Intimate ethics—As medics, social workers, water engineers, protection officers or livelihood experts, humanitarian workers frequently work on very personal matters of survival and dignity in intimate contact with individual adults and children, and with families and small neighbourhoods. This level of practice is concerned with the best interests of individual human beings who are suffering and with finding immediate solutions to their suffering. The intimate sphere of humanitarian ethics generates a succession of personal care challenges in which individual humanitarian practitioners must work face-to-face with affected individuals, and in their best interests, to find practical and often urgent solutions that best meet their needs.

- Operational ethics—As project managers, humanitarian leaders are required to make choices and decisions about whole areas of operation at the level of camps, districts and sub-regions. These choices involve organizational questions about what to do, how best to do it and with whom to collaborate. The operational sphere is more likely to involve organizational questions about the optimal organizational platform, appropriate resource allocation and more political questions of cooperation with government, armed groups, other agencies and local NGOs. It also involves important questions of staff care and security.
- Strategic ethics—As leaders of international organizations, humanitarian directors make global strategic choices around funding priorities, geographical coverage and political and commercial collaborations. This level is concerned with institutional interests and goals. The strategic sphere is the most remote but potentially most influential sphere of humanitarian ethics. Here, grand questions of institutional priority, goal setting, resource allocation, strategic focus and organizational culture are decided. These questions are combined with decisions around appropriate political partnerships, strategic relationships with funders and the marketing of human need.

These different levels of ethical practice are common to any large organization and business and show the range of different practical challenges involved in humanitarian ethics. Not the least of these is the requirement for humanitarians in each layer of practice to be sensitive to the ethical challenges of the other layers.

Political and Professional Reality

Humanitarian principles present humanitarian action in ideal terms as a way of saving and protecting human life in armed conflict and disaster. In many accounts of agency websites and in the Powerpoint slides of training programmes, it is suggested that humanitarian action's core moral values (human life and personal dignity) can be put neatly into practice by respecting the main principles of impartiality, neutrality, independence. However, as any humanitarian worker will tell you, once you leave the training session on humanitarian principles and start working on the ground, humanitarian ideals crash straight into political reality.[1]

Politics is the arena of humanitarian action, and humanitarian ethics are soon swept up into political process and not so easily applied according to principle. Within the political arena, humanitarian ethics also has to deal with the particular ethics of its various fields of practice. Alongside political judgements, and often because of them, there are difficult choices to be made about assisting individuals within particular fields of health, food security, water, sanitation, livelihoods, emergency education, protection and social work. Most humanitarian workers have to operate as politicians and technical professionals: negotiating political space and deciding how best to meet people's survival needs.

The political and inter-disciplinary character of humanitarian work suggests that humanitarian ethics is a more complicated field of ethics than is formally recognized in humanitarian action's declamatory ethical texts like the Code of Conduct, the Humanitarian Charter and the Sphere Standards. In reality, as it is actually practised, humanitarian action combines political ethics with medical ethics, economic ethics, social work ethics, supply chain and logistics ethics, and the ethics of any other field in which it responds to human need. Humanitarian ethics is also multi-layered. It operates at very different levels of society as it expands globally in large international organizations. The natural domain of humanitarian action reaches organically from UN headquarters in New York to a pit latrine in an IDP camp, from meetings in Geneva to the examination of wounded patients in field hospitals.

A Realist Ethics

Simone Weil felt passionately that "contradiction is the criterion of the real". When we find ourselves in an apparent contradiction, we are probably hitting hard upon reality because reality is seldom simply one thing or another but usually a difficult mixture of things. This is certainly humanitarian action's experience of the mix of ideals and political realism in every operation. Humanitarian ethics has long struggled with the contradiction that it seeks to be apolitical in the midst of some of the world's most extreme political environments. Naturally, humanitarians encounter a contradiction here—the hard knock of reality. Humanitarian action finds it impossible and undesirable to avoid politics. To be present and active on the ground, agencies must negotiate political space with political actors. It is impossible to be humanitarian without also working politically. It is a dream to imagine that humanitarians are allowed simply to be principled and to go and do as they choose wherever they choose. Instead, humanitarian action is routinely obstructed, restricted or manipulated by politicians; and humanitarians must do politics and make compromises to operate amongst them. Like politics, humanitarian action fast becomes "the art of the possible" and the art of the expansion of the possible.[2] Alongside its intimate care ethics, humanitarian ethics is all about political ethics. The political arena in which humanitarians operate requires them to be politically realistic if they are to deliver some of their ideals of compassion and care. Of all the agencies operating today MSF has been the most explicit and transparent about this fact.[3]

Political ethics has long involved a struggle between idealists and realists. Today this difference is discussed in political theory as a difference between ideal theory and non-ideal theory.[4] Ideal theory sets out how the world should be and can reasonably be, and then sets this vision as a target for politicians. For example, the ideal theory of democracy and human rights serves to be inspirational and prescriptive in politics. It sets out a blueprint for the kind of ideal liberal society that should be constructed on the ground. Non-ideal theorists reject the practical feasibility of such idealism as profoundly unrealistic. Instead of modelling perfect societies as a pattern of potential reality, they emphasize the importance of starting with the world as it actually is and theorizing about what is practically possible within it. In their political ethics, realists prefer to compare options within the "feasible set" of real world possibilities rather than go all out for a "transcendental" model of justice that is not feasible in the current situation.[5] For realists, politics is always about generating as many "instantiations" of good things as possible in an imperfect world. It can never be about pre-designing and ushering in the perfect world.

The British philosopher Bernard Williams has criticized idealist politics as an overly simple "enactment model" of politics in which politicians decide what is morally right and then expect to roll it out in practice. Williams notes that in the enactment model, "political theory formulates principles, concepts, ideals and values; and politics seeks to express these in political action, through persuasion, the use of power and so forth".[6] The weakness of the enactment model for Williams is that it gives "priority to the moral over the political" so that politics becomes simply "applied morality" when, in fact, politics is about a hard struggle for order, legitimacy and the "conditions of cooperation" which must precede moral agreements. Williams contrasts the enactment theory's "political moralism" with a more accurate and prior process of "political realism".

Humanitarian ethics lives in this tension between humanitarian ideals and political reality. It has its ideals but is soon thrust into reality. In most armed conflicts and disasters, humanitarian action is not a simple ethical goal that is routinely and easily applied or enacted as obvious political morality. Instead it is a fundamental moral ideal that must be struggled for in very non-ideal circumstances in which longer-range political goals or downright unethical objectives are being given greater priority by those in power. The enactment model of politics does not ring true in humanitarian action. The simple good of reaching out to save a life is soon challenged, constrained and compromised amidst the fierce passions of national politics and the calculating grand strategy of geopolitics. Williams points out that, although it relies on the same moral impulse, rescuing many thousands of people in a war sits in a different ethical paradigm to rescuing one person drowning in a canal.[7] William Galston, another realist, elaborates the point: "Individual rescue typically leaves everything else as it was: throwing a rope to a drowning man typically does not require or produce reorganizations of social relations and responsibilities outside of the rescuer–rescued dyad".[8] In contrast, it is clear that humanitarian ethics at scale is not a simple and unique form of ethics that exists and operates in isolation from politics as an intimate form of caring that we can just scale-up from a personal emergency to a public emergency. Instead, when expanded into international organizations, massive resources and extreme political environments, humanitarian ethics is as much about political ethics as it is about religious, humanist, medical and care ethics.

Humanitarian action is the pursuit of certain goals within the context of other people's politics and is consequently carried out in the political sphere above all others. It is in the realm of politics that humanitarian ethics finds its natural habitat and not simply the realm of medicine, nutrition, sanitation, economics or social work that make up the various fields of its practice. Doing humanitarian work at scale is doing politics. Like the political realists, the postmodern ethicist Zygmunt Bauman observed that "the problem of extending moral insights and impulses to society at large is a matter of politics not morality".[9]

An Ethics of Struggle

This means that struggle is perhaps the eleventh major principle of humanitarian action and the principle that is most predominant as it is practically applied. Thea Hilhorst is right to describe humanitarian action as an arena.[10] Humanitarian action routinely faces very real opponents who disagree profoundly or opportunistically with humanitarian ideals. It is for this reason that Rony Brauman says "that it is necessary [for humanitarian action] to remain in tension with whatever kind of power".[11] The fact that humanitarian action regularly meets resistance of some kind is an indication of the world as it actually is and a clear sign that political realism is the appropriate ethical stance for humanitarian work.

So, how can humanitarian ethics be better informed by political realism? The British political theorist and former psychiatric social worker Mark Philp has worked hard to define a form of political realism that remains firmly anchored in moral values.[12] Philp makes clear that the ethics of good political realism is "not relativist but contextualist". Realists do not drop or relegate values at will but struggle to find ways to bring them about as much as possible in situations that are bounded by hard and soft constraints of various kinds, like very real limits to agency and capacity, and clashes with competing interests. The whole emphasis of political realism is:

> on what the agent can realistically expect to bring about and at what cost. In making a judgement about what to do, the politician has to consider a range of contingent and non-ideal forces that constrain his or her choice.... While the constraints narrow the range of possibility, the values remain germane to decisions about which of the paths open to a politician, he or she should take.[13]

This understanding of realist political ethics seems to accurately represent the core struggle of applied humanitarian ethics. It describes the main way in which humanitarian ethics has developed in practice to engage politically but with only humanitarian interests. As honest discussions of humanitarian ethics make clear, humanitarian work is profoundly political. All humanitarians are bound to confront this contradiction and work outwards from it. What often sounds confusing about humanitarian realism is that humanitarians tend to use ideals as their main persuasive instrument in political struggles. They use morality (humanity and impartiality) to push hard in political negotiations. Therefore, they sound very idealistic when they are actually engaging very realistically to pressure and expose their opponents.

The political realism inevitable in humanitarian ethics means that humanitarian principles tend to act as constant markers of value or guidance and can seldom be implemented as precise prescriptions of practice. An agency's principles are always forced to conform in some way to the feasibility set of humanitarian possibility in a particular situation. This is why humanitarian action operates slightly differently in Syria, Haiti, the Kivus or Somalia. Humanitarian principles cannot be simply applied to a situation. Instead, they are typically interpreted from within a situation. Humanitarian ethics is, therefore, about struggling to interpret ethical limits and balancing various principles, rather than routinely enacting the Code of Conduct.

A Role Morality

If political realism and ethical struggle are core characteristics of applied humanitarian ethics, then the adoption of a role morality is another. Humanitarian principles define and guide humanitarian action as a specific role morality or role responsibility in armed conflicts and disasters. By professing these principles and seeking to realize them in distinctly humanitarian practices that are recognized in international and national law, humanitarian workers create the humanitarian profession. The profession then adopts principles like impartiality, neutrality and independence as role responsibilities.[14] This consolidates a very specific role morality for humanitarian action—a moral posture and particular behaviours that make sense when you are trying to achieve a very specific good, but which do not make sense as a general rule for all areas of life.

In practice, humanitarian professionals adopt a role morality much like a doctor, policeman, politician, nurse, soldier, priest or accountant. In their various official roles, members of these professions must act in line with their role responsibilities when they are on duty. A professional soldier cannot take his weapon on holiday and kill people who offend him. His arms-bearing role as a soldier is a special responsibility confined to particular circumstances. An accountant must be careful and exact with the bookkeeping he does for his clients, but might be relatively relaxed and disorganized in managing his family finances. A priest must share confidential information about a crime that he has overheard accidentally on a bus, but (in some countries) he is not bound to share privileged information he has heard professionally during a confession.

Humanitarian office carries the specific obligations and behaviours of humanitarian principles, but they may not be necessary or morally appropriate to humanitarian workers' personal lives when they are off-duty. In their humanitarian role, humanitarian professionals live certain virtues that are deemed distinctly humanitarian. They are obliged to be impartial and neutral in a way they would not necessarily be in their private lives, in which they might have strong political views or put their family first in a crisis. For example, if a fire breaks out in a cinema when a Lebanese Red Crescent paramedic is watching a film with his children, he would be entitled to save his children first without looking to see who was in greatest need. Similarly, a water engineer from Action Contre le Faim (ACF) might respect local customs that forbid the consumption of alcohol when she is in Mali, but happily drink wine with her friends at home in France. A more direct clash of values can occur around political associations which may need to be handled with discretion in particular countries. If a national humanitarian worker is regularly seen at the front of political rallies for a particular party in a country enduring an armed conflict, legitimate questions could be asked about her neutrality and independence when she is in her humanitarian role.

The Turn to Rights

Another new characteristic of humanitarian ethics in practice is its increasing tendency to adopt a theory of rights alongside, or even on top of, its more traditional principles and legal rules from IHL. The fundamental principle of humanity has been increasingly spelled out in human rights law over the last sixty years. In this process, it has become the norm to talk in terms of rights in humanitarian ethics. The Humanitarian Charter is explicit on this point and identifies three general rights which together encompass what constitutes humanity for people suffering in armed conflicts and disasters. These rights draw closely on a mixture of the UDHR and IHL; but, as the Charter points out, "while these rights are not formulated in such terms in international law, they encapsulate a range of established legal rights and give fuller substance to the humanitarian imperative".[15] These three aggregated rights are:

- The right to life with dignity
- The right to receive humanitarian assistance
- The right to protection and security

Importantly, these three rights are true to the essential value of humanity. In their concern for dignified bodily life they point clearly to the principle of human life lived as a person. Indeed, the Humanitarian Charter's explicit emphasis on dignity is only a beginning. Having acknowledged the principle of dignity in the Charter, the actual Sphere Standards that follow it have a further seventy-seven references to dignity in their various prescriptions of what counts as good humanitarian action.[16]

In natural disasters, the same move to rights has taken place in the development of International Disaster Relief Law (IDRL). Pioneered by the Red Cross and Red Crescent Movement and by a UN Special Rapporteur, draft articles on disaster relief law are now established, and several governments are officially recognizing and referring to their recommendations and incorporating them into domestic law.[17] The IDRL Guidelines and UN Draft Articles on Protection of Persons in the Event of Disasters are largely concerned with improved efficiencies in the provision and coordination of humanitarian aid.[18] They affirm respect for state sovereignty and the primacy of state responsibility in disaster response, but the UN Articles and Red Cross and Red Crescent Guidelines are also framed in terms of human rights. The Red Cross and Red Crescent resolutions make clear that the Guidelines are grounded clearly in the needs of the individual, especially "the safeguarding of basic human rights" and "the fundamental right of all people to offer and receive humanitarian assistance". This resolution and the Guidelines themselves explicitly recommend that states organize humanitarian action in line with the Humanitarian Charter and its Minimum Standards.[19]

The rights turn in humanitarian ethics is significant because it binds humanitarian ethics into international law, and also because it moves the moral emphasis on the principle of humanity from the virtue of the helper to the entitlement of the victim. Adopting a political theory of rights in humanitarian action is a shift of ethical paradigm away from a moral landscape of optional philanthropy towards a political contract of legally based obligation.[20] This political process of engaging state and non-state responsibility around individual human rights has been in train ever since the first modern laws of war were agreed in The Hague and Geneva in the nineteenth century. However, as it now stands, applying a theory of rights has created a certain political ambivalence in humanitarian ethics in four main ways.

First, a rights-based approach to humanitarian ethics involves a major change in the ethical mood of humanitarian action to shape its discussion in terms of politics rather than humanity. This development is both advantageous and problematic. Specifically because politicizing humanity is progressive. Just and peaceful states have usually become so precisely because of a political consensus that agrees to prioritize humanity, mutual aid and fairness. But such transformations are usually born from a deep political process that takes centuries. During armed conflicts, when the very basis of society is being contested, a political discourse of rights rather than a compassionate discourse of humanity can be seen as premature and *parti pris*. Wars are usually fights about rights, and any additional interference from outsiders can antagonize people further. Humanitarian agencies can sound politically partisan when referring to rights in a way that differs from discussions on humanity.

A second area of ambivalence concerns the potential proliferation of humanitarian entitlements. Trying to limit humanitarian discussion to key rights that relate strictly to the preservation of life and dignity is difficult even *in extremis*. Talk of rights tends always to cascade into a wider conversation about the whole spectrum of human rights. In liberalism, at least, it is intellectually and politically incoherent to talk as if only a few basic rights matter. If a person in war-ravaged Aleppo has rights to humanitarian assistance, she also has all the rights in the UDHR and every other relevant human rights convention. The natural proliferation of rights in any engagement with communities brings hard questions about the scope of humanitarian action.[21] How far does it go in addressing the full range of human rights? As Charles Beitz has well observed, the longer the list of rights, the greater that scepticism about human rights tends to become.[22] The use of rights discourse can then encourage scepticism around humanitarian action itself when it is seen as part of a contested human rights movement.

Thirdly, a system of rights explicitly politicizes humanitarian action to bring state responsibility centre stage in any humanitarian encounter. This is desirable because the state is often, but not always, best placed to influence the humanitarian conduct of conflict. However, it is also diplomatically testing because observations of rights violations frequently involve simultaneous criticism of the state. This explicit politicization of humanitarian responsibility can make it difficult for humanitarian agencies to argue an apolitical posture in armed conflicts and natural disasters in line with humanitarian neutrality and independence.

Finally, the politicization of humanity in a system of rights encourages and enables states to take full responsibility for a crisis and then to exclude international agencies as extraneous or interfering. This kind of humanitarian nationalism has been a feature of government policy in Sudan, Syria and Sri Lanka, where strong states have refused, coerced or expelled international humanitarian agencies on the logical legal grounds that humanitarian responsibility belongs to the state. Having rightly taken political control of the crisis, they have then wrongly failed to meet humanitarian standards of protection and care, sometimes deliberately.

This chapter has examined the shape and character of humanitarian ethics beyond the simple presentation of itself as a principle-based system of ethics. In its application, humanitarian ethics inevitably becomes more realist as an ethics of struggle that adopts a role morality and is increasingly turning to the theory of rights to buttress or perhaps even supersede its more traditional ethical claims. Moving beyond theoretical description, the next part of the book looks in more detail at the practice rather than the theory of humanitarian ethics.

PART THREE

THE PRACTICE OF HUMANITARIAN ETHICS

7

REASON AND EMOTION

In Parts One and Two, we have looked at the origins of our ethical consciousness as human beings and its particular elaboration into a humanitarian ethics for responding to suffering in armed conflict and disaster. Now we need to start thinking about what it means to make ethical decisions in practice on the ground in the full flow and ferment of humanitarian work as it really happens. What is it to actually practise humanitarian ethics? What parts of ourselves should we use to be ethical and make ethical decisions? How can we develop a consistent practice of ethics as humanitarian professionals that enables us to operate realistically and habitually by humanitarian principles, and so walk the talk of the first part of this book? This chapter examines the various parts of ourselves that we can draw on as we try to be ethical in humanitarian work and the various ethical traditions that guide the making of moral choices.

Our Moral Faculties

Our experience as ethical beings is a mixture of feeling, thinking and action. All three aspects of our person—heart, head and hands—need to come into play if we are to embody sound moral practice. We need to feel something, to reflect upon the problem posed by our feeling, to choose the best response and then to act in a way that best embodies our decision.

As ethical practice, this requires a good balance between emotion, reason and action. However, the history of ethics has all too often witnessed different ethical schools that over-emphasize the rational, the emotional or the activist element in isolation from one another. In his intellectual history of Western ethics, Alasdair MacIntyre describes a "long catastrophe" in moral thinking since the Enlightenment in which different philosophers have wrongly defined the practice of ethics in binary terms as either rule-based "calculations" or emotional "preferences". MacIntyre suggests that the fundamental dualism in this modern ethical tradition has left us with unintelligible and conflicting ethical "fragments" as our guides.[1] He argues for a return to a more integrated Aristotelian and Thomist approach that builds on the cultivation of virtues in which thought, feeling and habits combine as practical wisdom.

Despite humanitarian action's strong focus on principles, it is this integrated approach to ethics that I will pursue in this part of the book. For most humanitarian practitioners, applied ethics is most likely to involve humanitarian virtues which they develop over time and can apply routinely every day and in moments of major crises. Virtue grows from using all our moral faculties, so it is useful to look at each of them in turn in this chapter, before looking more specifically at humanitarian deliberation in the next.

Reason

Two highly rational and calculative schools of thought have tended to dominate ethical thinking about human welfare in modern Western culture and have influenced global norms accordingly. These are the ideas of duty-based ethics and utilitarian ethics. The first affirms absolute principles of good in human welfare, which have subsequently emerged as human rights in international law. The second is generally used as the proportionate rule with which to distribute resources fairly in efforts to fulfil these welfare duties and realize human rights.

Immanuel Kant, the great eighteenth-century German philosopher, nurtured human reason as the source of our moral judgements and developed the principle of the "categorical imperative". This states that "I should never act except in such a way that I can also will that my maxim should become a universal law".[2] In other words, Kant believed that we live best when we always do what reason dictates that everyone should do in our position. This strand of ethics became known as "deontology" (from the Greek word for duty) because applying Kant's categorical imperative created a series of absolute duties in particular situations. Insisting on a range of moral absolutes as universal principles led Kant to argue that we should never tell a lie, not even if it is to protect someone hiding in our house when his would-be murderers knock at our door and ask if he is inside.[3] This absolutism may be rationally coherent if we are to conserve a principle, but it strikes us as emotionally wrong if we want to save a life.

The second great calculative schema of European ethics emerged in the nineteenth century from the English philosopher Jeremy Bentham. He argued for a "moral science" that could be governed by a single rule: the principle of utility. This view of ethics, known as Utilitarianism, dictates that any moral problem should be resolved by calculating which course of action would be most useful to ensure the happiness, pleasure and wellbeing of the greatest number of people. In Bentham's words:

> By the principle of utility is meant that principle which approves or disapproves of every action whatsoever, according to the tendency which it appears to have to augment or diminish the happiness of the party whose interest is in question...I say of every action whatsoever; and therefore not only of every action of a private individual, but of every measure of government.[4]

If Kant's absolute duties are instinctively attractive to us for the consistent moral norms they help to shape, Bentham's absolute single rule of utility chimes with a very different ethical intuition within us. Utilitarianism confirms our deep moral sense that we must always weigh the consequences of our actions in a difficult situation. This is the idea of consequentialism or proportionalism in ethics, which determines the goodness of an action by its consequences, or in proportion to its wider effects.[5] It is consequentialism that makes many of us think that it is right to lie, in the scenario of the murderers at the door, and so breach Kant's principle of absolute duty. But in a different situation, it is Kant's sense of absolute duties that resonates with many of us when we feel that it is wrong to torture a captured enemy soldier to make her give up important information about her army's plans for a future attack.

Kant's absolute duties are insufficiently nuanced to recognize when lying might be the right thing to do. Bentham's single rule is vulnerable to its reliance on risky speculation about the future impact of an action. His requirement that we gauge the morality of an action by the "tendency which it appears to have" is full of uncertainty, inevitable speculation and guesswork. Standing in the present, it is not always clear what impact and side-effects our actions will have in the medium and long term. This is particularly true if we do not control events and if others, unbeknown to us, are making decisions of their own around the same problem. Medical science and engineering can sometimes know enough to make near certain choices about which drug or material to use. But other areas of human morality, especially politics, tend to be less certain. This means that raw consequentialism cannot routinely be applied with confident scientific precision. Typically, in political ethics, we neither know enough, control enough, nor can we predict enough about the outcome of our actions. Between them, Kant and Bentham confirm a deep moral sense in all of us that duties and consequences both have fundamental significance in ethics. But neither system seems to speak completely to life as it is felt and lived. Somehow we want to respect absolutes and consequences at the same time.

The unsatisfactory feel of a purely deontological or consequentialist approach indicates two other deep truths in our experience of ethics: the constant reality of moral risk, and the significance of emotion and intuition in ethics. Neither Kantian nor Benthamite ethics is without risk. Our ignorance about the future means that, in each system, a "right path" could still involve, and even initiate, bad things for people. There will be winners and losers in either approach. The insight here is that risk is an essential part of ethics and one that is very seldom overcome. Indeed, it is only by recognizing the central place of risk and uncertainty in ethics that we can move into a more balanced and truly reasonable approach to moral problems. The felt incompleteness of simple deontology or utilitarianism also indicates the important place we need to give to our emotions and our intuition in ethics. If we need to honour absolutes, consequences, risk and intuition as permanent concerns in our ethics, then we will also need a more human and less calculative approach to humanitarian ethics which at once respects the depth of our values and the range of our decisions. It seems it is too hard to resolve ethical problems with our intellect alone, so the emotion we bring to difficult moments is important too.

Emotions

Much of the modern European and North American tradition of ethics has been biased towards calculative or rational deliberation in ethical decision-making. Like many ancient Stoics before them, modern deontologists and utilitarians have been wary of our emotions as passionate and unreliable guides that might easily blow us off course in our ethical decision-making. Pure reason, they argue, is more likely to be a more stable and less biased guide. Immanuel Kant held clearly to the unemotional approach to ethics and encouraged "the duty of apathy" (non-feeling) in which "the feelings arising from sensible impressions lose their influence on moral feeling".[6] He regarded this process as essential if one is to be able to live in line with moral law, and he was very wary of the "momentarily glittering appearance" of emotions in our ethical practice. Instead, he argued that:

> A man [*sic*] should collect himself...and bring all his capacities and inclinations under his authority (that of reason)...and not let himself be governed by his feelings and inclinations. For unless reason takes the reins of government in its own hands, feelings and inclinations play the master over man.[7]

This suspicion of emotion means that ethics has often been practised as if it were a purely rational cognitive science. However, while Kant tried to minimize the impact of emotions on ethics in eighteenth-century Germany, in eighteenth-century Scotland David Hume was convinced that reason and emotion needed to work together in moral decision-making. Recognizing that human morality has its source in our emotions, he was adamant that "the rules of morality, therefore, are not conclusions of our reason...and tis vain to pretend that morality is discovered only by a deduction of reason".[8] Hume thought that our emotions should continue to guide our ethical decision-making; but he was in no doubt that our capacity for thought and reason should play a "correcting role" by verifying facts, assessing feasibility and avoiding bias in the choices and strategies we make. Because reason deals primarily in assessing truth and falsehood, Hume recognized that we must use it to gain a proper understanding of the situations that arouse our passions and our compassion.[9]

The recent "affective revolution" in psychology, sociology and political science has drawn on Hume and neuroscience to revive an important emphasis on the value of emotions and "emotional intelligence" in relationships, business, politics and ethics.[10] In political theory, the role and value of emotions is increasingly recognized too.[11] People's political judgements as voters and politicians are increasingly understood to combine the emotional and rational very closely together. It is our emotions like anxiety, frustration or fear which first alert us to political dangers, or our hopes and subconscious scripts which dispose us to certain political preferences.[12] It is the fact that we care about things that motivates our engagement with politics and ethics in the first place. The American political philosopher Sharon Krause has argued, therefore, that our emotions must be a central part of political discussion. She has importantly encouraged space for "civil passions" in democratic deliberations about changing values.[13]

In 2001, the American philosopher Martha Nussbaum put emotions right back at the centre of ethics. She argued for "the intelligence of emotions", suggesting that our emotions are "judgements of value in a world that we do not fully control".[14] This is similar to how Aquinas described compassion as "a felt evaluation".[15] When we feel things, we are detecting what is morally valuable or morally repugnant in events happening around us. Nussbaum shows how our higher emotions (like grief, wonder, anger, joy, fear, loss, love and compassion) are not merely animalistic or bodily parts of us limited to expressing pain and pleasure and likely to blow us off course from practical reasonableness. They are not just physical reactions that will pass. Instead, she encourages us to respect our emotions as "a kind of judgement or thought" that has a richness and density that is superior to purely rational and calculative thought; a textured thinking. Nussbaum argues that our emotions are evidently concerned with our flourishing and the flourishing of others, and so we are wise to take them seriously as moral prompts and guides to what is important and what is right to do. Our emotions can embody our deepest thoughts of what is good and bad, right and wrong. When roused, they are really "upheavals of thoughts".[16]

But, of course, we must not assume that all our emotions are good. Although our emotions can be evaluative and ethical in the best sense, they can also be immoral. As Nussbaum points out, "all emotions are not equal...there may be some that are per se morally suspect...and linked with self-deception".[17] For example, many of our negative emotions, like greed, if left unrecognized as such, are unethical. Other emotions can be immorally constructed by the society around us or by imbalance in our personality. We can be encouraged by our class to look down on poorer people and feel them to be less valuable than us. Hardened racism and scapegoating ingrains in us feelings of disgust, envy and hate about certain types and groups of people whom we then learn to de-humanize, disregard and despise emotionally.[18] Thus, while we are right to recognize our emotions as important ethical evaluations, we must also evaluate the ethical content of our emotions as part of our deliberation. So how are we to integrate the ethical insights from our emotions and our reason in an effective form of everyday ethical practice?

Virtue

A more nuanced approach than purely calculative or emotional schemes is best found in the ethics of Aristotle and the long tradition that has followed him in Christian and Islamic ethics. Alongside the Jewish Torah and Talmud, the Christian New Testament and Islam's Koran and Hadith, Aristotle's Nicomachean Ethics and Eudemian Ethics are the founding systematic texts of Western ethics. These traditions have a strong focus on the detail of particular problems, the cultivation of individual virtues, the importance of personal choice and a strong sense of moral absolutes. It seems possible to use this idea of virtue to develop a sense of humanitarian virtues.

Aristotle used the Greek word *arete*, meaning excellence, to describe good conduct and character in his ethics. This word was translated into Latin as *virtus*, which has its root in the Latin word for strength. Like prudence, the word "virtuous" has suffered some denigration in modern English and tends to be confused with ideas of piety and self-righteousness. However, as John Finnis points out, this is very far from its true meaning:

> Virtue is not some prim conformity to convention or rule, but excellence and strength of character involving a disposition and readiness to act with intelligent love in pursuit of real goods...and with successful resistance to the ultimately unreasonable lure of bad options.[19]

Fundamental to Aristotle's ethics is a search for the "golden mean" which sees virtue as a "middle state" between excess or deficiency in attitude and action in a given situation. So, the virtuous middle state between cowardice and foolhardiness is courage; between gain and loss it is justice; and between cunning and naivety it is wisdom.[20] For Aristotle, the cultivation of these median virtues and their application in difficult situations becomes central to acting ethically. The repeated practice of ethics also works to develop character (ethos), and the accumulated experience of moral problem-solving develops habits of practical wisdom and judgement in a person's life and choices that are based on intuitive reason as much as intellectual reason.[21]

Sound judgement and moderated behaviour are by no means the only aspects of Aristotle's ethics. He also has a strong sense of the goal of human life. He sets out some clear moral absolutes and espouses clear thinking about moral choice and moral responsibility. Aristotle is very clear that the goal of human beings is to live a good life, which is a largely virtuous life that will produce a meaningful and lasting happiness. This is what we are for as human beings. This is "our use" and the "work we have to do", just in the same way that a good cloak has the virtue of keeping us covered and warm, or a boat and a house each have something that is their intrinsic purpose. So, "the work of a good shoemaker is a good shoe...and the work of the human soul will be a virtuous life".[22] This is our goal as human beings.

Aristotle's idea of an overall goal in ethics and the virtues needed to achieve it are important to humanitarians and to humanitarian agencies. Like a shoemaker who is true to his goal in the work of a good shoe, a humanitarian agency must be true to its goal and create humanitarian outcomes for people affected by war and disaster. In pursuing a goal, Aristotle suggests we must cultivate wisdom, judgement and deliberation to find the golden mean in a given situation so that we can create "the goods achievable by action".[23] These achievable goods are the instantiations of value so prized by political realists in their ethics. After all, we cannot be judged for what is not achievable, but only for what is actually possible in armed conflict and disaster. So, while we should always have goals in any area of life, we are always limited by the feasible set of what we can actually bring about. Feasibility is an important aspect of ethics. It does not change the goal itself but determines the degree to which a goal can actually be achieved in a given situation and helps shape what is a "practical option" for action.[24] The virtues of practical wisdom and judgement help us find the appropriately virtuous route through a particular situation. Sometimes it may be a mix of daring and invention; at other times it may demand caution and restraint.

Not all goods exist as a middle state between extremes. Aristotle makes clear that "not every action nor every passion admits of a mean".[25] Some goods are absolute and basic goods like life, friendship, society and reasonableness.[26] And some things are absolutely and intrinsically bad like envy, spite, murder and theft. You cannot find a middle state for these intrinsic wrongs and, for example, murder someone in a right and balanced way. Humanitarian ethics with its absolute values of humanity, impartiality and the prohibition of indiscriminate killing and suffering shares this strong sense of a moral bottom line.

Choice

The purpose of reason, emotion and their cultivation in particular virtues is to make the best moral choices in our lives. These might be choices about the best attitudes, behaviours, strategies, partnerships or actions. Because of necessary judgements about feasibility, the virtuous mean, and moral absolutes in any situation, ethics is ultimately about choosing and deciding. All ethical traditions emphasize the importance of purposive and deliberate choice in our lives as individuals, and this must be true of organizations too. Choosing is inevitably a key part of humanitarian ethics too.

Choosing is often stereotyped as a sharp binary decision of some kind. One particularly dominant image of choosing is a person standing at a crossroads who must decide to go one of four ways: right, left, straight on or backwards. Sometimes we face these stark moments of extreme choice: to close down a humanitarian programme or to risk trying some emergency surgery that we have never done before. But these stark choices are relatively rare, even in humanitarian ethics. Most often our everyday choices are not dominated by sharp turns through 90 or 180 degrees.

More usually our choices are scalar rather than binary. We move up and down a scale of some kind that we are already on. For example, as we try to balance humanitarian principles with an authoritarian government or alongside a counter-insurgency, we decide to accept a relative loss in independence for an increase in access. We move up and down a scale of compromise. These choices are more like changes in ethical climate than dramatic decisions. This makes these scalar choices subtler and more pervasive than crossroads moments. If we are not conscious of making them, we can become dangerously path-dependent and soon be unwittingly hot, like the famous boiling frog.

Choosing can also be more exploratory and path-finding than scalar or binary. We may make choices with which we edge further up an uncertain pathway that has already been chosen for us. This might mean pushing the envelope a little more in our food security programming to increase the proportion of cash-based transfers and reduce direct food distributions. We are not sure it will work without making people vulnerable to inflation, but we choose to try it.

Action

Our ethical lives do not stop at making choices that are shaped by reason and emotion. Ethics is not just being rational and affective. Our choices must also seek to be effective. If reason, emotion, virtue and choice are essential to how we actually practice ethics, they remain incomplete without actions that attempt to deliver on the moral judgements and decisions we have made. Feeling and judging what is right and wrong, and willing good things, is important as a good in itself. But, wherever possible, we must translate this moral sense into specific practices. Acts are, therefore, the ultimate outcome of ethics. The practical field of humanitarian ethics is deliberately known as humanitarian action because of this basic moral insight that ethics without action is nonsensical.

8

HUMANITARIAN DELIBERATION

If ethical practice rightly includes reason, emotion, virtue, choice and action, then what is the process in which we combine all these to work through ethical problems in humanitarian operations? How should we best make stark decisions, adjust our positions along some moral scale, or choose wisely as we explore a variety of paths in the everyday ethics of humanitarian work? Deliberation is the word used in ethics to describe the process of evaluating and deciding upon a course of action. Moral philosophers and religions alike insist that "due deliberation" is a necessity in ethical decision-making. If we have not deliberated, then we have not given serious matters the attention they deserve. But what makes for a good process of deliberation in humanitarian action?

Aristotle defined deliberation very clearly as the application of practical wisdom to problems that we can do something about, but which involve high levels of uncertainty:

> We deliberate about things that are in our power and can be done... [and] we deliberate not about ends but about means.... Deliberation is concerned with things that happen in a certain way for the most part, but in which the event is obscure, and with things in which it is indeterminate. We call in others to aid us in deliberation on important questions, distrusting ourselves as not being equal to deciding.[1]

Aristotle rightly suggests involving others in our deliberation, because their expertise, experience and interests can add value to our decision-making. In addition, of course, the very process of telling people our problems and speaking them out loud to one another can help us to hear the problem better.

Deliberation is also best done with others because it usually concerns others. This is true for most ethical decision-making. A company chief executive who needs to find a new building for her expanding business will only make a good decision if she discusses the best location and building design with her employees. If not, she may fail to think about where most of her employees live and so how easy or difficult the new location is for their journey to work; or she may overlook what kind of access a new building needs for her disabled employees. As a caring profession, humanitarian deliberation typically involves the best interests and consequences of hundreds or thousands of people. Deliberating with them in some way will obviously lead to wiser and more ethical humanitarian strategy and decision-making. Articles 6 and 7 of the Code of Conduct make clear the importance of deliberation as an activity that is best done with people in the affected society.

Deliberation is also something that can be done individually as part of a wider process, or in situations where isolation is unavoidable. Sometimes we have no choice but to think things through on our own. Deliberation does not always have to be a long, slow and highly inclusive process. Sometimes circumstances require it to be quick and instinctive: more a sudden judgement than a thoughtful analysis. In a burning house with sleeping children still upstairs, we make ethical judgements fast, drawing on the moral prompting of our emotions, the judgement of our conscience and the virtues that have become our habits. In such a situation, it would obviously be wrong to sit down and have a meeting to deliberate the problem with as many stakeholders as possible.

In many situations—probably most situations—there is time for deliberation. Difficult humanitarian situations usually take shape gradually, changing and developing over time. For example, the Syrian civil war started first as a ferocious government crackdown in 2011, but it unravelled over time into an internationalized civil war, a regional refugee crisis and a mix of cross-border and cross-line humanitarian operations. In evolving situations like this, ethical deliberation is constant and forms a continuous reflection that informs what is best to do. The tragedy of the realpolitik around international humanitarianism is that there are thousands of burning houses in Syria today, but political obstacles prevent agencies from providing direct assistance. Instead, humanitarians are forced to deliberate on how to actually get near the affected people in the first place.

Good Deliberation

The distinctive characteristic of deliberation is that it should be reflective, considered and infused with care. Any deliberation must discover and reflect upon the true nature of the problem by appreciating the different needs and perspectives of the people concerned. It must then identify the responsibilities of those involved and the best action possible to address the problem. Good deliberation brings people together in a creative process of dialogue. Ideally, this dialogue then enables them successfully to find a common answer to the problem for themselves.[2] At its best, deliberation is not only an approach to moral problem-solving but also acts pastorally as moral support in a time of ethical crisis. Recognizing and working together on difficult moral problems acknowledges people's difficulty and moral stress, and sharing decision-making can be good for morale. But sometimes deliberation fails, or no decision is made; a leader is needed to step in to impose a decision, or has the courage to take one when others cannot.

Deliberation as Action

Good deliberation is not just a sedentary process of thought. It can and should involve thoughtful action too. Deliberation is not simply talking, thinking and scratching one's head. John Kay, an Oxford economist, emphasizes the importance of iterative decision-making that approaches problem-solving by deliberate interaction with the problem instead of stepping back to imagine the problem and solve it from a distance through planning and target setting. Constant experimentation in deliberation is creative because "the problem, and our understanding of it, changes as we tackle it".[3] In humanitarian work, deliberating will regularly involve trying things out on the ground in this way. In the language of modern management science, this is "reflective practice" in which we reflect on what works well as we do things, and adapt and innovate accordingly.[4] One does not have to stop to deliberate. Deliberation can be very active experimentation. Often, the best way to start deliberating is to try something and see if it works.

This principle of active deliberation recognizes that our technical knowledge is never enough at the boundaries of our professions and that we can often learn more by doing new things than by simply thinking and planning with our current knowledge. In situations of uncertainty, in particular, when it is not clear what is possible and what will work, we have to try things out and innovate as part of our deliberation. This might mean piloting a network of mobile phones among IDP communities to see if this improves protection early warning. It may mean courageously driving a relief convoy up a road to see what happens at a checkpoint belonging to an armed group with which we have no contact. In very fast-moving practical work, we cannot always live by the maxim "Ready, aim, fire"; we may have to invert it a little and operate by a more interactive deliberative rule, "Ready, fire, aim", and then reflect and fire again. We have to start somewhere and deliberate as we work outwards from that point. This is what urban activist Nabeel Hamdi calls "working backwards". Sometimes we just have "to start where we can" in order to understand what is happening and to get our imagination going around what is possible and best.[5] In many situations, our process of deliberation has to be more emergent than prescriptive. Only by experiencing or disrupting a situation can we begin to think reasonably about the problems it sets us. Deliberation often involves starting, not pausing.

Humanitarian Deliberation

Active deliberation will still require methods of discussion and reflection. In forming a distinct approach to humanitarian deliberation, humanitarian ethics can usefully draw on three different traditions of deliberation. Each one has a particular contribution that can inform humanitarian practice.

- Decision-making theory—concentrates on the psychology of decision-making in individuals and organizations. It can guide us on positive forms of decision-making within humanitarian institutions, so supporting intra-organizational deliberation.
- Political theory—discussions of deliberative democracy in political ethics offer insights into inclusive forms of discussion that struggle to resolve problems of power and justice between different sections of society. This offers insight into how humanitarian agencies can delib-

erate outwards in their political relationships with authorities and affected communities. This theory may help us with external collective deliberations with diverse stakeholders.

- Medical and social work ethics—specialize in very intimate forms of deliberation between a professional and a vulnerable patient or client and their family. This body of ethics can add real value to deliberation at the intimate face-to-face level of humanitarian practice that is concerned with individual needs and options.

Each one of these deliberative fields can contribute to humanitarian ethics. This chapter examines their particular relevance in an effort to shape a clearer practice of good humanitarian deliberation.

Decision-Making Within Organizations

The purpose and outcomes of deliberation should be decisions of various kinds: either a decision to continue to do what you are already doing, or a decision to try something new. This means that a good understanding of decision-making is important to the deliberation process as it helps humanitarian agencies make the best possible decisions within their respective organizations.

Modern decision-making theory rightly distinguishes between a judgement and a decision.[6]

- A judgement is an evaluation of a situation and the options involved. To make a judgement, we weigh evidence against all available data. Because of the frequent impossibility of ever knowing or understanding enough, good judgement is best seen as an art or a gift. Those who have good judgement seem almost to transcend the data, to feel the texture of a problem like a potter feels her clay, sensing just how it is and how best it can be shaped.[7]
- A decision is a choice between two or more alternatives. It is informed by judgement of the situation and the possible alternatives. Typically, alternatives are characterized as fixed and well-defined or uncertain and ill-defined. They are also risky or relatively riskless. In humanitarian action, as in business, politics and government, decisions are made either by an individual, a team or by a whole organization. Decisions are also made at different levels of an organization, typically frontline or headquarters.

Like Aristotle, the modern psychology of decision-making notes that significant decisions are commonly made in imperfect situations. This is certainly true in many humanitarian operations. The psychology of most individual or group decision-making at any level of an organization is routinely characterized by "bounded rationality"—situations of limited understanding in which all possible information, alternatives and outcomes are rarely known.[8] As well as problems of incomplete knowledge, decision-making is frequently pressured by time and is often crowded out by other decisions. The ability to prioritize which decisions are the most important to make is a rare skill. We tend to be preoccupied by decisions that are closer to us somehow: the person who keeps knocking at our door, or the email at the top of our inbox. We are also tempted to defer or deny difficult strategic decisions and to opt for easier ones instead. Contrary to public expectation, this means that some important humanitarian decisions are made far too slowly or not at all, rather than too fast. Hesitation and reluctance to respond to early warning and to "call" particular crisis points in slow onset disasters can be instances of such deferral.[9]

Psychology also suggests that we instinctively use a number of set-piece cognitive approaches in our judgement and decision-making. It is important to be aware of these mental shortcuts because they can sometimes inform careful deliberation and sometimes undermine it. Unless we are very disciplined in our judgement and decision-making, our brains will tend to follow the four main strategies set out below: categorization, simplification, anchoring and storylining.[10] These serve as psychological coping mechanisms in our routine decision-making and particularly kick in when we face a lot of decisions at once or intense time pressure.

- Categorization—when we encounter a particular situation or problem, we immediately try to fit it into an existing schema of similar things that we have faced before. In short, we try to recognize it as something we know already. Sometimes we are right and our previous experience will help directly with this new problem. At other times, we risk stereotyping problems and actually misconceiving them. So, in a security incident in which a relief convoy is aggressively showered with stones from a hill above the road, we might mistake a deeper acceptance problem for a one-off rogue threat because the incident was similar to the last security problem we faced which was a rogue stone thrower. But this time the causes might be very different and more entrenched.

- Simplification—there are various ways we tend to simplify our decisions. Decomposition involves breaking the problem down into component parts and only solving the easiest parts. By editing a problem we may deliberately ignore or discount uncertainties or difficulties. We may draw on certain rules of thumb that dictate simple maxims like "keep it simple" or "ask Geneva" or "never negotiate" or "what did we do last time?" Or we may use an endorsement or role model strategy and copy another agency or humanitarian that we admire. Sometimes this is wise; sometimes it may be inappropriate as a short cut.
- Storylining—is a particularly powerful form of simplification in which a dominant group edits events and motives to produce a particular and satisfying story about the situation which others will then be made to recognize as true. This storyline is then "sold" as the explanation of a problem (which it may be in part or not at all) and decisions are made in line with the story. Storylining is a term used in film and TV drama. It was also in vogue in management studies as the best way for a leader to communicate a company's challenges and goals. But it fell out of fashion when many of these stories proved profoundly inaccurate and businesses failed.[11] Humanitarian agencies must also treat certain "stories" that are told to explain ethical problems and justify humanitarian decisions with care. Such stories may be over-simplified and vested with the self-interest of key actors.
- Anchoring and adjusting—in which we tentatively or experimentally adopt a certain response and adjust it or abandon it as things develop. If done well with a genuinely open mind and a readiness to pull in the anchor, this is more like the interactive deliberation recommended above by John Kay and Nabeel Hamdi.

Deliberative cultures are as significant as deliberative psychologies. Decision-making is strongly influenced by an organization's culture as well as by the personal psychology of decision-makers. Whether made by an individual or a team, decisions lean towards certain cultural norms in every organization. These norms can be positive values, like inclusion and transparency, or can involve cultural norms that act as cultural trumps or habits in any decision-making. For example, some organizations have instinctively commercial cultures that prioritize "bottom line" considerations and make the criterion of financial loss and gain paramount in their decisions. Others might have pragmatic cultures that trump values and transparency with a total commitment to "getting the job done", team loyalty and confidentiality. For example, studies in police ethics suggest that in some units there is an unofficial ethical culture described as the "blue code" or "Dirty Harry" beliefs. These agree that a certain amount of rule bending is acceptable to get the job done and that team loyalty is absolute, even in covering up a colleague's wrongdoing.[12] Some organizational cultures are deeply risk-averse. In humanitarian agencies, this may involve excessive emphasis on staff security and operational procedure. In contrast, other organizational cultures might prioritize a culture of daring, bravado and independence that drives their deliberation accordingly. Such companies value risk-taking as a mark of commitment and action. MSF can project this culture type in the humanitarian sector. Sexism, racism or ageism may also be powerful forces in certain organizations and consistently bias decision-making processes and outcomes. Some organizations are more consequentialist and utilitarian than others in their ethics, more focused on end-states than values and means. The power of organizational culture means that the ethical culture of a humanitarian organization is very important in shaping its decision-making.

Judgements and decision-making are usually best made when deliberation is as inclusive as possible, with the exception of burning house scenarios. As ALNAP's recent studies of humanitarian leadership have shown, collaborative leadership and decision-making frequently delivers better decisions that also attract more buy-in.[13] By including all relevant stakeholders and some constructive critics or sceptics, participatory decision-making can avoid some of the "cognitive blinders" and elite "group think" that inevitably restrict the knowledge and views of a single group.[14] A variety of people and groups see different angles on a problem, have different interests, own particular information and understand different things. At its best, therefore, strong participatory decision-making involves a four-phased process: seeing the problem as widely as possible by involving a range of people to get near to a 360-degree view; seeking out as much information as possible, particularly contradictory evidence; sharing this information widely; and using it together to make judgements and take a decision.

However, group decision-making is not always wise in an emergency. Collaborative leadership can be slow and there is evidence that when making a decision in an ambiguous situation, individuals are more decisive than groups. When the same ambiguous problem is given to an individual for a decision without any discussion, a person usually makes a judgement and takes a decision. But when the same person is asked to join a group to discuss the problem, that person tends to retreat from the earlier decision and stall. The same stalling happens when a group is asked to make the decision as a group around an ambiguous problem. The group becomes indecisive or neutral on the subject.[15] This so-called "convergence to neutrality" confirms how important it can be for agencies to leave room for individual leadership and personal discretion at all levels of a humanitarian operation. Some important deliberation and decision-making will need to be done by leaders alone without resorting to a mobile phone, a conference call and inter-agency cluster meetings that seek consensus more than strategy.

Open, exploratory and participatory deliberation in organizations is one kind of decision-making process. Other types of deliberation are more closed loop and explicitly based on rules, decision-making trees or checklists. This sort of framework-based deliberation is very popular in business ethics, medical ethics and social work ethics, especially for routine procedures like site safety, supply chain ethics or recruitment procedures. Frameworks are also popular in codes of "ethical fitness" as pioneered by Accenture with its fifty-eight action statements that specify particular kinds of behaviour or virtues that show their staff putting their values into practice. So, for example, one of the Accenture statement affirms: "our best people understand different points of view and foster and inclusive environment".[16] These kinds of action-guiding statements serve as rules in an ethical checklist. However, there is evidence that in more complex situations there is a low use of frameworks in actual practice. They can be abandoned early on as people move to a deeper discussion of problems that are embedded in a very particular context.

Framework processes have their place in humanitarian ethics where international humanitarian law (IHL), the Code of Conduct and Sphere all lend themselves to a checking approach. For example, some moral problem-solving will be usefully informed by checking a situation and its options against the six main questions below. This checklist will only give closed answers (yes or no) but these can be used to identify the humanitarian strengths and weaknesses in different options for further deliberation.

1. Are we respecting fundamental humanitarian principles and the Code of Conduct?

2. Are we likely to increase actions that are in accordance with or in breach of IHL, refugee law and disaster law?
3. Are we likely to increase or decrease the ability of humanitarian actors to meet Sphere Standards?
4. Are we likely to improve or worsen our target population's dignity and conditions?
5. Are we likely to increase or decrease our ability to abide by principles of good humanitarian management?
6. Are the affected population likely to understand and respect our decision?

Decision-Making Contexts

Decision-making frameworks can also be useful in humanitarian ethics by broadly distinguishing between different types of contexts in which deliberation and decision-making need to take place.

As we have seen in the example of the burning house at the beginning of this chapter, different types of ethical challenge call for and prioritize different kinds of deliberation and decision-making processes. The so-called Cynefin model is a useful way of modelling the different types of deliberation that are likely in four different types of context.[17]

The model usefully shows how different types of deliberation or decision-making are appropriate to different types of situation and problem. Relatively orderly conditions can be deliberated conventionally by categorizing and analysing. In more complex and chaotic situations, more rational approaches fail and "sense-making" requires more engaged approaches that require you to experience the problem: probing into complexity or jumping in and acting in chaos to discover what is best to do. This is similar to Nabeel Hamdi's advice of starting somewhere and working backwards from experience to reason.

The appeal of this model is its reliance on sensing. This chimes with Aristotle's virtue of practical wisdom and Nussbaum's emphasis on feeling. It protects against an overly rational or calculative form of deliberation. A more unordered situation of chaos and complexity plays to the strengths of those who may not be overly analytical but have developed strong humanitarian intuitions and virtues. With these, they can feel their way to design aid programmes that innovate and operate effectively in extreme or unconventional settings. Examples of these settings would be the extreme devastation and humanitarian overcrowding of the Haitian earthquake, or the new challenges of low access, mid-conflict humanitarian action in urban areas of Syria. In these conditions, probing and sensing is likely to be more productive of effective practices than programme design by categorizing based on precedent and detailed attempts at analysing the situation.

Deliberative Legitimacy

Good deliberation must also be marked by a legitimate process and so be respected as an ethical form of discussion that has the respect of those involved. In their study of deliberation in international organizations, Millewicz and Goodwin found that to be effective and have any credibility, deliberation must be an empowered space where decisions stick and deliver results.[18] They identified seven key characteristics in the successful deliberations they examined:

- Authenticity—deliberation is real, not token
- Inclusion—all relevant people are involved
- Efficiency—deliberation is decision-orientated, not a talking shop
- Legitimacy—deliberation is recognized as official and powerful
- Discursive discipline—people know how to talk well together
- Empowered decision-making—deliberation will lead to action
- Feedback loops—deliberation continues, learns and adapts

Political Deliberation with Wider Society

In most humanitarian organizations, people are aligned around common goals and generally have a common language in which they can sufficiently share. Political deliberation with external parties is a much more subtle and challenging process across wide gaps in culture, class, life experience, intentions and interests. These distinct political dynamics are usually in play when humanitarian agencies try to deliberate on difficult programming options with affected communities, national authorities, armed groups and donors.

Some form of public deliberation is imperative in most difficult instances of humanitarian ethics. Article 7 of the Code and its emphasis on participation demands it, and wider and diverse discussion will tend towards better decisions and greater legitimacy for humanitarian agencies. These discussions will usually involve a structured dialogue of some form in community meetings, regular inter-agency meetings and private discussions at senior level. Deliberation of this kind typically involves asymmetries in power and big differences in political objectives. Discussing aid options with communities of destitute people usually puts a humanitarian agency at a political advantage. Discussing humanitarian access with a government or armed group tends to see power tip away from agencies.

Humanitarians do not usually talk about "deliberating" with authorities. Instead, they use the terms "humanitarian negotiation" or "humanitarian diplomacy" to describe their discussions with state and non-state authorities.[19] But in both these processes, ethical deliberation is in play as humanitarian workers make the humanitarian case and discuss optimal ethical arrangements for humanitarian action in a given context. In their definition of humanitarian diplomacy, the Red Cross and Red Crescent definition makes clear that humanitarian deliberation around ends and means is at the heart of humanitarian diplomacy: "humanitarian diplomacy is persuading decision-makers and opinion leaders to act, at all times, in the interests of vulnerable people, and with full respect for fundamental humanitarian principles".[20] Both diplomacy and negotiation have a more persuasive element than pure deliberation, and humanitarian diplomacy is often played out on a very uneven political field in armed conflicts and disasters.[21] Nevertheless, a process of ethical deliberation by humanitarian professionals certainly needs to precede diplomatic and negotiation efforts, and the best diplomatic meetings or negotiations are the ones in which all sides deliberate openly, empathically and constructively to find the most ethical strategy for humanitarian action.

The principle of deliberation has been at the heart of democratic politics since classical times. In the last twenty years the distinct idea of "deliberative democracy" has had a renaissance in political theory, largely in the wake of the new emphasis on discourse ethics inspired by the German philosopher Jurgen Habermas.[22] Deliberation is one important way in which political communities or their elected representatives can make decisions. It is recognized as a form of arguing and reflection that is distinct from other forms of democratic decision-making like bargaining or voting. Bargaining is essentially competitive and compromising, whereas voting is the simple adding up of preferences. In contrast, deliberation is a form of constructive argument that is intended to be transformative, leading to creative and co-generated options that are ethically acceptable to all parties.[23] In politics, deliberation typically happens in open spaces like parliaments and formal meetings, while bargaining and deal-making takes place in backrooms, corridors and private lunches.

The main advantages of public deliberation as a democratic process are summarized by Diego Gambetta, Italian social scientist, and James Fearon, Stanford political scientist, in the list below. These advantages also stand as sound reasons for public humanitarian deliberation.

Advantages of Public Deliberation in Political Decision-Making are:

It distributes information and reveals private information of concerned parties
It lessens or overcomes bounded rationality
It spurs the imagination and incentivizes people to create new options
It introduces a demand to justify options and preferences in public
It shares risk and instils the courage to try daring options
It dilutes self-interested claims and injects principles into public consideration
It can make better and fairer decisions in terms of distributive justice
It can generate wider consensus
It produces more legitimate decisions
It improves the ethical and intellectual qualities of the participants
It increases public accountability[24]

But public deliberation has its risks too. As Gambetta points out, there are problems with deliberation.[25] First, as we have seen in our burning house scenario, "if the quality of outcomes declines rapidly over time, deliberation may simply waste precious time". Secondly, political rhetoric and sheer eloquence during deliberations can lead people to be duped, or can promote conformism in any deliberative group. An important variant of this emerges when elite lobbyists push propaganda or false information into a discussion. This can deceive and create what Susan Stokes calls "pseudo deliberation" and "pseudo preferences".[26] Finally, "the subtlety that deliberation may bring to a discussion can have a paralyzing effect", as we have seen in the tendency towards neutrality in collective discussions of ambiguous situations.[27] This is the so-called paralysis of analysis. Michael Walzer marks a wider note of caution about exaggerating the feasibility and significance of deliberation in politics. He points out that reasoned and impartial deliberation (similar to the objective and socially diverse deliberations of a criminal jury) is only a small part of how politics actually functions. Its significance should not be overstated alongside other political activities like campaigning, protest, elite bargaining, manipulation and sheer power play.[28]

Public deliberation today is not just face-to-face discussions. Most societies are constantly humming with much wider forms of deliberation, particularly in the new information age of blogs, tweets, internet news and other virtual discussion spaces. Sharon Krause, a political scientist at Brown University, rightly observes that there is a larger "deliberative system" at play in every society that is much wider than officially organized discussions.[29] This system includes: the talk and emotions of protests, campaigns and influential movies; the discussions of expert advisory bodies; the preaching of religious officials and media commentators; and the "everyday talk"[30] of people puzzling through burning issues for themselves around the dinner table, during car journeys, on Facebook, Twitter and around the office printer. Krause notes that all elements of this deliberative system play a critical role in the formation of sentiment, opinion and will towards particular moral problems. Humanitarian agencies play a big part in this wider deliberative system around armed conflict and disaster with their advocacy, campaigning and fundraising. Increasingly, they need to inform this public deliberation but also listen to public reaction as they draw ethical conclusions for their own operational decisions. In some situations, agencies might be wise to use public polling and public meetings not just to ask for money but to canvas public views on the ethical strategy their agency is taking. A two-way conversation with the public rather than a one-way "ask" could give agencies ethical guidance and legitimacy at particularly difficult moments, like the decisions to stay in the Goma camps or go cross-border into Syria.

All humanitarians will have experienced the different benefits and risks of deliberation when talking with local authorities and affected communities. Dialogue that happens across different cultures, languages and classes is always hard. Developing good quality deliberation is especially hard in polarized societies or in emergency situations when time is short. Sometimes it is extremely dangerous for local communities or government staff to be seen talking in depth with humanitarian agencies. But there are important moments of frankness and constructive discussion when valuable deliberation is possible with local authorities, affected communities, armed groups, donor agencies and donor publics. These moments need to be sought and seized.

Empathic Deliberation

Deliberation theory tries to be conscious of power imbalances and cultural differences, and tries to find ways through them by emphasizing dialogical skills. Modern political theory understands formal deliberation as a sophisticated dialogue in which listening is active and transformative. To convey the intensity of this listening, Habermas uses the idea of "reciprocal reversals" to encourage each party to reverse into the experience of the other party and so understand from where they are speaking. This requires each party to make a considerable effort to understand the situation of other parties, so that all parties can think together to come up with solutions that are morally acceptable to all. But his is still a very rational process. Following Hume, Sharon Krause, recognizes the role of emotions in deliberation too, noting that "we must feel with others to arrive at legitimate decisions" and that "our minds are changed when our hearts are engaged".[31] For Krause, reversals or "perspective-taking" involves emotion and reason together. She argues that most of our reasons "are constituted by the things we care about".[32] In proper perspective-taking that imagines the point of view and experience of the other, we must "consult not our own personal responses but the sentiments of those affected".[33] We need to imagine what it feels like to be them.

Humanitarian deliberation requires empathic reversals in three main directions:

- Humanitarian agencies need to feel and understand the goals and reasons of authorities and affected communities.
- Authorities need to feel and understand affected communities and humanitarian agencies.
- Communities need to connect with the goals and reasons of political authorities and humanitarian agencies.

Agreement on the justice of each party's experience and goals is usually neither feasible nor necessary, but recognizing them is essential to shaping a humanitarian negotiation strategy that is ethically and operationally acceptable to all parties.

Building Humanitarian Will

An important part of the deliberative process of reversal and perspective-taking is its ability to help build a position of humanitarian impartiality around a problem from which various stakeholders can make better and joint decisions. Krause knows that total impartiality is never achievable in deliberations across diverse groups, but deems some level and ambition of impartiality as an essential component in due deliberation.[34] Humanitarian ethics would agree with this. A main purpose of deliberation in humanitarian action must always be to gather evidence and understandings that enable humanitarian agencies to be as objective as possible as they identify human needs and the best operational means to reach affected people. Encouraging humanitarian impartiality in the authorities and communities affected by the problem must be a core purpose in public humanitarian deliberation. Building humanitarian will and humanitarian impartiality becomes critical in strategies of deliberation and negotiation. Only through a deliberative process that contributes to impartiality formation and the formation of wider humanitarian will in all parties, can agencies and authorities make effective decisions that work on the ground and succeed over time.

Intimate Deliberation with Suffering Individuals

Alongside these forms of public and collective ethical deliberation around humanitarian grand strategy, humanitarian deliberation also needs to take account of much more intimate instances of joint deliberation in which a humanitarian worker discusses very personal options with an individual or family. This might involve a patient in a clinic, an older sibling caring for her baby brother in a therapeutic feeding centre, a prisoner in detention, a family seeking their lost relative, a family requesting a cash grant or a person recovering from sexual violence. These very personal discussions should be at the heart of humanitarian action and are the intimate frontline of humanitarian ethics. Empathic communication, reciprocal reversals and perspective-taking are integral in this intimate deliberation too, but the context of this deliberation is a more immediate relationship of care. This is different to the organizational and political deliberations of humanitarian strategy described above. Instead, it is the face-to-face encounter of personal responsibility emphasized by Levinas, Ricoeur, the religious traditions and medical ethics.

ICRC medical doctor Paul Bouvier has described how these intimate deliberations need to be truly "human encounters" in which a "relationship of humanitarian care is at the core of humanitarian action".[35] In his powerful paper on ICRC's work with detainees, Bouvier emphasizes how intimate humanitarian work needs always to involve "moments of shared humanity" and "mutual recognition" in which the humanitarian worker and the affected person both present themselves openly, giving something of themselves and receiving something of each other. These individual or family discussions are the repeated instantiations of the principle of humanity in action. In them, all parties are seen as human and seek to be humane. Bouvier tells several stories of small things given and received between detainees and ICRC delegates, including a drop of perfume. Once a male prisoner asked an ICRC delegate if she could bring him some perfume. She borrowed some eau de toilette from a male colleague and brought it into the prison the next day with the approval of the authorities. Bouvier continues:

> The detainee sprayed himself generously and joyfully with the perfume, on his face, his hair and his clothes. The man was radiant and said with gratefulness: "You know, today for the first time since I am here, I smell good. I feel I am a human." Then he went to the courtyard to see his comrades, sharing his joy, and rubbing his clothes on theirs to share the perfume. When we saw them later in the day, they came to us joyful and proudly sharing the good smell.

Importantly, Bouvier also tells of detainees giving small presents of their own to delegates, and stories of detainees insulting and yelling at delegates as the only people on whom they could safely vent their pent-up anger. And he tells of delegates crying as they hear stories of suffering and torture face-to-face.

In its understanding of intimate deliberation, humanitarian ethics can usefully draw on Paul Ricoeur's notion of solicitude and Simone Weil's emphasis on attention that we examined in the earlier discussion of humanity. Both these ideas capture the professional focus and individual concern that must embody humanitarian action at its most intimate point of impact. This is the closeness and proximity that humanitarian ethics has always prized. Belgian philosopher Gaelle Fiasse has summarized the medical ethics of Paul Ricoeur in a way that is perfectly suited to guide the face-to-face deliberative encounters of humanitarian action in health projects, but also in all other humanitarian projects like food security, livelihoods, education, psycho-social, water and sanitation, shelter and advocacy gathering that involve individual relationships of humanitarian care.[36] Fiasse shows how Ricoeur's emphasis on narrative, imagining, translation and mutual fragility can create the right relationship between patient and carer, a deliberative relationship that can be applied at the heart of humanitarian action.

Listening is the first step in a careful deliberation with someone about the best options in their suffering.[37] Ricoeur's insight into narrative identity (the idea that we are our individual story and its "entanglements" with others) means that a good way to listen is to attend to a person's narrative of what has happened in their lives, and what they want to happen. It is to pay attention to the story they have made of their lives and to understand the next chapter or the ending that they seek. Real listening is not just hearing but requires imagination. Simone Weil described the importance of listening as part of her doctrine of attention: "to listen to someone is to put oneself in his place while he is speaking".[38] As humanitarian workers know well, listening across large gaps in culture, class, gender, experience and pain is not easy. It requires imagination of the kind that Weil recommends and a certain translation too. For Ricoeur this translation means learning "to speak the language" of the other person. This fluency is really the ability to resonate with the lived experience of the other person and so understand where they are and what they need. Our translations are never perfect and are always undertaken "with some salvaging and some acceptance of loss".[39] However, this process of imaginative translation, which is often mediated to international humanitarian workers through actual linguistic interpreters, is essential if deliberation is to be real and meaningful.[40]

The importance of letting people speak must not be underestimated in humanitarian deliberation. Speaking out is an act of power and the act of listening shows respect for the speaker. Speaking can, therefore, be a particularly important experience for people who have lost much or are routinely ignored and maltreated in armed conflict and disaster. As one Egyptian widow told the Cambridge anthropologist Helen Watson:

"Words from the heart are more alive than your scribbling. When we speak, our words burn."[41] In the same way that people are right to talk of their lives, humanitarians need also to speak powerfully of the value of humanity in all their public and private deliberations with authorities and communities. Humanitarian deliberation with others must prioritize humane speech if humanitarian values are to respond to people's needs and burn holes in brutal ideologies that seek to reject them.

This kind of solicitous dialogue happens best when we humanitarians recognize that we are all fragile and that, in some ways, we may be more fragile than the person before us. People are also resilient and able to work out the best options for each other in a given humanitarian situation. As Fiasse observes: "sometimes a suffering person can be more actualized in other dimensions of her being than the person treating her".[42] This is certainly a common experience for humanitarian workers who regularly stand in awe at the dignity, resilience, practical wisdom and goodness of people deeply affected by armed conflict, famine and disaster.

Ethical Competence

All these different ways of deliberating need to combine with the technical knowledge of humanitarian workers and the values and expertise of their organizations to develop a sufficient level of ethical competence in every humanitarian worker. Ethical competence is a very practical notion that has been developed by Ann Gallagher and others in nursing ethics. Gallagher defines ethical competence as the trained manifestation of a strong sense of moral agency, which is "the capacity to recognize, deliberate and act upon moral responsibilities".[43] Moral agency and ethical competence stand in stark contrast to moral blindness or moral complacency, in which people will not or cannot scrutinize the ethics of a situation.

Ethical competence is a good level to aim at for all humanitarian workers, and an equally good way to gauge and evaluate the ethics of humanitarian programming as a whole. Gallagher's model involves a fivefold ability set. First is knowledge, in particular the ability to know something about ethics, the technical field in which you are working, rules and guidelines, people's options and the wider socio-political situation around you. This knowledge can then inform ethical problem-solving. Secondly, there is a perceptual dimension—the ability to perceive and recognize ethical problems as they arise. A good sign of ethical competence is that people develop a "moral eye" which enables them to spot moral problems. This perception is also the space of intuition and moral sense that guides right analysis and action. Third is ethical reflection, the kind of deliberative competence we have discussed. Fourth is ethical doing and action; this is the competence, and often the permission, to act in the right way in a given problem. Finally, "ethical being" is the gradual "habituation" of ethical awareness and competence that eventually becomes second nature in the humanitarian professional.

This chapter has examined three types of deliberation—organizational, political and intimate—that have important parts to play in humanitarian ethics. At any one time, a humanitarian agency and its people are likely to be engaged in every one of these deliberative spaces: thinking about what is best to do among themselves, in public meetings, and privately with individuals in their care. The next chapter looks more precisely at the typical structure of moral choices that will often be the contexts of humanitarian deliberation.

9

MORAL CHOICES

Humanitarian action presents a range ethical choices and predicaments. We now need to look in more detail at the way these choices tend to be structured. Humanitarian professionals face the same fundamental types of moral choice as everybody else. The detail of particular humanitarian problems may be unique, complicated and extreme; but underneath the peculiarities of a situation, the essential structure of moral problems is often one of several main types. This chapter looks at these typical structures of moral choice.

Making choices is often difficult, however some people find this process more challenging than others. Once again, it may help if we do not think of choosing as a purely rational and calculative procedure that requires particular philosophical expertise, but recognize that choice has important emotional elements as well. One great test of any choice is if we can make it and then actually carry it out after we have reasoned that it should be right. Often we make big choices in a rational discussion: to take a new job, to get divorced, or to close down a humanitarian operation. We go to bed resolved, but then we sleep on it. In the morning we awake uneasy about the choice and tend towards another option. Sometimes this hesitation can arise because of fear and a lack of moral courage, but often it is the gentle pressing of our will and our desire. Quite simply we cannot go ahead with it because we do not feel right about it.

This moral swaying comes about because we are not moved by our reason alone, but also by our will and our emotions. A choice that is voluntary and freely willed will also be truly desirable to our conscience and our intuition. We will want to do it. Thomas Aquinas encapsulates this emotional aspect of choice when he says: "Therefore, choice is substantially not an act of the reason but of the will: for choice is accomplished in a certain movement of the soul towards the good which is chosen."[1] That a choice is the combination of reason and will is informative, because we usually feel real dissonance if we start doing something that we do not desire to do. Alternatively, we feel in tune with our actions when we are moving with our will rather than against it. The presence of "the soul's desire" in our choices is theological language for the part played by emotion and conscience in our moral reasoning, which can help tell us if we are on the right track in our ethical decisions.

As we saw earlier, not all ethical decisions are binary choices. Many are scalar and more a matter of degree, while others concern iterative moves as we gradually explore a particular path. It is, therefore, unwise to frame every situation as a stark choice. The way we frame situations is very important in ethics as in everything else. Making every problem into a dramatic choice can bring a fatalistic tone to humanitarian programming: "we have to do A or we have to do B". Instead, good ethical practice is more often about adjusting the scale of your relations with one party or exploring new options that are not A or B to see if you can tweak the situation or create a more ethical climate to your programming. In agencies not used to talking ethics, the appearance of a problem as an "ethical problem" can tend to catastrophize the situation and render it unnecessarily into a predicament of extreme options. Ethical concerns need to be something routine and not used only to mark something extreme and exceptional in an agency's thinking. Nevertheless, humanitarian situations do regularly come to a tough point of decision that involves a hard choice.

Different Types of Choice

The range of different situations faced by agencies and individuals in their work usually boils down to a few common types of choice. These different choices are distinguished by four main factors that shape the choice in a given situation:

- different levels of knowledge and certainty
- different levels of feasibility

- competing values and principles
- different levels of loss from choosing one thing over another.

In other words, some choices are difficult because they are not entirely clear. Some are hard because it is not possible to do what you really want to do. Other choices are difficult because choosing one good thing inevitably leaves other good things undone. Some choices are hard because they enable bad things by others. These generalizations will make more sense if we look at particular examples of each type of choice.

An Obvious Choice—High Levels of Certainty

This is the best choice to have. In this choice, both moral certainty and practical feasibility are high. In other words, it is clear what one should do and one is clearly able to do it. For example, in a humanitarian operation, this might involve a simple impartiality choice where a nutritional survey shows clearly that children in district A are much more malnourished than children in district B. Your agency is politically and logistically able to operate easily in either district. In this choice, the evidence makes clear the area of greatest need and indicates the best choice with a good degree of certainty. Your humanitarian programme should focus on district A.

In obvious choices, moral certainty is high so that a range of alternatives can easily be ranked as best, good or bad. Agency ability to take the best course of action is also high, meaning that operational feasibility is not in question. Some moral philosophers like to use equations and might represent a choice of this kind as:

$A < B$ *so OA (where O = ought to do)*

In this situation, because of high levels of certainty and feasibility, it is clear that doing A is better than doing B and so you ought to do A.

Compromise—A Certain Choice but with Clear Moral Losses

Some choices may be clear to see and feasible to make but involve a heavy loss regardless. A may be better than B or C but the choice itself may still involve bad things. Losses may involve matters of principle, material interests or humanitarian impact. These choices are frequently posed and solved as moral compromises. In humanitarian action, they often emerge in judgements and decisions around political and operational association. So, for example, it is common in humanitarian politics to trade independence for access in areas where there are powerful government or armed group authorities. In many armed conflicts, humanitarian agencies choose to compromise complete independence of action by accepting operational restrictions from authorities that have very clear vested interests in the way aid is distributed. Agencies compromise because the choice is between restricted operations or no operations at all. This kind of choice is a common feature of humanitarian action. It was the case when working with the Ethiopian government and rebel groups in the Ethiopian civil wars of the 1980s. It has also been the case with the government of Sudan in the civil wars in South Sudan and Darfur, and is also the case for humanitarian agencies working in Rakhine state in Myanmar today. This kind of compromise has also happened when agencies cooperated with NATO counter-insurgencies in Iraq and Afghanistan. Compromise is also usually at the heart of relationships with government donors. Agencies often have to tilt their programmes towards donor priorities in order to win funding.

Tony Coady, Australian philosopher, defines compromise as follows:

> A compromise is a sort of bargain in which several agents who see advantages in co-operative efforts of some sort agree to proceed in a way that requires each of them to surrender, perhaps only temporarily, some of their ends, interests or policies, in order to secure others. There is nothing immoral in compromise, as such.[2]

In their excellent book *On Complicity and Compromise*, MSF doctor Chiara Lepora and philosopher Robert Goodin usefully distinguish between three types of compromise: substitution, intersection and conjunction.[3]

> Substitution
>
> Where one party wants a,b,c,d and the other party wants e,f,g,h. They opt instead for a third possibility x,y,z. This kind of compromise is based on finding a jointly acceptable new option.
>
> Intersection
>
> Where one party wants o,p,q,r and the other wants q,r,s,t, they will settle for q,r. This kind of compromise is possible when you can trim your own prefer-

ences and find overlap with the other party's preferences, so creating an agreement from existing options.

Conjunction

Where one party wants o,p,q,r and the other wants not-o, not-p, not-q, not-r. Both parties settle for o,p and not-q, not-r. In this situation, each party agrees to settle for something it wants and something it certainly does not want. This is usually the worst kind of compromise because it involves not just diluting preferences but actively including unacceptable ingredients.

In many compromises, the main purpose of the choice is to opt for non-ideal but acceptable common ground, or opt for the so-called "lesser evil" in a decision between two options.[4] Compromises are always made to secure an "on balance good" and are characterized by being voluntary, negotiated and essentially fair and proportionate so that no one side does obviously worse than the other. Every compromise leaves people feeling some sense of moral discomfort, hence the difficult sense of "being compromised". But overall, a good compromise is essentially acceptable because it enables other goods. However, a compromise that is forced and distinctly disproportionate against one side is coerced. This kind of compromise is rightly felt to be a "rotten compromise" in which one has paid too high a moral price and in which an excess of bad things has come about. A rotten compromise is, therefore, usually a wrong decision, or was never a proper choice because of coercion and duress.

An Uncertain Choice—Epistemic Veils

Many choices involve high levels of uncertainty. This is essentially what makes them moral problems rather than simple ethical choices. These uncertain choices are often described as being shrouded in an "epistemic veil" or an "epistemic cloak", meaning that people do not know enough or cannot know enough to make an informed choice between various alternatives.[5] These terms in moral philosophy are equivalent to the cognitive blinders of psychology.

In humanitarian action, uncertain choices may involve programming choices around what kind of aid and protection is likely to work best or security decisions about when it is safe for a team to continue to work in a high risk area. New information can sometimes improve the structure of these choices by introducing higher levels of certainty. However, making these choices usually involves the virtues of courage and practical wisdom. Uncertain choices carry high levels of moral risk, but even when a decision has a bad outcome it may not have been an unethical decision. For example, sending a humanitarian team back, with their own consent, into a dangerous area to continue to provide primary health care for IDPs can be an ethical decision even if two members of the team are then kidnapped two weeks later. The decision may well have been a good one because it was rightly weighing a variety of different goods—people's health, staff safety and a principled stand for continuing health provision. Outcomes and consequences alone do not determine what is responsible ethical behaviour.

Slippery Slopes—Uncertain Dynamic Choices

Many problems of moral uncertainty are particularly difficult because they are "dynamic choice problems". This means they spread out and degrade over time. The choice you make now may become the first in a series of choices over which you have less and less control and which add up to become increasingly bad choices that lead you up an undesirable moral path that is not entirely clear from where you now stand. These future pathway dynamics latent in a choice are often described as "slippery slope" problems. What may be right to do now may set you on an irreversible course that goes increasingly wrong.

For example, in a child welfare programme it may be absolutely right to gather unaccompanied children together in a temporary orphanage to protect them and save their lives. However, over time this strategy can change the emotional incentives of parents and extended families. Within three months these children could become less and less likely to be claimed by family members who see life in an NGO institution as a very positive start in life for their children. The good thing you did three months ago has created a slippery slope and a moral hazard. It is playing a part in encouraging family break-up, institutionalization and involves expensive organizational running costs. These costs now soak up funds to care for 1,000 children that could be invested in community programmes to improve the lives of 10,000 children.

Like uncertain choices, decision-making in slippery slope problems can be painful. The pain in these types of choice arises from an awareness of future moral risk and the inability to predict or control them. One does a good thing now despite not being sure if it will involve a bad thing later. Or, one makes a harsh decision now to prevent suspected moral degradation arising from the soft option and ensure wider goods in future. Such uncertainty is morally stressful.

Apples and Oranges—Conflicts of Incomparable Values

Many moral conflicts are not between the relative certainties of equal goods (choosing between three ripe apples) or equal bads (three rotten apples) but are difficult choices between different goods (a ripe apple and a ripe orange).

Conflicts between incomparable or incommensurable values preoccupy moral philosophers, especially ones who are analytically or mathematically minded. They struggle to see if a poet and a novelist could be assessed equally for a literary prize, or if it is better to grow up to be a great violinist or a great lawyer. Can you compare the genius of Mozart and Michelangelo and decide who is the greater artist? Are these things "roughly comparable", or is there such discontinuity between them that they are essentially arguing between "incommensurable" values? Is it possible to say when we should make a choice between life and liberty, privacy and national security?[6] How do we weigh different goods?

Problems of incomparable or incommensurable value often emerge in humanitarian ethics. For example, people often question whether humanitarian agencies should stay on and feed people in camps when the authorities are simultaneously using these camps as a convenient way to coerce them and violate their wider civil and political rights. In another example: is it better to invest in a programme of school repair and teacher training or post-conflict counselling and economic support for women who have been raped? These moral problems seem to present difficult choices for humanitarian agencies between the different values of human life and political justice, or education and personal dignity. For many multi-mandate agencies, these choices create ethical tensions between different aspects of their mission: relief and development, long-term poverty reduction and immediate humanitarian need, advocacy and discretion.[7]

If it is impossible to find a way that different values like life and freedom can trade off against one another, then one philosophical solution is to find a moral equation that always allows you to "trump" one value with another. James Griffin recommends trumping in conflicts of value "if a small amount of A is always better than a large amount of B".[8]

Humanitarian ethics with its fundamental value of humanity probably accepts this trump most of the time, thus putting human life temporarily above wider rights. But the way many philosophers discuss value differences and frame them as "clashes" and "conflicts" can be a mis-representation of these problems. It makes them unrealistically binary as either/or choices, when sometimes it is possible to address both moral claims on an agency in creative humanitarian programming. It is usually possible to smooth these moral conflicts by addressing different values together in one programme, or separately in two programmes. For example, it is not inevitable that an agency should have to choose between a project for women recovering from rape or a project of school rehabilitation. The two can be finessed. Rape survivors can be trained as staff, teachers or pupils in a school rehabilitation programme, thus recovering their dignity in an empowering social role. Humanitarian agencies that are committed to food distributions in coercive IDP camps could also try to protect people from the worst dangers of this coercion, and also discreetly campaign for national and international action to stop it. If it is impossible to resolve this incompatibility smoothly and completely, then it becomes yet another part of humanitarian action's inevitable and continuous struggle for elements of success in difficult situations.

Perhaps Simone Weil has the most realistic approach to the problem of incomparable values or, as she puts it, "the incompatibility of duties". Discussing the problem, she notes: "Consciousness of [our] various obligations makes it impossible for us to resign ourselves to situations in which obligations are incompatible with one another."[9] We must never be resigned to this problem, but we have to keep trying to meet these various obligations whenever and in whatever way we can. We may never have complete success, but we may get instances of success. The very fact that we keep trying ensures that all the values we hold remain alive in a given situation, if not sufficiently fulfilled. The restriction of women's rights in Afghanistan under the Taliban is one of the most obvious cases of this incompatibility of duties in recent humanitarian history. The Taliban policies restricting women's participation in education, work and health examinations by male medics constructed a situation of incompatible obligations for humanitarian agencies. Humanitarians felt bound to help everyone, but could not help everyone. They also wanted to work against the Taliban's violations of women's rights and to change Taliban policy. In this situation, humanitarian agencies were really the victims of coercion, and they could not be sure that they would be in a better moral position by leaving the country and "focusing on advocacy" to change Taliban policy. The best way to mitigate this moral outrage was probably from within by doing what they could for men and boys while gradually finding innovative and perhaps subversive ways of reaching women and girls through the illegal underground network of girls' schools. From this operational base, agencies could then also inform public advocacy by others.

Dirty Hands—Choosing a Wrong to do a Right

The option of supporting underground schools deemed illegal by the Taliban raises the question of "dirty hands" in ethics. Some difficult choices seem to be structured between the need to break one moral rule in order to fulfil another. In other words, the best thing to do in some situations is to do something that would usually be wrong. This type of choice has come to be understood as the inevitable ethical problem of getting dirty hands, and is particularly common in emergency ethics when the stakes are very high.[10] It is similar and sometimes interchangeable with the idea of choosing a "lesser evil" in a difficult situation, or the change in morality that can occur in a "ticking bomb" scenario when some argue it is permissible to derogate from a moral absolute. Notoriously, the ticking bomb example frequently engenders the scenario of suspending the prohibition of torture in order to extract information that could save lives. Humanitarian choices are never as immoral as this, but certain situations do present the logic that suspending some moral norms is necessary for wider humanitarian goals.

Despite its relatively recent name, the challenge of dirty hands in ethics has a long history. Many ancient legends and religious texts have stories that celebrate deception, lies, misinformation and the murder of unarmed people as legitimate moral strategies in pursuit of a greater cause. Famously, Odysseus and the Greeks deceived the Trojans with the gift of a wooden horse filled with armed men. Rebecca and Jacob deceived Isaac to steal his paternal blessing from Esau, his rightful heir. Many tales also justify sex and seduction as a means to information or assassination in a just cause. Judith murdered the drunken Holophernes, an Assyrian general who was planning to destroy her city. Queen Esther used her sexual influence over the King to undermine the plans of his Vizier, Haman, to massacre the Jews in Persia. Throughout Shia history, this much persecuted branch of Islam has held to a doctrine of *taqiyyah* that allows them to disguise themselves and lie about their identity and beliefs if this will save their lives. Most commonly, these breaches of the normal moral law are understood as necessary cunning for the preservation of a greater good.

In Michael Walzer's classic paper on dirty hands, he explores how Niccolo Machiavelli, the great political theorist and courtly adviser of Renaissance Italy, recognized the occasional need for "necessary immorality".[11] Importantly, as Walzer points out, choices of this kind do not signal moral relativism: an "anything goes" or "whatever works" approach to ethics. To talk of dirty hands decisions is not an extreme utilitarian position that argues that the end always justifies the means. Instead, Machiavelli himself was highly conscious that these choices involve a very real breach of moral rules. In his discussion of such practices, he still upholds the standard involved in the breach, but is clear that political realism requires some breaches to take place:

> The fact is that a man [*sic*] who wants to act virtuously in every way necessarily comes to grief among so many who are not virtuous...taking everything into account, he will find that some of the things that appear to be virtues will, if he practises them, ruin him, and some of the things that appear to be vices will bring him security and prosperity.[12]

Walzer shows how Max Weber and Albert Camus felt similarly about such breaches, but more so. Weber observed how the politician with dirty hands is a hero, but always "a tragic hero" who has lost his soul. In his play on the theme called *The Just Assassins*, Albert Camus is in no doubt that his assassins put themselves beyond the realm of justice in choosing to murder. Despite the good that may follow, they must accept punishment and execution for the crime it involved.[13]

In humanitarian action, dirty hands choices are obviously not about assassination, but they routinely emerge around problems of corruption, armed protection, dangerous associations and deception of various kinds. Sometimes it makes sense for an agency to speak only of assistance when negotiating humanitarian access, so being silent about the advocacy and protection role it also plans to play. Sometimes a toleration of food diversions is the only way to reach vulnerable communities. Sometimes hiding people is important to do and it is necessary to deceive those who seek to harm them. Exaggerating the importance of his agency's diplomatic immunity proved a good way for ICRC delegate Frederick Born to achieve this during the Holocaust. This is how he managed to preserve the immediate safety of hundreds of Jewish people in the centre of Budapest in 1944, although his protection was to prove tragically temporary and ultimately insufficient.[14] Deception of this kind can be morally important and justified as "emergency ethics". The notion of emergency ethics has been developed by Michael Walzer in relation to the use of force, but remains under-developed in humanitarian ethics.[15] One situation that may demand such emergency ethics is what Coady calls "moral isolation" in which, as described above by Machiavelli, everyone around you is breaking all moral norms, so creating a perverse situation in which acting normally and virtuously renders you and others extremely vulnerable to immoral acts.[16]

In humanitarian ethics, the main concern in any strategy of dirty hands seems to turn on the gravity of any moral breach and the likelihood of dangerous slippery slopes that may emerge from half-truths, dishonesty, bribery or misinformation. Alex Bellamy has rightly pointed out that most dirty hands or lesser evil problems are really challenges of the incomparable and incommensurable values (apples and oranges) discussed above.[17] Resolving a situation's simultaneously different demands for humanitarian access, absolute honesty and impeccable food distributions may simply be impossible. The key question becomes whether dirty hands choices have humanitarian legitimacy even when they may not align strictly with law or morality. In other words, can such acts make moral sense and be broadly acceptable to the fundamental concerns of humanitarian ethics? Here, humanitarian workers have to decide and choose.

Tragic Choices—Moral Dilemmas

The structure of a moral dilemma is particularly grim. Proper moral dilemmas have a terrible symmetry about them. Whichever path you choose will inevitably involve serious moral losses of some kind. These losses also result in significant pain for the person making the choice. Moral dilemmas (or trilemmas if there are three options in the choice) are structured by high but competing levels of certainty. In obligation dilemmas, the conflict is between opposing good things, like life-saving, in which you are obliged to do both. In prohibition dilemmas, the tension is between opposing bad things, like killing, where norms prohibit you from doing both and yet you must choose one.

The particular characteristic of a pure moral dilemma is that it is a forced choice that is not possible to evade and so involves imperatives of some kind. One is forced to choose in a situation in which one would rather not choose at all because the losses in either choice will be extreme and live with you forever. Ethicists call this continuing pain the "residue" or "remainder" of the choice that continues as significant badness, sadness and moral distress.[18]

In obligation dilemmas, the various alternatives might all be good but there is no way to rank them or to mitigate the costs of choosing only one. Hard triage situations are an example of these dilemmas. So, for example, a nutrition survey shows that child malnutrition is equally bad in three districts—A, B and C—but you are the only agency in the region and your agency only has the resources to deliver significant impact in one district at a time. It would be good to work in A or B or C but you have to choose one and cannot do anything significant to minimize the effects of not choosing the others.

This moral conflict could be reversed and you could be choosing between bad things. Programme cuts could be an example of a tragic choice between equally bad options. As funding declines in a region where maternal mortality and neonatal death are very high, you have to cut your midwifery programme in either district X or Y. The most extreme kind of moral dilemmas are, therefore, posed in a choice between things of identical value in a situation in which you cannot choose both. This has been most cruelly illustrated in Ruth Marcus' scenario of a mother who sees a pair of identical twins who are unable to swim, each falling into different sides of a wide pond equidistant from where she is standing. The time and distances involved mean she cannot save both. Whatever she does by saving one twin will somehow be unfair and incomplete.[19] A particular version of this tragic choice and its devastating residue was famously elaborated in William Styron's novel and film, *Sophie's Choice*. Once again, there is an equation for an extreme moral dilemma of this kind, in which $-C$ = cannot do:

$$OA \text{ and } OB \text{ but } -C(A+B)$$

In other words, you ought to save Twin A and you ought to save Twin B but you do not have the capacity to save A and B together.[20] In prohibition dilemmas in which all feasible options are prohibited by one or more moral principles, the equation would have a similar structure but look a little different, with N = not and C = can only do:

ONA and ONB but C(A or B)

Many moral philosophers feel that the actual complexity of moral dilemmas is overblown. Philippa Foot insists that the extremity of a dilemma lies in the intensity of its residue and pain, rather than in the technical difficulty of the choice itself. In most cases, a right choice can be made and justified while also acknowledging the inevitable loss and being conscious that it is a terrible choice to make. A person would be right to save one twin. A doctor would be right to triage *in extremis*. An agency would be right to focus on one district. And everyone involved in these choices would be right to feel sadness but not necessarily guilt at the badness of the situation. "So acting for the best in a moral dilemma, while it can entail sorrow, and in serious cases even horror, does not, if we have no doubts about the rightness of the action, make a place for regret but only explanation."[21] Foot suggests that there is no "inescapable wrongness"[22] in the choice you make and so no need to feel guilty unless you have deliberately brought about the situation yourself. In an obligation dilemma like the twins, the sadness comes not from doing the wrong thing but from the tragedy that in doing one good thing you could not do both things.

This chapter has looked at the basic structure of various moral choices that typically present themselves in humanitarian work. The next chapter looks at how we understand individual and agency responsibility in making these choices.

10

MORAL RESPONSIBILITY

Philippa Foot's point about guilt and regret after difficult choices leads us naturally into a discussion of moral responsibility in humanitarian ethics. How can humanitarian professionals and humanitarian agencies gauge their own moral responsibility in the various situations they face? What are they responsible for in difficult conditions and what is the responsibility of others? These questions need to be at the heart of humanitarian deliberation of all kinds: public, private and organizational.

Ethics has always pondered the question of responsibility as one of its original problems. Determining who should be praised for good things and who should be blamed for bad things has naturally preoccupied philosophers and theologians. If ethics is all about developing good character and doing the right thing, then it becomes essential not only to decide what is good but also to know when someone has done it, or not. In law, all criminal proceedings turn on proving or disproving a person or a company's responsibility for certain things. In humanitarian ethics, agencies and their staff also need to consider where moral responsibility lies in humanitarian operations and in the politics around them. This is particularly important in situations when many human lives are at stake. Analysing and understanding moral responsibility in humanitarian action is important for three main reasons:

- Understanding and taking responsibility is an essential part of an individual's professional accountability and an agency's mission accountability.
- Allocating humanitarian responsibility correctly among the many state, non-state actors and international actors in armed conflicts

and disasters is essential if these actors are to face up to their precise responsibilities, and not pass off responsibility wrongly onto others.

- Having a clear sense of the extent and limits of personal responsibility in extreme situations is important for the morale and mental health of humanitarian workers, and the management of moral distress. Humanitarian professionals can carry an inappropriate and disproportionate sense of their own responsibility for bad things that happen around them.

Reflecting on moral responsibility in particular situations of humanitarian action, therefore, becomes important for political and legal reasons as well as for humanitarian, organizational and personal reasons.

This chapter elaborates a basic framework of moral responsibility that has proved useful to humanitarian agencies.[1] The framework will then help to inform the next chapter's discussions of particular moral problems in humanitarian work. This framework focuses on eight key factors that are deemed essential to any careful deliberation of moral responsibility in humanitarian work: agency, intention, motivation, knowledge, ignorance, capacity, mitigation and deliberation.

Levels of Agency

As moral agents we can act in various ways: we can do things directly; we can fail to do things; and we can contribute to things. The first area of scrutiny in any assessment of moral responsibility needs to examine the level and quality of our own or others' agency in a particular situation. Traditionally, ethics has distinguished between two main types of action: acts of commission and acts of omission. These general categories recognize that the things we do and the things we do not do are both subject to moral scrutiny. But moral philosophy also recognizes more nuanced forms of these two types of agency that are manifest in ideas of permission and "bringing about".

Acts of Commission

Acts of commission are actions that we commit directly ourselves or as part of our organization. We actually do them. A humanitarian agency delivers health supplies to a local partner that is running primary health care clinics in a particular place, or organizes a cash distribution in a certain way, or advocates on Al Jazeera for particular changes in international policy. In one country, a President mobilizes the armed forces to help rescue people threatened by floods. In another, a Minister of the Interior incites hatred against a minority group and encourages his police forces to evict them from their homes. In a certain civil war, one armed group imposes harsh taxes on the vulnerable population under its control, another enables humanitarian agencies to distribute seeds and tools in areas it controls. These are all direct acts of commission in which people actively do certain things, some good and some bad. When we actively do things, we are responsible for the deeds we commit and must give moral reasons to explain why we did them.

Acts of Omission

Acts of omission are things we do not do. Sometimes we choose not to act and so leave the world as it is. A humanitarian agency decides not to launch an operation in the Central African Republic because it is so preoccupied in Syria. In a humanitarian assessment, NGO workers make nutritional surveys of children under five but do not ask people about their protection risks. In a government-run IDP camp, a Ministry of Health nurse does not pass information about a recent series of rapes to a human rights agency. A government refuses to respond to calls for help from citizens affected by increasing food insecurity. An armed group has trained its forces in IHL but omits to respect it in the way it attacks government-held areas. These are all things that are left undone. As direct actions of not-doing, the people concerned are responsible for their omissions and would need to justify why they did not act in these particular cases.

Conscious and Unconscious Agency

Moral philosophers have long realized that the consciousness of what we do and do not do can vary. In old English, people used to talk of doing things wittingly or unwittingly. Sometimes we consciously make decisions not to do things. We may decide not to help certain communities, or a government may decide not to increase humanitarian budgets. In these choices, we consciously act upon a situation. At other times, we remain unconscious of the impact of our actions. A humanitarian worker driving fast through the countryside in his Toyota may not be aware that its tyres are spraying dust into the eyes of children walking to school. Hurrying past the same beggar every day and not speaking his language, an NGO manager will not understand that this desperate man is repeatedly asking her if she can help him find his family in the IDP camp where her agency is working. Unwittingly, she ignores his pleas for help. More strategically, a humanitarian agency may be unaware that its cash transfer programme has been infiltrated and monopolized by a local clique, which is now diverting funds from people who need it and are entitled to it. In each case, unconsciously, or unwittingly, people fail to show others respect and care. More positively, we can be equally unconscious of good things that we do. By just turning up and walking round an IDP camp to look for the notebook she left behind that morning, a Red Crescent volunteer may deter a husband from beating his wife out of ill-founded jealousy. A few words of encouragement from a teacher in an emergency school may be the first time a teenage boy has been praised for his intelligence. These words have a disproportionately positive and transformative effect on the boy's self-esteem, while the teacher remains forever unaware of the positive long-term impact of his words.

This distinction between our different forms and levels of moral agency is very important to any assessment of moral responsibility in and around humanitarian operations. Understanding that we may be judged equally for things we do and things we do not do is essential in moral reasoning. So too is the understanding that we are not always aware of what we do and do not do to others.

Permission

Permission is another slightly different level of agency. We can aid other people's actions and inactions by permitting them, or not. Permission takes various forms. In some situations, we can simply let things happen. In this rather indirect way, we can create a generally permissive environment in which a range of actions by other people is free to thrive. For example, a government can be generally permissive of corruption by its civil servants in humanitarian operations. A humanitarian agency can be permissive of insensitive behaviour in international staff that offends national staff and the local community. In other situations, we can target our permission more actively to encourage or forbid specific things from happening. An armed group can give explicit permission for a pattern of hostage-taking in the area under their control, even if they do not wish to be directly involved. Permission of various kinds feels one level removed from direct responsibility, but it often plays a very big part in shaping the moral culture of a situation or shaping (for good or ill) the particular strategies of individuals and organizations under your influence or control. A general atmosphere of permissiveness is much more than unconscious commission or omission, because it usually communicates itself in a nod, or a wink or a meaningful silence.

Entanglement and Bringing About

Ethicists also talk about the actions of individuals and organizations indirectly "bringing about" good or bad things. Here we are even further removed from simple acts of commission, omission or permission but are faced with indirect actions that are still involved enough to be the subject of moral scrutiny. One example of bringing about a bad situation would be the road designer who is designing a new coast road high above the sea on a Mediterranean island. In his efforts to maximize the view and create a wonderful panoramic route for the island's tourists, his design follows the curve of the cliffs very tightly at one point. The view is spectacular and the road is a significant engineering achievement. However, British tourists, who are not used to driving on the right hand side of the road and are also prone to drinking too much alcohol, do not have the expertise to drive such an unexpected bend. As a result, in the first year there is an exceptionally high incidence of British tourists losing control on this bend and crashing to the rocks below. Although the designer was not driving any of these cars or selling their drivers cheap wine, he did have some role in bringing about a situation that had an impact on British tourists. He might have anticipated the particular weaknesses of British drivers and tended more towards safety than elegance in his design. In a similar way, in their programme choices and design, humanitarian agencies can sometimes be deemed to bring about unintended and probably unforeseen consequences for people in and around their projects.

Bringing about good and bad things can be even more oblique in human relationships that involve no design at all. Paul Ricoeur talks about the natural "entanglements" of every human life. As we encounter so many different people in so many different ways, our lives inevitably become morally complex and full of small acts of commission and omission of various kinds that affect other people. These encounters are many and various: some are deep and some are superficial; some last for a long time and some for a moment; some are done in anger and malice and some in gentleness and love; some are conscious encounters while in others we are acting unaware. We know from the analysis of global supply chains and the intricate ecological footprint of a single product like a Kenyan green bean that our entanglement spreads outwards well beyond the intimate locus of our lives. Like the mythic butterfly of chaos theory that flaps its wings in South America and makes a hurricane in Asia, we too can have a moral effect for good or ill on people in areas far out of sight. And we may never know it. The coffee drinker in New York is the last in a chain that exploited the coffee grower. The farmer in Afghanistan nurturing his poppies plays his cruel part in the graveside grief of a family mourning a son in Paris who lost a decade of his life to heroin addiction and died alone.

In his famous morality play *An Inspector Calls*, the English playwright J. B. Priestley gives a tragic illustration of our intertwined responsibilities that all add up to bring about something terrible.[2] A cascade of little things done or not done by different members of a rich industrial family brings about the suicide of a young and pregnant mother. When the police inspector pieces together the sequence of actions and inactions by every family member into a single narrative, it becomes clear how each one of them has played some part in creating the conditions that shaped the young woman's desperate act. They are all responsible in some different way, and their unmet responsibilities towards the young woman are all tragically entangled.

These different forms and levels of agency in our lives and our inevitable entanglements make our intentions as moral agents all the more important. If we are not always aware of what we do and the impact it has on the lives of others, then it becomes vital that we have a clear sense of what we intend to do and the impact we desire to make.

Intention

The second element to be scrutinized in any analysis of moral responsibility (our own or that of others) is, therefore, the intention of the actors involved in any situation. Thomas Aquinas stressed that our intentions are the most fundamental part of any moral project because they define the object of our actions.[3] In our intentions we deliberately "tend towards something" and set ourselves a particular end or goal.[4] An intention is purposeful and is "an act of the will in relation to the end".[5] This means that a first question in any analysis of moral responsibility runs as follows: what is this particular actor and action aiming to achieve? For example, why is this humanitarian agency distributing cash to destitute people? Or why is this country director speaking out about violations of international humanitarian law on BBC World? What do they want to achieve? What is their intention? The first place we must be judged as ethically responsible or not is in our intentions and our will.

Immanuel Kant placed a similar emphasis on intention in his idea of moral will. Kant set the highest store on the goodness of what we "will" in our moral life. Even if we fail and do not manage to achieve the thing we will, "our good will would, like a jewel, still shine by its own light as something which has its full value in itself".[6] So our intentions count for a lot and are the first locus of moral judgement. To have good intentions is a good thing in itself, no matter how hard it is to realize them in practice. Because of this, any deliberation or evaluation of moral responsibility in humanitarian operations must be clear about its fundamental intention: what do we intend and what we do we desire to achieve? Is our intention good and in line with humanitarian ethics?

Sequential and Multiple Intentions

In an evaluation of humanitarian responsibility, we need not look simply for a single intention and a single objective. It is clear that we can intend various things along the route to our ultimate end. As Aquinas puts it, "in the movement from A to C through B, C is the last terminus, while B is a terminus, but not the last. And the intention can be of both."[7] So, as we aim towards some final goal we are likely to have a series of intermediate goals. This is important for humanitarian ethics whose goals are often inevitably incremental because of people's desperate conditions. An agency may intend a food security programme to ensure people's recovery to a point that is as good as or better than their lives before a crisis, but it cannot make this happen without passing through various intermediate goals. First, people may need to regain a sufficient level of health and nutrition; then they may need to recover their means of production or income; and finally they will seek to develop a new level of resilience that prevents them from suffering so badly again from any new political, economic or environmental shocks. The overall intention of improved and resilient food security is bound to pass through a series of proximate goals on the way to its ultimate end. This means that humanitarian work can often have a sequence of goals along the trajectory of a single intention. This passage of sequential intentions needs to be understood in any evaluation of humanitarian responsibility. While a programme's ultimate intention is important, it would be wrong to judge a programme harshly for not meeting its final goal if this were dependent on difficult intermediate goals.

Equally, humanitarian work can operate a range of divergent intentions across a single programme at the same time. These are intentions that are not sequential towards the same overall goal but involve a multiplicity of distinct goals. This principle of multiple (as well as sequential) intentions is structurally important in humanitarian ethics. Agencies may, quite rightly, be trying to achieve several goals at once. In a simple analogy, Aquinas illustrates that we can have more than one intention and that a single thing can have different intentions at the same time: "Nature often intends two purposes by means of one instrument. Thus the tongue is for the purpose of taste and speech. Therefore, for the same reason, art or reason can at the same time direct one thing to two ends; so that one can intend several ends at the same time."[8]

The most constant way in which humanitarian ethics may be operating multiple intentions in a single programme concerns the various goals of its own principles. A medical agency may be working hard intending to preserve human life and dignity, but is also naturally trying to combine this goal with wider intentions to involve people in running their own health programmes, offering donors value for money, and respecting people's culture and customs. Because of the validity of multiple intentions, evaluations of humanitarian responsibility and performance need to appreciate the full range of agency intentions in any operation. The plurality of humanitarian intention means that it would be unfair to judge an agency on just one single intention (for example, value for money) when its additional intention to increase participation is also ethically valid.

Many humanitarian agencies not only do humanitarian work but are "multi-mandate" agencies that have much longer-term goals around poverty eradication, political change and social justice. These agencies have multiple and sequential intentions in the very texture of their mission. This is not at all a bad thing in itself, but it is likely to make their operational choices and their programming more complicated. The most important thing for such agencies is to own their multiple intentions and to discuss them accordingly in a given situation.[9] It is their particular responsibility to be explicit about the variety or sequence of their wider intentions, and to account for them accordingly.

Motivation

Motivation is a little different from intention and not always a positive thing. A motive is something that may not exist at the root of good intention but could help guide us toward an act of good. Often these motives are positive. So we help people because we love them and our affection for them spurs on our good intention. But sometimes our motives are negative and more self-centred. We care for an elderly relative because we seek a place in their will or fear a bad reputation if we are seen to abandon them. We are often driven by both positive and negative incentives and so are described as acting well but with "mixed motives".

Humanitarian agencies and humanitarian workers are influenced by various motives in their work. Their intention to save lives in a major famine may also be driven by fundraising and brand-building objectives. In big emergencies with a high media profile, agencies need "to be seen to be there" and can leverage large funds if they are there. They sometimes act as much out of a concern for their reputation as for the emergency itself. This is not necessarily bad, because the world needs large humanitarian organizations. Any director of such an organization has a responsibility to ensure its survival so that it can continue to provide valuable humanitarian relief in future. Having mixed motives in this way is perhaps inevitable and not unethical. However, it can become unethical when it reaches a certain tipping point. An agency which chooses to site its operations near a main road and within easy reach of the world's media may breach more fundamental principles of impartiality as it begins to tilt its programmes more towards the cameras than towards people's actual needs.

Coercion

One of the most extreme forms of motivation is coercion: when we are forced to do something. As we have seen, free will is essential in the creation of genuine intention. Our intentions are what we want to do. Something that I do under coercion, and so against my will, can never be a true intention. If I am forced to do something, then I cannot be held responsible for my actions in the same way. My level of responsibility must be discounted. For example, if I decide to rob a bank and work with a small group to plan the raid, prepare for it and carry it out, then it is obvious that my intention was to rob the bank. However, I could also be forced to become involved in the raid against my will. If I am the bank manager who is taken hostage by the group and forced to give them information because they are threatening to kill my family, then my role is coerced. My intention (my deep desire) was never to rob the bank but to save my family.

Coercion can be a significant factor in humanitarian ethics. Humanitarian agencies can be coerced to do certain things by various authorities. They can be made to focus on certain places or be forced to avoid helping certain groups. Threats against humanitarian staff can be direct or veiled. Affected populations can also be coerced and so prevented from cooperating honestly and openly with humanitarian agencies. They can be deterred from giving important information or frightened into giving false information. Sometimes, they can simply be forcefully prevented from using humanitarian services. Leading members of affected communities can also coerce humanitarian agencies into prioritizing particular interventions. When coercion is in play, a person's level of responsibility is significantly diminished. In the face of force, threats and fear, we cannot be held as responsible for our actions and inactions as when we are free to choose our goals and shape our own intentions.

Knowledge and Ignorance

One of the most significant factors affecting moral responsibility is what we know, or could know, in a given situation. Humanitarian agencies and humanitarian workers can only really be deemed fully responsible for a decision on the basis of what they knew when making that decision or what they could have found out at the time. Knowledge is a central issue in questions of moral responsibility and blame. So too, therefore, is ignorance. It is morally negligent to be ignorant if you could have discovered important information about a situation. Because of this, moral philosophers have traditionally distinguished between vincible ignorance and invincible ignorance in calculations of moral responsibility. Vincible ignorance is a state of ignorance that can be conquered or overcome. Sufficient information is reasonably available to a humanitarian agency so that it can become better informed and overcome its lack of knowledge of the likely risks and impacts resulting from its decisions. Invincible ignorance is a lack of knowledge that is impossible to overcome at the time when decisions need to be made, strategies designed and operations implemented.

For example, if a humanitarian team wants to design a food distribution strategy that is culturally acceptable, nutritionally effective and poses no new security risks to a particular community, then they are duty bound to explore options with the community, gather as much relevant information as possible and to analyse protection threats. The members of the team need to know as much as they can. If this kind of information gathering is easy to do, then they have a responsibility to do it. Their current ignorance is vincible and can be overcome. If, however, there is extreme time pressure, a lack of easy access to the community and no immediate possibility of knowing the intentions and patterns of violence in the area, then, in the circumstances, the agency may be judged a victim of invincible ignorance that it could not reasonably overcome. It must try to get whatever information it can and then proceed on the basis of low information. Its responsibility for any negative consequences will be diminished by its inevitable lack of knowledge.

Capacity

The next aspect of moral agency to have an important bearing on moral responsibility is the capacity of an actor in a given situation. A humanitarian agency can only truly be held responsible for what it can actually do. This reflects the famous dictum derived from Kant that "ought implies can". We are only required to do what we can realistically do. Aristotle makes the same basic point that a person is only responsible for those things "that are in his power if they occur or not".[10] Therefore I am not morally negligent if I see a person being attacked by a gang of ten armed men and do not rush to his aid to fight them off. It would be physically impossible for me to protect him this way and I would as likely be killed or beaten up myself. I would need to find better ways to help him. This illustrates the reality of what Kant described as problems of imperfect power. An agency is only culpable for doing something badly if it could have done it better, or if it would have been better to do nothing at all. In the same way, a humanitarian agency cannot be rightfully criticized for not stopping some abuses against civilians if it simply lacked the capacity to stop them.

Mitigation

Problems of imperfect power lead naturally to mitigation, the next key factor in assessing moral responsibility. Even if we do not have the perfect power to stop something bad or do something good, we retain a responsibility to mitigate the worst effects of our weakness and do the next best thing that lies within our power. In short, we always have a responsibility to mitigate a situation that we cannot totally control. In the example of the ten armed men, it would obviously be wrong of me to stand by doing nothing or simply walk away. Confronted with the suffering of another, I must do what I can. In this example, therefore, I should use my mobile phone to call the police, or create a distraction that might divert the men from their crime.

In humanitarian work humanitarian power is seldom perfect, so the duty of mitigation is a strong one. When faced with violations it cannot stop, a humanitarian agency has an obligation to protect people as much as it can and use what knowledge and influence it has to enable authorities or inter-governmental agencies to use their power to change the situation. In another example, any agency making a narrow strategic choice to work only on health within an affected community needs to encourage and cooperate with agencies working on related sectors like water, shelter and livelihood. Without improvements in these wider areas, the value and sustainability of health work will be compromised. Or, if an agency is forced to evacuate an area, it needs to do everything it can to leave its precious resources in the best possible hands and to protect the national staff it leaves behind. Sometimes mitigation is inevitably damage limitation, but a great deal of mitigation in humanitarian work is also about ensuring effective collective action and complementary programming.

Deliberation

Finally, the other key factor that is an essential ingredient in any evaluation of moral responsibility is the duty to deliberate in every situation. As we have seen in Chapter 8, deliberation takes many forms. An agency who is not able to show that they have made every effort to deliberate well in a given situation is rightly vulnerable to ethical criticism. Without such effort, a humanitarian agency or a humanitarian worker cannot be regarded as giving serious thought to a moral decision. Feeling uneasy and agonizing about a moral problem is not the same as giving it due deliberation. A formal commitment to ethical deliberation as part of responsible programme design and operations management is a vital part of being morally responsible.

This chapter has examined the different aspects of moral responsibility that make humanitarian actions worthy of praise or blame. The next chapter examines some persistent ethical problems faced by humanitarian agencies and uses the principles and approach set down in this and earlier chapters to explore responsible decision-making in these more practical contexts.

11

PERSISTENT ETHICAL PROBLEMS

Humanitarian workers, academics and a succession of anti-aid critics have long observed a range of ethical problems that arise in humanitarian work.[1] This chapter looks in more detail at five main types of moral problem that routinely occur in humanitarian work: the potential harmfulness, or maleficence, of humanitarian action; difficulties of association; complicity and moral entrapment; duties of care towards humanitarian staff; and the potential problems of humanitarian growth and increasing ambivalence of humanitarian power. On the last point, it examines the moral problem posed by many postmodern theorists that humanitarian action now exercises unjust biopower over vulnerable people and colludes with predatory liberal power as a force of structural harm in international relations.[2]

All these ethical problems are persistent in humanitarian work. They tend to rise anew in every humanitarian operation and seem to be integral rather than occasional problems in humanitarian ethics. In some way, these challenges are the core ethical problems of humanitarian action. They cannot be solved once and for all but must be lived through again in each new operation, albeit differently configured with new actors and settings but essentially the same. These main moral risks were effectively identified by Mary Anderson in her important 1999 book, *Do No Harm: How Aid Can Support Peace or War*.[3] In 2002, Fiona Terry highlighted the potential paradox of humanitarian action enabling harm in her seminal work, *Condemned to Repeat: The Paradox of Humanitarian Action*. Terry identified a point in many humanitarian operations at which she felt humanitarian action "loses its sense".[4] Responding to these perennial moral risks, humanitarian principles can provide guidance and moral boundaries to inform humanitarian strategy. Deliberation can help to identify and think through particular cases as they arise. But it is likely that these challenges will always arise. The most important thing is that humanitarian workers are conscious of these moral risks and able to account ethically for the choices they make around them.

Problems of Maleficence (Harm)

This range of moral problems is concerned with the potential maleficence in humanitarian action: its ability to do harm instead of or as well as its intended good. Sometimes humanitarian action can do harm directly by treating people badly. At other times, it can contribute indirectly to harm by enabling or bringing about the wrongful acts of others. Either way, humanitarian aid can run the risk of making things worse for the people it intends to help. As Shakespeare's Friar Lawrence reminds us in *Romeo and Juliet*: "virtue itself turns vice being misapplied".[5]

The Moral Hazard of Indirect Harm

Many ethical problems in and around humanitarian action concern the harmful unintended consequences of humanitarian aid in the wider context of an armed conflict or disaster. The potential for these indirect effects is best described as the moral hazard of humanitarian action. Ethical critiques of humanitarian action cited above identify many specific areas in which humanitarian aid may cause indirect harm. They suggest that humanitarian aid can prolong war, create dependency, destroy the local economy, legitimize and empower abusive regimes, and facilitate the creation of concentration camps. They argue that aid distributions in volatile areas can bring about violence by increasing the incentives for armed raiding that steals aid from vulnerable communities, or increases corruption as local authorities exploit or tax people because of the aid they receive. More structurally, several critiques suggest that prolonged humanitarian aid is corrosive of proper political contract between a government and its people because humanitarian agencies take de facto responsibility for people's needs. Government abdicates its social responsibilities and people make demands on international agencies, not local politicians.[6]

This legitimate ethical focus on the wider negative effects of humanitarian action is naturally consequentialist in its concern. It places significant weight on indirect harm that may arise as a consequence of humanitarian action. It rightly worries that while humanitarian action may make some things better, it may make other things worse; or that it may make things worse overall in the long run for the people it is trying to help. These consequentialist concerns represent genuine moral problems for humanitarian work; but before we address them in more detail, it is necessary to dispel a couple of myths in the ethical discussion of humanitarian action. First, that humanitarian aid is so powerful that it can have extraordinary structural effect. Secondly, that humanitarian workers are the only people who have moral responsibility in a given situation. Neither of these ideas is empirically true, but sometimes they feel true and they certainly tend to make a good story.

Two Moral Myths About Humanitarian Aid

The first myth is about humanitarian power. Several claims about wider humanitarian maleficence assume extraordinary power in humanitarian action. A good example of this is the frequently repeated anti-aid mantra that humanitarian action prolongs war. No comprehensive and credible evidence has ever been produced to prove this point. On the contrary, all recent studies of war economies regularly report that the drivers of entrenched conflict are to be found in the predation of natural resources, horizontal inequalities and the dysfunctions of governance.[7] Humanitarian aid never really gets a walk-on part in these empirical studies. This is not surprising, because minerals, timber, national taxes, arms trading and ministerial budgets have a much greater strategic value than the food, medicine, vegetable oil and latrines of aid distributions. The structural significance of humanitarian aid in a war economy is marginal at best. It can and does create fights at a local level but is not the main reason for the armed conflict or the main resource with which to prolong and win the war. Wars are prolonged by the greed, grievance and violence of their protagonists. Even the explicit aid strategies of liberal counter-insurgencies in Afghanistan and Iraq did not prolong war. These two wars lasted because they could not be decisively won militarily and because the real high-value resources in both wars were oil, minerals, sectarian hatred and political power. For their part, humanitarian agencies can consistently show that they have saved hundreds of thousands of lives in all these modern wars.

The second myth is about humanitarian responsibility. Anti-aid critics also routinely exaggerate the moral responsibility of humanitarian agencies while simultaneously discounting the moral responsibility of more powerful political actors in a war or disaster. Because it is usually easier to visit humanitarian projects and interview humanitarian workers, many story-telling journalists and qualitative researchers become mesmerized by humanitarian agencies and humanitarian power. They lose their wider focus on the military or political ethics of the armed groups and governments who shape the conflict and who naturally prove less forthcoming as interviewees. In the structure of many of the ethical problems they face, humanitarians only ever bear a secondary responsibility for the devastation around them. In armed conflict in particular, humanitarian agencies are always responding to the frequently immoral choices of others who have decided it is best to kill, forcibly displace, rape and starve people. Because they can quite literally end up holding the baby, humanitarian agencies can seem especially morally responsible in situations which are not of their own making and in which primary responsibility belongs to others. As we shall see, the charge of "complicity" is the laziest moral label that is used to over-emphasize humanitarian responsibility in situations that are more ruthlessly controlled by others.

The classic "Goma scenario" is a case in point.[8] The moral problem of running food distributions and paying staff salaries in a refugee camp that is being brutally controlled by armed men who are diverting food and cash to rebuild their genocidal armed forces is a problem inflicted upon agencies not created or brought about by them. They are not responsible for this situation. The armed group is responsible, and so too are the national government and UN Security Council who should be separating combatants from refugees. In such a situation, humanitarian action is severely coerced and constrained by the power and decisions of others. By virtue of their limited capacity, the responsibility of humanitarian agencies is one of mitigation only: to find the best way to minimize the worst effects of aid theft and taxes, while still continuing to meet their primary responsibility to save lives and protect people. It is ethically incoherent to frame humanitarian agencies as the moral centre of such a problem. Their responsibility is secondary, their capacity is low and the source of the problem lies with others.

Making Things Worse—the Ambiguity of Aid

Humanitarian power and responsibility may be exaggerated structurally across a conflict or disaster. However, indirect humanitarian effect is still real and important locally and needs to be taken into account as a matter of humanitarian responsibility. Any attempt to help people carries risks. Help may go wrong or it may introduce new problems. In the fourth century, Abba Paphnutius, one of the desert hermits of the Egyptian church, was consulted about the injunction of Christian charity to help one another. Sagely, he observed: "I have seen a man on the bank of a river buried up to his knees in mud and some men came to give him a hand and help him out, but they pushed him further in up to his neck."[9]

In an essay on ethics, Michel Foucault makes a similar point about the dangers in any human enterprise. For Foucault, the main challenge in organized solutions to human problems is that perfect solutions do not exist and any solution always involves new risks: "My point is that not everything is bad, but that everything is dangerous, which is not exactly the same as bad. If everything is dangerous, then we always have something to do."[10] There are obviously dangers in humanitarian action that can bring new problems to people and places that humanitarian action is trying to help. In the language of the Code of Conduct, these are the "negative effects" that can arise in humanitarian work. The Sphere Standards' first protection principle worries about the same thing: "Avoid exposing people to further harm as a result of your actions."[11]

There are many ways in which aid can go wrong or create perverse incentives—no different from any other human activity that is prone to ambiguity. For instance, cars are a wonderful invention that serve many good purposes; but their speed can encourage people to drive too fast and so cause fatal accidents, and their fumes pollute the world. Smartphones can prove extraordinarily beneficial in many ways; but they can become addictive both in themselves and for offering permanent online gambling. These indirect effects were not the original intention of the car or the smartphone, but they have become related sources of indirect harm. So it is with humanitarian aid sometimes. For example, humanitarian services are often most quickly and easily delivered to a dispersed and hungry rural population in a camp of some kind; but, as Alex de Waal discovered in his doctoral thesis, the spread of disease within these camps killed more people than hunger in the Darfur famine of 1985.[12] During the civil war in Liberia in the early 1990s, armed groups deliberately ambushed people returning from food distributions in order to steal their aid, kill men from opposing groups, rape women and terrorize the population. Encouraging hungry people to humanitarian distributions was obviously exposing them to terrible new risks, and created perverse incentives for armed groups eager to show their power and increase their wealth.

These kinds of moral hazard in humanitarian aid are programmatic. They concern the immediate moral responsibility of programme staff whose duty is to know as much as they can about a situation and design the best possible programme accordingly. As we saw in the last chapter, knowledge, capacity, deliberation and mitigation become central in such situations. In both these scenarios, the moral burden on the humanitarian agency is to develop as much knowledge as possible about the situation and to think through their best options, all things considered. If the agencies concerned in Darfur in 1985 did not know enough about the public health dangers of densely populated camps, they should have been able to find this out and redesign their programme accordingly. But agency knowledge may not have been the key issue in this situation. As professional agencies, they probably knew the risk of camps but could not control or influence the behaviour of a desperate population. Or perhaps the agency simply did not have sufficient onward transport to set up a network of hub and spoke services that could extend to meet people where they lived. If this were the case, the problem was one of capacity and imperfect power, plus the additional agony of knowing that they were forced to pursue the least best strategy. Such an imperfect strategy would then require agencies to mitigate its worst effects in the best possible camp planning, disease control and options for people to return to their homes.

Similar issues of knowledge and capacity were in play in the Liberian example. In this scenario, if humanitarian workers genuinely made every effort to find out about the presence of local armed groups, examined previous patterns of violence and noted the success of recent distributions, they might have gone ahead with the distribution with a reasonable expectation that it would be safe enough. Perhaps they could never have known that an armed group was traversing the area en route to somewhere else and spontaneously decided to make an unplanned and purely opportunistic attack on the distribution. In this situation, the agency's ignorance would have been truly invincible and their responsibility much diminished. They could not have reasonably known about the presence of the group or its sudden intention to attack. But if an agency had done none of this information gathering and could easily have discovered that an armed group was nearby and had a history of attacking distributions, then its ignorance would have been vincible and its conduct would be judged as morally irresponsible. A constant concern to identify and mitigate potential indirect maleficence is essential in humanitarian work.

Risks of Association

Humanitarians need to deal with everyone. In order to reach people affected by war and disaster, humanitarian agencies are required to talk and work with all kinds of people and all kinds of power. They need to talk and cooperate with governments, armed groups and civilians representing a range of different political and religious views. Many of their interactions are with political and military representatives who are explicitly pursuing inhumane policies. The main purpose of the principle of neutrality is to ensure that humanitarians can talk across the various factions in a conflict or disaster. Inevitably, however, the need to liaise and cooperate with all sides in an armed conflict brings potential problems of association for humanitarian agencies. Coordinating closely with an armed group or a government, or working through their line ministries for health, water or education, poses two main risks: the potential erosion of agency impartiality, neutrality and independence; and a risk of conferring undue political legitimacy on the parties to the conflict.

Substantive risks to humanitarian principles from political association are only severe if the party concerned seeks to influence humanitarian programming. If, however, a warring party clearly leaves an agency free to pursue its own needs assessment and programme design, then problems of impartiality, neutrality and independence will be low. This, of course, is rare in armed conflicts and disasters where political authorities usually retain strong control and have definite agendas of their own. In such cases, the greater risk becomes one of complicity discussed below. The lesser risk with mere association concerns the potential for an agency's relationship with a warring party to imbue new levels of legitimacy on this armed group. This issue is alive on both sides of the armed conflict in Syria at the time of writing. On the government side, agencies worry that by being confined to a partnership with the Syrian Arab Red Crescent (SARC) they may be falsely legitimizing the humanitarian intent and decision-making of the Syrian government. On the rebel side, NGOs worry about giving undue political legitimacy to resistance groups with very little popular legitimacy but who can offer a humanitarian partnership.

Not all associations with warring parties are negative for humanitarian legitimacy. Some bring a wider increase in humanitarian values across a conflict. Earlier in humanitarian history, when church agencies discreetly set up the Emergency Relief Desk (ERD) in Khartoum in 1981, they were making a clear decision to work cross-border into the Ethiopian civil war in cooperation with the humanitarian wings of the two main rebel groups opposing the Ethiopian government: the Eritrean People's Liberation Front (EPLF) and the Tigrayan People's Liberation Front (TPLF). In the cross-border programme, agencies provided and monitored food, cash, medical and agricultural supplies to the humanitarian wings of these armed groups.[13] In doing so, they naturally brought some unintentional reputational allure and international recognition to both parties. Naturally, this possibility of humanitarian cooperation adding political legitimacy to armed groups has always worried states. Because of this, Common Article 3 of the Geneva Conventions, which guarantees the impartial provision of humanitarian services in non-international armed conflicts, is also determined that "the application of the preceding provisions shall not affect the legal status of the Parties to the conflict".[14] In other words, just because an armed group is being humanitarian does not make it any more politically legitimate.

While the law is clear, the reality is that humanitarian associations can indeed change political perceptions and increase the moral legitimacy of armed groups and governments. Perhaps they should. If one or both warring parties are doing everything in their power to respect IHL and organize effective humanitarian relief for the civilian population, then this does genuinely increase their ethical legitimacy, if not their political status. In situations when the warring parties' intentions and actions are good, humanitarian agencies need not worry about enhancing the humanitarian legitimacy of warring parties. Indeed, a core principle of IHL, expressed in Common Article 1 of the Geneva Conventions, requires states "to respect and ensure respect for the present convention in all circumstances".[15] Geneva Call, the Swiss NGO, has also made impressive efforts to encourage and support non-state armed groups to respect IHL and human rights law acts in the same spirit of Common Article 1.[16] Inevitably if warring parties do abide by IHL and cooperate well with relief agencies, their humanitarian legitimacy rightly increases. This is not a moral problem but a moral success. It is also a basic requirement of international law and need not be considered politically scandalous in any way.

The real risk of association arises when a warring party uses humanitarian associations more cynically to gain undue legitimacy. Commonly in armed conflict and disasters, warring parties and politicians will seek to manipulate humanitarian associations to boost their public image without any deep respect for humanitarian principles and law. They will be truly opportunistic and manipulative in their humanitarian associations. In these cases, agencies face hard questions about coordinating and cooperating with authorities that are more akin to the complicity dilemmas discussed below. For example, in 2009 the Sri Lankan government requested humanitarian agency help in the large internment camps for displaced Tamils that it had established after its ruthless final offensive against the Tamil Tigers; this posed genuine problems of association. There was little doubt that the government's intention was to create an impression that these fenced and militarized camps were normal IDP camps, complete with humanitarian agencies, in an effort to regain some international legitimacy.[17] Cooperating with North Korean authorities in the famine of 1995 posed even starker problems of association about working with a government which had zero humanitarian conviction and was concerned with the survival of its regime rather than its citizens.[18] In both these situations, an association with humanitarian agencies could be used cynically or perceived as immoral by outside critics. In these situations, agencies must weigh the greater good of each association in an effort to establish the best course of action, all things considered. If they decide to engage with risky political intermediaries and partners, they should work hard to mitigate the worst effects of the association, both in their community relations on the ground and in public or private statements at international level. They should also agree clear red lines within their organizations and negotiate these with the associate if possible. These red lines must be set around what is feasible to achieve, but can take months and years to be negotiated and respected. MSF's experience of negotiating neutral and independent humanitarian assistance in district hospitals without a government military escort during the conflict in Swat province of Pakistan took months of constant negotiating, with a succession of advances and withdrawals.[19]

A good example of placing moral limits around risky associations can be found in ICRC's detention work. This is one of ICRC's most important areas of work and involves private visits to security detainees and the prison authorities to understand the terms of people's imprisonment, the nature of their treatment and the physical conditions of detention facilities. ICRC then works with the relevant authorities to improve detention practices and conditions, while also providing a message service between detainees and their families. ICRC's work and recommendations on detention remain confidential between them and the detaining authority. Their presence in prisons has sometimes been criticized for lending undue legitimacy to very harsh regimes, which in turn exploit ICRC presence to give a misleading impression that their detention system must be good because they are working with ICRC. The opposite is, of course, more usually the case. ICRC is usually present because of serious concerns about detention practices.

ICRC has clear parameters and red lines around their detention work. Significant or potential signs of improvement in detention have to be one criterion for ICRC's engagement if it is to tolerate the ambiguity of the legitimacy that can be gained from its presence. In two recent cases, it drew a line and stopped its detention work. In a statement on Myanmar in 2007, ICRC publicly dissociated itself from efforts with the government to improve the conditions of detainees who were consistently being exploited as military "porters". ICRC's statement noted that: "The ICRC has repeatedly drawn attention to these abuses but the government has failed to put a stop to them...and consistently refused to enter a serious discussion about these abuses."[20] In Uzbekistan in 2013, ICRC publicly withdrew from its detention work stating that: "In Uzbekistan we are unable to follow our standard working procedures when we visit detainees to assess the conditions in which they are being held and the treatment they are receiving. As a result, we cannot address humanitarian issues and that renders any visits pointless."[21]

ICRC's ethical judgement on the rights and wrongs of a dubious association hinged on their operational freedom and practical effectiveness. These two criteria have been weighed against the risk of a potentially misleading impression created by these governments, and the false legitimacy that ICRC's presence and association might create. The criteria of feasibility, autonomy and effectiveness make good sense. Fundamentally, they relate to capacity and intent. In Kantian terms, ICRC's decision was taken because they could not meet their humanitarian goals so they ought not to lend undue legitimacy to authorities that do not deserve it. Ought implies can and, in this situation, ICRC could not so ought not.

In recent years, ethical questions of association have arisen acutely around cooperative relationships between humanitarian agencies and military forces. There is nothing intrinsically unethical about humanitarians professionally associating with military forces. Indeed, such relationships are central to humanitarian action as agencies negotiate their operational presence, advocate for the conduct of hostilities to abide by IHL, and treat military personnel who are wounded or *hors de combat*. Military forces have particular humanitarian obligations in armed conflict and also in their supporting logistical role to governments in natural disasters. As a result, contact and association with military forces is professionally normal and ethically desirable for humanitarian agencies.

Moral risks arise in military association most frequently around the question of military protection for humanitarian convoys and infrastructure like offices, warehouses, staff houses, distribution points, refugee camps and health facilities. In these situations, with the presence of a particular armed force so obviously aligned around a humanitarian agency, the military association potentially undermines agency neutrality and independence in the eyes of other warring parties and the civilian population. The problem is not a legal one of military protection itself being wrong; rather it is an ethical problem, because protection by one side in a conflict tends to undermine trust in that agency's neutrality, independence and, therefore, its impartiality. Such perceptions may indeed be right. Perhaps the agency is genuinely biased and more aligned with one side than another.

Military protection for civilians and civilian objects is by no means anathema in IHL. Every state has the responsibility to protect its civilian population from attack. Preferably, in doing so, armed forces should be positioned far away from civilians and civilian infrastructure so as not to draw enemy fire towards these protected areas. Sometimes, however, when civilians have quite obviously become the main target of the enemy, troops need to be placed close to the endangered population in some way. Refugee and IDP camps must not be "militarized" by being infiltrated with members of armed forces who control the population and exploit humanitarian aid for themselves, but they can and should be militarily protected by the responsible state. So what about military protection for objects essential for civilian survival, like food convoys? IHL is not against this in principle, but in practice it risks further endangering civilian objects by attracting legitimate fire towards the convoy or buildings, as well as introducing serious problems of perception and humanitarian trust.

Once again, agencies have to judge how best to manage these military associations and their consequences for wider humanitarian trust. Agencies like ICRC and MSF tend towards an absolute position that armed protection is always ultimately self-defeating. In certain situations, other agencies might find a different moral calculus. For example, armed protection may enhance their capacity from zero to something very significant. It could mean the difference between them reaching nobody or reaching 100,000 people. Perhaps the military protection comes with no strings attached around their independence and autonomy of operation and they can still choose where and how to work. The price they pay is one of overall impartiality by recognizing that they must limit themselves to the area of the conflict currently controlled by one warring party. If other agencies are reaching into the other side of the conflict, this is by no means an unethical decision. Even if it is currently impossible to reach the other side of the conflict, this is still a morally legitimate strategy because it reaches some people.

In the long term, there are wider risks that include some slippery slope dynamics. The war may change. Perhaps the warring party currently protecting this agency is knocked back or defeated and the agency is left exposed and mistrusted. Also, the protagonists of one war always observe and study other wars. If the agency has accepted the military protection of one side in a conflict with global dimensions—Western, Islamist, capitalist, socialist—then the agency's reputation for neutrality will suffer globally. More internally to the organization, a tendency to go for military protection in one case may be habit-forming and become a first resort rather than a last one. The agency and its staff will lose the values, will and skill required to negotiate neutral and independent humanitarian action. But there are risks the other way too. Agencies who refuse military convoys may take casualties and find themselves stuck at checkpoints for days, unable to reach their target areas. Building the trust and confidence of warring parties to let them move safely through their territory can be slow. In a crisis, this might be immorally slow if faster armed options are available.

Similar problems of association come with humanitarian financing, both state and corporate funding. Funding relationships with particular donors can give agencies significant conflicts of interest that threaten their perceived neutrality and operational autonomy. Taking funding from one or more belligerents in a conflict can affect the way opposing belligerents regard the political orientation of an NGO or UN agency. But the reality of such links always needs to be examined, not assumed. MSF's absolute determination to refuse belligerent funding from European and American governments is a principle that may help them sometimes and in some places. However, it has not stopped their staff from being murdered in Afghanistan and Somalia and the subsequent closure of their programmes in these countries. This proves that extremists usually have more than one reason to kill humanitarian workers. It also shows once again that ethical deliberation and decision-making need to rely on evidence. If belligerent funding is not the key variable in violence towards humanitarian agencies, then naturally it does not become as ethically salient in humanitarian strategy-making.

More problematic in funding associations is the ability of a donor to skew agency intention. Many humanitarian NGOs are significantly reliant on government funding, and some donors are less guided by humanitarian conviction and principle than others. All governments have their own geopolitical priorities which shape the geography of their humanitarian spend. As agencies are naturally inclined to follow the money, so they also follow these donor priorities more than they might otherwise be ethically guided to do. Inevitably, and without malice, donors also develop specific funding policies which they prioritize. Large tranches of money then dictate spending in priority areas. Often these policies are needs-based, progressive and far-sighted; but they always involve agencies adapting their programming to fit donor preferences and requirements. Agencies may have to adopt policies like resilience and public–private partnerships, or vertical programming around special interest groups like the victims of sexual violence and child soldiers.

Big funding, therefore, brings significant influence that carries potential conflicts of interest and identity. NGOs, in particular, can feel under pressure to lose their mission identity and become something they are not. We are all inevitably interdependent and necessarily accommodating of partners of different kinds; but humanitarian agencies need to reflect regularly and hard about their mission integrity and their autonomy to be true to their values. Similar ethical considerations about funding associations need to be made around corporate funding. In 2013, the BBC alleged that Save the Children had been reluctant to advocate on fuel poverty in the UK because British Gas is one of their major corporate donors.[22] Funding associations can involve conflicts of interest and problems of "pollution". They need to be made with clear ethical agreements about an agency's mission autonomy.

Inferring legitimacy on a warring party or a donor is not the only perceptual risk in humanitarian associations. American philosopher Larry May has examined a more general psychological and social problem of "pollution" in people's dealings with people or organizations with blood on their hands. Drawing on powerful ideas from Greek tragedy that are akin to many ideas still prevalent in traditional and modern societies, May notes how "one could lose one's innocence by being polluted or tainted due to being associated with something that is bad or wrong, and yet in which one is not even complicit".[23] The aura of pollution can hang over humanitarian agencies and individuals who have contact with political parties, armed forces, donors and individuals who are involved in killing and violence. Not surprisingly, people who themselves, or whose family members, have been hurt, raped or dispossessed by a group will find it hard or unbearable to deal with an agency who is touched by physical contact with the perpetrators of these crimes. In many situations, it seems to be a sense of pollution rather than a strict ethical logic association that influences people's attitudes to humanitarian agencies' association with political powers of various kinds.

Risks of Complicity

The dangers of association pose moral problems of perception, trust, reputation and neutrality because of the risks of undue influence, political bias and conflicts of interest. The ethical problem of complicity takes humanitarian agencies a step beyond the unintended consequences of moral hazard or the potentially tainting problems of association. Graver than these, complicity is concerned with actual cooperation in serious wrongdoing. Throughout its history, humanitarianism has repeatedly been accused of complicity by anti-aid critics, the media, war victims and warring parties. Agencies have been criticized for complicity with forced resettlement in Ethiopia, with communist insurgency and capitalist counter-insurgency in Central America, with ethnic cleansing in Bosnia and Darfur, with genocidal Hutu extremists in Goma, with liberal counter-insurgency in Iraq and Afghanistan, and most recently with Al Shabaab's insurgency in Somalia and with anti-government rebels in Syria. This is to name just a few of the many allegations of complicity against humanitarian action. The list is long and the cry of complicity is usually raised by one or more parties at some point in every armed conflict and natural disaster. Routinely, humanitarian agencies are also accused of complicity with corruption of some kind in their field operations as they make access deals with political authorities and community leaders, or procurement deals with local merchants.

In their excellent study of complicity in humanitarian action, Chiara Lepora and Robert Goodman rightly point out that the word "complicity" is often used lazily as a loose catch-all term to describe simplistically what is often a more subtle range of roles and positions.[24] Their study brings important precision to the idea of complicity. It recognizes that complicity involves a sliding scale and is not simply black or white. Complicity with wrongdoing involves many different gradations of intention, involvement and behaviour. Most importantly, Lepora and Goodin make the point that in certain situations it can be right, and inevitable, to be complicit with wrongdoing in some sense in order to achieve a greater humanitarian good. In humanitarian tradition, Oscar Schindler is iconic of this kind of complicity. Schindler maintained a level of involvement and association with Nazism that enabled him to save the lives of 1,200 Jewish people in the midst of the Holocaust.

Lepora and Goodin's scale starts clearly at one end with the extreme form of complicity: the idea of "full joint wrongdoing" in which two or more parties act as deliberate "co-principles" in a wrong.[25] They share the same intentions and work actively together to conspire, cooperate and collude in the construction of intended wrongdoing. Together, their actions are "constitutive" of this wrong. They want it to happen and together they make it happen. In the middle of the scale, various parties may not be so closely aligned and involved. Some may play roles that contribute to the wrong in a more secondary way. They may collaborate, condone or consort with those who are engaged in it, and they might be physically close to the process of wrongdoing. As such, they play a "contributory" role as secondary agents not co-principals. Moving to the far end of the scale, there are parties who play a "non-contributory" role but whose presence and actions are contiguous with the wrong. These parties might be condoning or tolerating the wrong.

This scale of complicity is helpful to humanitarian ethics. Moving beyond simplistic understandings of the word "complicity" to a more finely grained analysis of what Lepora and Goodin describe as complicity's "conceptual cousins" (like consorting, condoning or contiguity) is important for any evaluation of humanitarian ethics. Humanitarian agencies should obviously never be co-principals in the deliberate construction of genocide, crimes against humanity, ethnic cleansing, war crimes and disaster. If they are, they have stopped being humanitarian agencies. However, they often find themselves in difficult contributory or non-contributory roles that can be intentional or unintentional to varying degrees. Here, the next move in Lepora and Goodin's approach helps to clarify things further as they move from identifying different types of contribution to grading the seriousness of these contributions.

An agency's contribution to specific wrongdoing, or to a wider context of wrongdoing, is best judged according two main areas of any contribution. Lepora and Goodin distinguish between "mental stance" and very practical "doing". An agency's mental stance concerns its commitment to planning and supporting the wrongdoing. Here, the level of an agency's "responsiveness" to the plan is what counts, and so the extent of their shared purpose or reluctance. In short, does the agency respond favourably or unfavourably to the planned wrong? Did the agency have a role in "plan-making" as a designer of the wrong? Or was it more "plan-taking" as a party who actively "adopted" or more reluctantly "accepted" the plan, or part of the plan, in some way? Or, more coercively, were agencies forced to "comply" with the plan? As we have seen in Chapter 10, intentions matter in moral responsibility. The question of responsiveness in mental stance relates to the legal notion of *mens rea* and criminal intent, which is so central to judgements of intention and culpability.

Alongside mental levels of an agency's intention and responsiveness to wrongdoing, Lepora and Goodin point to the different dimensions of actual doing. Here they weigh the particular gravity and significance of any contribution to a wrong according to five particular "dimensions" of the practical contribution: essentiality, centrality, temporality, proximity and irreversibility.

- How essential is the contribution to the perpetration of the wrongdoing? Is it mission critical and a "necessary condition" without which the plan could not go ahead? Or is it more peripheral?
- How central is the contribution? The dimension of centrality is more about scale than necessity. The contribution may be necessary to the wrong, but how much was needed and how much was supplied by the contributor? How central was their particular contribution in the grand scale of the project? Did the humanitarian agency contribute a lot or a little of what was needed for the wrongdoing?
- What was the timing of the contribution? Was it before, during or after the wrongdoing? Temporality matters because knowledge and impact change. So, if a significant contribution was made before the wrongdoing, it can be deemed causal, although it might be unwittingly and unintentionally causal if the contributor had no knowledge of the plan. During the wrongdoing, when it is public knowledge, any contributions are more likely to be in the realm of condoning, accepting or complying with the wrong in some way. After the wrong, an agency may be contributing the same items into the situation but they may no longer have any wrongful part to play. Or, more seriously, they might be contributing to a situation that is likely to encourage the same wrong to be repeated.
- How irreversible was the contribution? The irreversibility of a contribution is another important criterion. Is the contribution an agency makes somehow "locked in" with the wrong, or do they retain an option to withdraw their contribution so that they can reverse the consequences of the wrong? In other words, is the contribution running through a one-way or two-way valve? This obviously makes an important difference for parties who may be forced to comply in a wrong but are able to structure their contribution in such a way that they can control and reverse it the moment they are free to do so. Their foresight in mitigating the worst effects of their contribution would then diminish their responsibility. If they were able to do this but did not, they would be open to charges of negligence for a failure of mitigation.
- How close was the contribution to the wrongdoing? Lepora and Goodin's final dimension is proximity to the wrong. This is not just the physical closeness of a contributor but their place in the causal

chain. Physical closeness itself is obviously not a consistent measure of complicity and criminal responsibility. If it were, the victims of a crime could be viewed as significantly responsible, which is of course absurd. Physical closeness, as we have seen, is only significant if you are at once close and capable in some effective way. In complicity, a contributor's proximity in the causal chain is more significant than physical proximity. If my contribution is right up there as one of the first few links in the chain which enables the rest, then my contribution is significant. In other words, I may have had an early "turnkey role" at some point or a "last clear chance" role to stop the wrong. Alternatively, my contribution may be very low down the causal chain, a distant link in a long chain in which my role is subject to the vagaries of chance and the choices of many other people that precede me. In other words, my contribution is very unlikely to count because the situation will probably change or others will intervene before my link comes into play as a meaningful factor. Therefore, I may be at risk of complicity but it is a low risk, and even a responsible risk depending on what else I am trying to achieve.

Combining judgements of shared purpose, knowledge and mental stance with these specific ingredients of complicity means that the high end of complicity in wrongdoing "must always involve a certain sort of act together with a certain sort of mental state".[26] But there is also a weaker version of complicity: "knowingly contributing to the wrongdoing of others", even if you are a reluctant or low-level contributor.[27] This weaker version is the challenge more likely to face humanitarian agencies and still requires an ethical justification of some kind. There are probably two main justifications: the argument of a different or a greater good, and the frequent difficulty of moral entrapment. These are best explored in the following examples.

Darfur 2004–13

Humanitarian agencies have been criticized for enabling ethnic cleansing and sustaining dramatic demographic change in Darfur over the last few years. In a surreal twist, the Sudanese government has sometimes blamed the humanitarian sector for actually creating the IDP problem. The more usual critique is one of agency complicity and self-interest. It suggests that by servicing camps the humanitarian sector has created incentives for people to become permanently relocated and increasingly urbanized. This means that the wider land grab and demographic reorganization in Darfur envisaged by government hardliners can proceed as planned. This criticism of humanitarian complicity is underwritten by an additional critique of agency self-interest, which argues that agencies have a business interest in creating and sustaining victims and so want to perpetuate the camps. What levels of mental stance and what dimensions of contribution would need to be in play in humanitarian strategy to make these charges stick?

In October 2013, there was still a registered long-term IDP population of 1.2 million people living in humanitarian camps in Darfur. The wider informal and unregistered figure for IDPs of all kinds was 3.2 million people, and there were also about 350,000 people who had crossed over into Chad as refugees.[28] Together, these people make up a very large proportion of the estimated population of 6 million people in Darfur at the outset of the war in 2003. The majority of displaced people had been forced to flee by violent counter-insurgency against a rebel uprising. How much were humanitarian agencies complicit in all or any of this?

For a charge of complicity to ring true in its strictest sense, humanitarian agencies, the Sudanese government and the Janjaweed militia would have had to conspire, collaborate and cooperate around a shared purpose to displace and reorganize Darfur society. Or humanitarian agencies would have had to conspire and cooperate in a joint plan with the rebels to lead people to safety in IDP camps with a longer-term view of their permanent resettlement in peri-urban areas. This obviously did not happen and humanitarian agencies played no deliberate constitutive role in the violence, forced displacement, flight and encampment of people in Darfur. For a weaker version of complicity to hold, humanitarian agencies would have had to contribute to this wrong in some way by adopting or accepting a government or rebel plan for major demographic change in Darfur. To meet the charge of self-interested opportunism, agencies would need to have created their own plan that prioritized long-term humanitarian work in Darfur and colluded with the wider political strategy of displacement to meet these goals for lucrative long-term work in Darfur for years to come. Much more likely is that humanitarian agencies have had no choice but to comply reluctantly with a policy of violent displacement with which they radically disagree, and make the best of this situation for IDPs, many of whom would otherwise have died. In this case, as in most humanitarian operations, agencies have little choice but to conform their actions to the much more powerful violence around them. They can seldom stop it, and only mitigate some of its effects. It is the stuff of fantasy to suggest that humanitarian agencies had a positively responsive mental stance towards the strategy of violent displacement in Darfur and so share intent as co-principals in a joint wrongdoing.

What about the weaker form of complicity involved in a knowing contributory role? Here there is a genuine moral problem. Humanitarians understand enough about political violence and counter-insurgency to know that it often prefers to concentrate its enemy population in camps or protected villages where it can control them better, and more easily screen out militants and isolate them from their populist base. This is usually the strategy of choice for governments and armed groups who cannot, or prefer not to, concentrate their enemies in mass graves instead. This knowledge of counter-insurgency puts humanitarians in a moral bind: they can either do nothing and watch displaced people die in large numbers; or they can provide resources for camps and urban hosting arrangements that will save people's lives but also build the new concentrated zones that risk playing into some warring parties' violent political objectives. Humanitarian ethics will always rightly prioritize human lives in a situation like this, because of its fundamental moral goal of preserving and protecting the human person.

But how do we ethically resolve the problem that the action of building IDP camps serves a double function without it automatically being regarded as contributory complicity? There is a very important principle in ethics that critics of humanitarian aid often overlook and which humanitarians need to hold dear in the face of simplistic consequentialist critiques of agency complicity. The principle is this: that identical acts may be ethically different.[29] This is obvious when one thinks about it at a more mundane level. Imagine you are a car park attendant at a supermarket. As you look around, you see a young man reaching into the open handbag of an older woman who is struggling with her shopping and you watch him take out her car keys. Five minutes later, you see the same thing happening again in another corner of the car park. In one corner is a pickpocket intent on stealing a woman's car. In the other is a son helping his mother to find her car keys while she is holding the shopping and unable to reach them. The hand movements and actions of both young men are exactly the same. These are two identical acts but each has a very different ethical content. As we saw in Chapter 10, the moral content of these actions is determined by the intention and object of each act. The principle of identical acts being differentiated by their objects holds true in the case of IDP camps in Darfur. When humanitarian agencies contribute to the building and servicing of IDP camps, they do identical activities to when an authoritarian regime does the same thing. They put up shelters, build latrines, run clinics and create food distribution centres. When the regime does these things, it may be for cruel political purposes. When a humanitarian agency does these things, it does them to save lives and mitigate some of the cruelty of political violence and oppression.

The insight into the moral difference of identical acts suggests a clear differentiation of moral responsibility in Darfur. The simple charge that agencies are complicit by merely contributing equipment and services that construct IDP camps is not enough to prove a contribution that condones, encourages or enables permanent displacement. Humanitarian agencies are doing something that is ethically distinct from deliberate and self-serving ethnic cleansing or demographic change. But, of course, the ambiguity created by the situation in which an identical action is driven by two different intentions must not be brushed away. If humanitarian agencies know the Sudanese government's intention of demographic change behind the IDP camps, then they must mitigate the worst effects of the ambiguity. Ideally, this would mean starting early recovery programmes that support people returning home or advocating against permanent displacement. But if agencies are not capable of sufficiently mitigating the ambiguity, they are still not responsible for it and they are right to keep preserving and protecting people's lives. This remains the best thing to do unless the camps become killing grounds or depots for even greater forced resettlement.

Korem 1985

In 1985, a policy of forced resettlement by the Ethiopian government took place around the IDP camp at Korem in northern Ethiopia, an area that was severely affected by war and famine. Destitute people seeking humanitarian services came to live in the camp and began to be forcefully rounded up at night and deported south against their will in the government's national resettlement programme. The programme ostensibly aimed to relocate people from the drought-stricken northern highlands to the wetter southern lowlands. It also seemed to aim at the removal of some of the rebels' natural popular support base. The situation in Korem was the founding moment of MSF's moral commitment to humanitarian "abstention" in extreme situations of this kind. Rony Brauman was President of MSF at the time and a frequent visitor to Korem. Interviewed many years later in 2008, he recognized the need for agencies to withdraw aid and abstain in certain situations: "If we accept that aid could be used against the people it is meant to assist, we must accept the possibility that in certain cases abstention or withdrawal may be preferable to action."[30] The problem of aid being used in this way as a bait or magnet to attract people to deportation or even death is truly problematic. It became still more intense in the Bosnian war when people complained of becoming the "well-fed dead", fattened up at aid distributions only to be killed in sieges or ethnically cleansed. But would it, therefore, have been right for agencies to withdraw from Bosnia, and were people ready to starve to death in preference to ethnic cleansing? More likely, their complaint was urgent propaganda to encourage military intervention than it was a condemnation of food aid and a desire to die hungry.

Brauman must be right in principle about the ethics of humanitarian abstention, but it is a hard principle to enact without genuine consent from the affected population. Even in Korem, hungry people still felt bound to risk the camp. During bouts of resettlement activity IDPs fled to the surrounding hills but would then gradually return. Many severely malnourished children stayed in Save the Children feeding centres and adults remained in MSF's in-patient facilities. Save the Children was also running a large dry ration distribution programme deliberately intended to support people living away from the camp. This was serving two or three villages per day from the surrounding area that was militarily contested in frequent fighting. Agencies could not yet move further into the Sekota area to extend distributions and people were walking for up to two days to reach Korem and collect their family ration. Even with the threat of resettlement, people were still prepared to move in and out of Korem because their survival options were still so limited. Gradually, international pressure was building against the resettlement programme, partly thanks to MSF, which meant that round-ups operated in erratic bursts rather than continuously.[31] All these conditions combined to make abstention and withdrawal unethical for Save the Children, not least because there was also no guarantee that strong advocacy and programme suspensions by all agencies would stop resettlement. Instead, it might just make existing agency working conditions subject to more punitive bureaucratic reprisals involving travel restrictions, threats to local staff and a reduction in aid.

Save the Children's mental stance was not positively responsive in any way that adopted and accepted sustained forced displacement and deportation. Neither abuse was ever condoned by Save, who routinely advocated against them. But working with and alongside the Ethiopian authorities was accepted as a necessary condition to save lives. In both cases, MSF and Save the Children were doing more than merely consorting with potential wrongdoers: they had also to cooperate with political authorities and with line ministry officials. Some of these ministry technicians as medics, engineers or administrators were political moderates and sensitive to people's suffering. Privately, they too did not condone wider policies. But others were hardliners and were organizing resettlement directly. In this case, compliance and coercion seem more accurate ways to describe agency responsiveness.

In situations like Korem and Darfur, humanitarian agencies often seem to be faced by implicit conditional threats of the kind that Oxford philosopher David Rodin describes as setting traps for people with good intentions.[32] Like a robber who stands with a gun and shouts "Your money or your life!", so does the inhumane government or armed group seem often to say "Your aid or their lives!" This is coercive extortion and explains why humanitarian workers often feel blackmailed somehow. In Darfur and Korem, the mental stance of humanitarian agencies might best be characterized as reluctantly tolerating a wicked ambiguity that was forced upon them and that, partly but not wholly, distorted some of the consequences of their actions. In view of these consequences, how grave were the various dimensions of their contribution? How essential was their aid to the wider wrongdoing?

It is easy to think that humanitarian aid was a necessary condition of forced displacement in Darfur and deportation round-ups in Korem. But this is doubtful. If there was no aid in either place, the authorities would most likely have continued with their strategies regardless. Without rescue in IDP camps in Darfur, people would have eventually died, informally regrouped (only to be attacked again) or would have kept walking for Chad. The current Sudanese government has consistently shown a very high tolerance for large death rates among its own civilian population and would probably have accepted tens of thousands more deaths from destitution. In Korem, the Ethiopian government had other more significant means of collecting and coercing civilians for resettlement, and the majority came from non-displaced communities.[33] Aid bait in Korem was not essential or significantly central to the whole programme of forced resettlement. The relief camp at Korem certainly did play a contributing role in the deportation of hundreds of people, but the government also ran its own food distributions at Korem. It could have continued to do so for some weeks with additional food requisitioned from NGOs if both agencies had left. The role of international agencies in Korem was not so central as to be determinative. In Darfur, agency resources were much more central. The proximity of agencies in the causal chain of creating displacement was weak. The temporality of their response was long after original political and military decisions to create displacement and the irreversibility of agency response was not high. The humanitarian system has repeatedly shown its preference for policies of return over policies of long-term encampment, and would be able to help finance and implement return whenever it is permitted. Humanitarians could and would reverse their role in the problem. They had not played a "turnkey" role at the outset and were not "locked in" by their own actions and intent.

Complicity needs to be taken seriously by humanitarian agencies as they evaluate the morality of their role and impact in the many wrongdoings created by others that form part of their operational environment. When working in the midst of wrongs it is an ethical requirement to have a good sense of one's place and rationale within them, and set appropriate strategies of prevention, mitigation and remedy to one's contributions. It is, however, foolish to overstate one's contribution because it allows the parties who are truly responsible to take cover behind a smokescreen of blame that circulates around humanitarian scapegoats rather than themselves.

Moral Entrapment

It seems genuinely wrong to say that in cases like Darfur and Korem agencies are strictly complicit with wrongdoing. They are certainly knowingly contributing to a structure of wrongdoing and so, as Lepora and Goodin would insist, they "have a case to answer". So what is the answer to this perennial problem in humanitarian ethics? Most agencies seem to argue a greater good. They decide to continue to concentrate on their main mission to save people's lives and mitigate the risk of their presence by creative aid strategies that reduce people's risks (in Korem this was dry food distributions) and advocacy. This justification seems right and, in most cases, is not the logic of a lesser evil argument but the commitment to sustain a good in the midst of wrongdoing.

However, it may also be fairer to nuance the weaker variant of complicity with one of entrapment. Most agencies that decide to stay in these situations are morally entrapped rather than simply complicit and morally irresponsible. In such circumstances, it seems fair to suggest that they are acting rightly for someone who is entrapped. The moral philosopher David Rodin has elaborated the notion of moral entrapment in his discussion of just war theory.[34] As Rodin observes, "a trap is something that it is easy to get into and hard to get out of". Rodin's thinking can be usefully applied to humanitarian entrapment too. Most human endeavours—whether in politics, business, marriage or medicine—are characterized by one persistent variable: that things will change once you start upon a venture. Some of these changes will be enabling, others will not. The Prussian general Helmuth von Moltke coined the famous military adage that "a battle plan never survives first contact with the enemy". The same is true in humanitarian work. Various things can happen that begin to construct a moral trap. Other parties in a conflict or disaster have their own plans and will often want to block humanitarian action or exploit it somehow as a part of their plan.

What may start as a simple health or feeding programme can soon be distorted by the actions of others intent on diverting or restricting food supply. A project that sets out as a development programme may be compelled to transform into an emergency operation as conflict or flood happens around it. A fuel wood project needs to become a protection project. An initial decision to integrate displaced children into local schools suddenly becomes untenable as numbers escalate and local resentment rises. But how do you change course without letting down those to whom you are already committed, or increasing social discord?

These changing contexts, creeping commitments and difficult exit choices are the norm in humanitarian work, as in many other human activities. They manifest themselves in what moral philosophers like C. A. J. Coady call "extrication problems" in which "whether they stop or persist, an agent will cause harms".[35] These problems are, therefore, traps of one kind or another. Traps are often what Rodin calls "dangling" or "aggravation" dilemmas. He defines an aggravation dilemma as a paradoxical situation in which you are left morally dangling: "in an aggravation dilemma the only way to avoid aggravating an offense is to continue to prosecute it". Rodin notes that most aggravation dilemmas are associated with exit decisions of some kind. "Very often there will be issues of extrication from immorality that will require wrongdoers to continue (and perhaps even to escalate) the immoral action prior to its termination." As above, I am not suggesting that agencies are acting immorally in these situations, but Rodin's specification of this predicament is useful. The party left dangling in a potentially immoral situation seeks an exit from it; but the best way to achieve that exit is—paradoxically—to keep doing what they are doing until rescue of some kind arrives or a better solution emerges. This seems to fit the bill for many humanitarian predicaments. It is another reason why agencies are usually right to stay until international action, new aid strategies or a change in the warring party's unethical policy transforms the situation.

Silence and Speaking Out

The problem of silence in humanitarian work is often related to complicity in the minds of humanitarians and their critics. The question of when it is best to speak out and when it is best to keep silent is a hotly debated subject in humanitarian ethics.

Humanitarian agencies and their staff often learn about or directly witness human rights violations, war crimes, ethnic cleansing and even genocide. Silence around atrocities is usually brutally imposed in situations dominated by strategies of terror or ruthless authoritarian rule. Violence is hidden, hushed up or people are too afraid to talk. In such settings it can become important for humanitarian voices to pierce this silence with descriptions of the truth. Humanitarian advocacy is now a highly developed practice and it is normal for agencies to speak out in some way about the atrocities and conditions they see, speaking either singly or together for greater protection. But sometimes they stay quiet. When they do, their silence is often interpreted as a form of complicity or at least a serious act of omission. Sometimes it might be one of these two things, but often it is not. Humanitarian silence may be chosen for ethical and other reasons. Silence can be a means to humanitarian action in difficult situations. It can be a quiet form of condemnation. But at other times, silence can simply be a wrong decision.

ICRC's decision not to speak out about what it knew of the Holocaust in World War Two remains an iconic lesson for the humanitarian profession and has been deemed a moral failure by those who have examined the case in retrospect.[36] Humanitarian agencies have spoken out powerfully about subsequent genocides in Cambodia and Rwanda. The principle of truth-telling is an essential one to ensure that suffering and violations are properly known about and brought to the attention of the authorities and the wider public. Sometimes, regardless of impact, it is morally necessary to make public note of extreme wrongs. Even if such public note can deliver no immediate effect, it still lays down a moral marker for humankind to build on later as morality evolves and when a capacity to act is positively increased. Many people rightly spoke out against slavery when there was still little moral desire or capacity to abolish it. Naming wrongs is an early step in finally recognizing and preventing them.

However, truth-telling is not always best done in truth-yelling by humanitarian workers, especially when others are better placed to communicate the truth. It is important that humanitarian silence and discretion are not pathologized in humanitarian ethics. Speaking out can be right, but it can also be unwise for a variety of reasons, a fact well known to most agencies. Obviously, members of the community at the centre of humanitarian agency advocacy can face serious reprisals if they are thought to have informed the agency about war crimes or other violations. These reprisals can be brutal and fatal. Staff in the humanitarian agency concerned and other agencies in the area can also face reprisals. As we have seen in previous examples, an agency's advocacy and campaigning can also mean the closure of its programmes, which can then have a direct effect upon people's safety, survival or recovery.

These are immediate life and death reasons why humanitarian silence may be wise, but there are other reasons related to the potential success of speaking out which are ethically significant too. Speaking out can rightly and importantly feel like the proper carrying out of a moral duty by humanitarian workers. Even if it has no obvious effect in ending or limiting the wrong, it is evidently the right thing to do in itself if all other things are equal. But in situations where other important goods are put at risk by speaking out and there is no reasonable certainty of a positive effect from doing so, then speaking may be reckless and silence be wiser. This is especially the case if there is no particular value added by a humanitarian agency joining in an already loud chorus of truth-telling. Means as well as ends are important in humanitarian truth-telling. The idea of "speaking out" has become a core doctrine in the practice of human rights, but there are other ways of telling and communicating atrocities and suffering. Speaking loudly and publicly is not always the best means of humanitarian advocacy if it risks hurting others or may have no positive effect and may be better done by others. In such cases, more discreet forms of information-sharing are legitimate alternatives to high-volume methods. Perpetrators and people in authority can be talked to directly and privately in the kind of "démarches" favoured by ICRC. Information can be passed to third parties on condition of anonymity and with due care taken to protect sources from danger. It may also be best to find discrete ways to support direct advocacy by the victims themselves or their representatives and families. This will always require their consent to the likely dangers arising from such action. In the end, judgements must hinge on the likelihood of success. The advocate's personal moral satisfaction in speaking out must be tempered with wider concerns about risk and success.

Finally, it is important to respect the meaning and eloquence of silence in certain situations. In her early work on the philosophy of silence, Lisa Schwartz, a current pioneer of medical humanitarian ethics, analysed our understanding of silence.[37] She noted that silence is not always meaningless. On the contrary, a person's silence or an organization's silence often sends a powerful challenge to interpret their silence. Schwartz remembers the two ancient Graeco-Roman gods who were the guardians of silence. One of these, Harpocrates, was the god of mystical and meditative silence providing a space in which meaning could only be created by people sharing in that silence. Larunda was a goddess who talked too much and had her tongue torn out by Zeus for revealing one of his secrets. Larunda still had much to say but had to say it in silence. Hermes, the messenger of the gods, fell in love with her and learned to interpret her silences.

This kind of "Larundic silence" seems to me a powerful image of humanitarian silence on occasion. Communities, warring parties, the media and public opinion may see the ICRC or other humanitarian agencies being silent. Sometimes this silence will feel intolerable to those around it, because they cannot understand it. But at other times this silence may be powerful, pregnant with meaning and legitimate. Such Larundic humanitarian silence will always be open to interpretation, not all of which will be inherently negative. Often humanitarian silence will be interpreted rightly as a reluctant stance that reflects quiet condemnation, operational patience and the hopelessness of speech having any effect. It will be recognized as a decision to act quietly whilst others speak. As Schwartz reminds us, "silence sometimes contains and transmits meanings". These meanings need not always be signals of complicity and moral weakness. Silence can also speak as quiet judgement. In his history of silence in the Christian Church, Diarmaid MacCulloch describes the silent look that Jesus gives to Peter who has just betrayed him for the third time as "one of the most eloquent quiet stares in human history".[38] A stopping of the voice does not necessarily mean a halt to moral engagement. Speech is only one way in which we embody our ethics. During the later stage of the civil war in his native Algeria in the 1950s, Albert Camus deliberately adopted a position of silence. He stopped speaking and writing publicly about the terrible violence of the war and the search for a just peace. He felt that there was no more that could be usefully said. At the ceremony to mark his Nobel Prize for literature in Stockholm in 1957, a young Algerian challenged Camus repeatedly about his silence over Algeria. Eventually, Camus responded by saying: "though I have been silent for a year and eight months, that does not mean I have stopped acting".[39] In many situations this is true for humanitarian agencies too.

Direct Maleficence—Humanitarian Cruelty and Disregard

Forms of indirect harm are not the only moral risks in humanitarian work. There is also maleficence in humanitarian action that is directly attributable to humanitarian agencies. These are patterns of harm inflicted in the very process of humanitarian action by humanitarian staff. Several ethical critiques of aid note that humanitarian action can itself be harmful in the way it treats the people it is aiming to help. This type of harm can be inflicted structurally in the way aid is organized in long queues and degrading practices that show a lack of personal care. The behaviour and attitudes of humanitarian workers can also be offensive and hurtful. These risks of direct harm require a constant focus on the personal ethics of humanitarian workers and the potential structural violence of humanitarian action.

Barbara Harrell-Bond, the anthropologist and pioneer of refugee studies, has consistently throughout her career criticized the structural and behavioural aspects of humanitarian work. In particular, she has objected to the central place of "the camp" in humanitarian practice. Correctly in many ways, Harrell-Bond sees the humanitarian camp as a locus of authoritarian humanitarian control that reduces the autonomy of refugees and displaced people and tempts the "humanitarian regime" to become domineering in its relationship with suffering communities.[40] Citing research by Jennifer Hyndman and others, Harrell-Bond gives many details of "inhumane humanitarianism" in refugee and IDP camps.[41] She describes how people are "rounded up" or "herded together" to be counted and fed, and how they are suspected by aid workers of being "bogus" or "scroungers". In Kakuma refugee camp for Somalis in Kenya, she observed that people were even subjected to collective punishment in 1994 when food distributions were suspended for fourteen days after the deliberate destruction of the food distribution enclosures by unidentified refugees.[42]

Not surprisingly, this critique of the humanitarian camp as a space more resonant of a prison, lunatic asylum or concentration camp has been taken up with enthusiasm by the new wave of critical theorists influenced by Michel Foucault's important work on European institutions for punishment and madness. The rise of immigration into Europe and the detention of many people as illegal migrants has similarly encouraged Italian professor Georgio Agamben and his followers to create an almost unified theory of humanitarian oppression in "zones of exception" around the poor margins of the world.[43] Michel Agier's exaggerated critique of the unkind dynamic of care and control in humanitarian camps set up for the purpose of "managing the undesirables" expresses a similar concern.[44] These wider theories of humanitarian oppression are discussed later. In the meantime, it is important to focus on more intimate acts of harm that aid workers can inflict and to examine the source of their disregard.

Harrell-Bond is not alone in finding a certain brutality in the actual organization and discourse of humanitarian work. As we have noted already, the label "beneficiary" is de-humanizing enough. The inevitable need to respond to large vulnerable populations can lead to a form of collective thinking in which aid workers think more in terms of crowds, numbers and lists than of the personalized faces of particular human beings living through terrible times. Without constant vigilance, the humanitarian ethic of personal care can slip into a more collectivist culture of management, logistics and control. A spirit of order and superiority can then supplant a more humane ethos of compassion and equality.

Elizabeth Dunn, the American geographer, has a more forgiving and probably more accurate analysis of the dynamics of humanitarian unkindness than Harrell-Bond.[45] Based on her observations of humanitarian operations in Georgia in the wake of the Russian–Georgian war of 2008, Dunn charts a three-phased passage in humanitarian governance. This moves from an initially "affective modality" in its primary ethical concern, through a "bureaucratic modality" which transforms (and reduces) human suffering into an organizational and logistical challenge; in its final move, humanitarian action takes on a "material modality" to become all about giving people objects. Dunn rightly observes that people lose some of the richness and dignity of their person when they enter the humanitarian system and become "*homo humanitarius*", as she calls it. But where Harrell-Bond senses malevolence in humanitarian systems, Dunn finds chaos and "adhocracy" that creates carelessness and confusion rather than wickedness: "Life inside humanitarian bureaucratic order was less about oppression and disempowerment than it was about disorientation and bewilderment. As an elderly woman in a Tserovani said: 'To put it simply, we are just confused'."[46]

The moral risk that humanitarian action can create confusion, unkindness and a reduced sense of self is a very serious one. Humanitarian workers must make every effort to create programmes that embody humanitarianism's dignity principles of inclusion, participation, capacity-building and accountability. This can help to ensure that people have meaningful choice, involvement, agency, transparency and understanding in the aid strategies designed to support them.

The Risk of Pity and Paternalism

The potential for humanitarian action to degrade into unethical authoritarian structures, insulting discourse and unfeeling managerialism is a constant challenge. We have all seen (or been) the humanitarian worker who gradually loses respect for the mass of people we are trying to help, or been infuriated by the staunch group of complainers who always want more. For some humanitarians, the feeling is a temporary frustration. In others it is a lasting turn that renders them angry and embittered and signals that it is time for them to quit. As Harrell-Bond and many before her have understood, the source of this moral risk lies in our attitudes to others as we try to help them. In many helping relationships there is potential for a dangerous asymmetry between a powerful helper and a powerless victim. Left unchecked, this asymmetry can erode the proper humane bonds of equality and respect that form the basis of humanitarian ethics. It is often a dysfunctional pity that spreads this creeping disrespect. Such pity can then grow into paternalism, to flourish finally in various gradations of disdain towards those who suffer.

The virtue of humanity that we discussed in Chapter 2 is grounded in compassion that is distinct from pity. A sense of pity forms part of this compassion, but it is only an initial emotional prompt that causes us to reflect on a person's suffering and extend our compassion. An ill-formed pity that persists without compassion can be profoundly patronizing, self-interested and even sadistic. Paul Ricoeur reminds us of the egotistical element in pity "in which the self is secretly pleased to know it has been spared" and begins to feel superior to those it pities.[47] This superiority is the beginning of paternalism, which infantilizes people's suffering and advocates a right of control. We have all seen instances of people becoming aggressive, interfering or strangely unsympathetic when they "help". We have also seen people become profoundly patronizing as they assist people. Both attitudes are misguided and a dangerous insult to people's dignity.

There is increasing evidence from neuroscience that our empathy can take two forms: one functional, and the other dysfunctional. Empathy can take the path of genuine compassion, which focuses on the person suffering and encourages positively connected and pro-social motivations; or it can turn inwards to become what Polish neuroscientist Olga Klimecki calls "empathic distress".[48] This is a self-obsessed emotion that internalizes the suffering of others. It takes their pain upon oneself to create negative feelings within the carer or observer. Empathic distress is then not surprisingly associated with burn-out, withdrawal and a feeling of being personally overwhelmed by the suffering of others. As Mark Walkup observed in a seminal paper on coping strategies in humanitarian organizations, this sense of being overwhelmed or disappointed that humanitarian work has not given us the good feeling we expected (and needed) starts a cycle of emotional decline in aid workers. Overwork with hints of martyrdom soon resorts to detachment and transference and reality-distortion. In the last two stages in particular, some aid workers spread blame for the dissonance between their personal expectations and the professional failure they feel. Some of this blame is imposed upon affected people themselves, who come to be regarded as the opposition rather than the goal of humanitarian work.[49]

The moral challenge in humanitarian relationships is to stay focused on the person, not one's pity and self-pity, and to resist all feelings of superiority. Even *in extremis*, compassion should seek to act with people, not on them. This is the proper solicitude of which Ricoeur speaks, and the love to which every religion calls its followers. Such love and solicitude do not subject people to our power, but respect others as subjects in their own right and with their own rights. It is an attitude of accompaniment started in equality, which respects a person's autonomy just as humanitarians are asked to do in the Code of Conduct. Moses Maimonedes, one of the greatest of all Jewish scholars, was unwavering in his suspicion of paternalism and championed autonomy as the most important way in which we can help others. Writing in the twelfth century and himself a victim of violence, dispossession and forced displacement, Maimonedes identified eight levels of charity, with the highest being one of respect and genuine "strengthening" of the other person:

Maimonedes' Eight Degrees of Charity

There are eight levels of *tzedaka* (charity), each greater than the next.

1. The greatest level, above which there is no other, is to strengthen another by giving him [*sic*] a present or loan, or making a partnership with him, or finding him a job in order to strengthen his hand until he needs no longer beg from people. For it is said, "You shall strengthen the stranger and the dweller in your midst and live with him," that is to say, strengthen him until he needs no longer fall upon the mercy of the community or be in need.
2. Below this is the one who gives *tzedaka* to the poor, but does not know to whom he gives, nor does the recipient know his benefactor. For this is performing a *mitzva* for the sake of Heaven. This is like the Secret Office in the Temple. There the righteous gave secretly, and the good poor drew

sustenance anonymously. This is much like giving *tzedaka* through a *tzedaka* box.

3. Below this is one who knows to whom he gives, but the recipient does not know his benefactor. The greatest sages used to walk about in secret and put coins into the doors of the poor. It is worthy and truly good to do this if those who are responsible for collecting *tzedaka* are not trustworthy.
4. Below this is one who does not know to whom he gives, but the poor person does know his benefactor. The greatest sages used to pack coins into their scarves and roll them up over their backs, and the poor would come and pick the coins out of the scarves so that they would not be ashamed.
5. Below this is one who gives to the poor person before being asked.
6. Below this is one who gives to the poor person after being asked.
7. Below this is one who gives to the poor person gladly and with a smile.
8. Below this is one who gives to the poor person unwillingly.

Moses Maimonedes, 1135–1204

The important insight in Maimonedes' sliding scale is that the helper should be as irrelevant and invisible as possible, or engaged on the equal terms of a partnership. Helpers are not heroic or superior. They are simply necessary intermediaries of justice rightly redistributing goods without controlling and humiliating those who need them. Interestingly, recent research into the impact of cash transfer programmes in humanitarian work after hurricanes in the USA and famine in Somalia confirms Maimonedes' ranking and shows that men and women feel high levels of respect, autonomy and agency when part of a cash relief programme.[50] People who feel less comfortable with it tend to be humanitarian workers who feel they cannot trust people to spend money wisely and fear they are losing control.[51] These, of course, are paternalistic anxieties.

Systemic Moral Risks of Humanitarian Power

Most moral hazards discussed so far affect humanitarian action at the programme level, but there are wider systemic hazards around the global culture and political economy of humanitarian work as it has developed and expanded as an international field in the last sixty years. These systemic professional and political hazards are rightly seen as new Foucauldian dangers from the bureaucratizion, institutionalization, hierarchy and vested interests of humanitarian action. They are the dangers of international humanitarian success.

Many critics of international humanitarian aid regard the expansion of the humanitarian system as a significant corollary of Western liberal power and a deliberate and essential form of liberal influence in the post-colonial era. Michael Agier borrows Pierre Bourdieu's phrase to describe humanitarianism as "the left hand of empire" and is one of many academics to postulate the idea of "humanitarian government" experienced by many vulnerable people around the world.[52] Agier's view is that the current system of humanitarian action functions as the "healing hand" of a hegemonic Western power that "follows on the heels of and smoothes over the damage wrought by military intervention, the latter conceived of as a police operation enacted simultaneously in different places on earth".[53] This combination of political and humanitarian power is therefore "a global and consensual apparatus" that helps Western power to govern unruly, vulnerable and oppositional parts of the world.[54] Similarly, Didier Fassin formulates the idea of "humanitarian reason" as a new and disempowering force in Western political power.[55] Humanitarian reasoning creates "humanitarian government" as "a mode for governing precariousness". It is "the deployment of moral sentiment in contemporary politics...which always presupposes a relation of inequality...[and] which is based on a fantasy of a global moral community and the secular imaginary of communion and redemption".[56] Humanitarian reason is then credited with "imagining" and "inventing" emergencies in order that the wicked West can take humanitarian control over large high-risk areas of the world.[57] For these and other critical theorists, therefore, humanitarian government and humanitarian aid are extremely dangerous for the people cast as victims in these "imagined" catastrophes. Laurence McFalls sees humanitarian government as "benevolent dictatorship" and decides that much humanitarian action is actually "iatrogenic violence". In medical theory, this is harm and violence induced by doctors in their attempts to heal and is brought about either by incompetence or as unintended side effect. For McFalls, much humanitarian action by NGOs is nothing more than "therapeutic domination".[58]

This kind of academic deconstruction by critical theorists is exceedingly binary and overblown. It represents the dualistic anti-Western fantasy of some postmodern thinkers and shows a tendency to discount the political power and brutality in non-Western societies. Most emergencies are constructed by these powers, not imagined by Western powers. Also, in much of this critique by critical scholars, humanitarian agencies are foregrounded as powerful and central actors in a way that is not really true on the ground where power is primarily held by governments, armed groups and local communities.[59] There are more grounded and realistic ways in which to criticize humanitarian power.

Alex de Waal is more nuanced and less ideological in his view of the global humanitarian system. Like Dunn's sense of humanitarian adhocracy and chaos, de Waal sees a less malevolent and more disorganized intent behind the recent emergence of humanitarian power. He talks of a "humanitarian imperium" but one that was built "in a fit of absent-mindedness". Surrounded by weak and conflicted political power in many African and Asian states, humanitarian agencies ended up taking disproportionate responsibility for people's lives. As such, "the mandate for humanitarian imperium has been acquired by default, driven not by grand designs in the metropolis but more by the incremental logic of trying to address these complex emergencies without appreciating the endpoint".[60] Antonio Donini, professor at Tufts University, has spent more time leading empirical studies of people's perceptions of humanitarian aid than most humanitarian academics. His view of the risks of the international humanitarian system clearly recognizes that while humanitarian action works to a universal ethos, it does so with "a western apparatus". This apparatus and its culture thrive on isomorphism, which demands that any new initiatives or partnerships operate in its image and on its terms. Humanitarian action also acts as "a powerful vector of western ideas and modes of behaviour". His general conclusion from studies of recipient perceptions in many countries is ethically challenging but avoids the dualistic apocalyptic melodrama of many postmodern theorists:

> Humanitarian action is a top-down, externally driven, and relatively rigid process that allows little space for local participation beyond formalistic consultation...this is sometimes exacerbated by inappropriate personal behaviour, conspicuous consumption and "white car syndrome".[61]

Donini's criticisms chime with that of another scholar engaged in empirical research, Dutch professor Thea Hilhorst, whose work also shows a tendency of international humanitarian aid to overwhelm or bypass local government and local institutions.[62]

There is no doubt that humanitarian action is now a major part of people's lives in many parts of the world, and that humanitarian agencies can achieve significant power in the everyday government of some communities affected by war and disaster. The arrival of humanitarian aid, which has also been described as an unruly circus or caravan coming to town,[63] can be deeply disruptive in different ways to the initial disruption of disaster and war.

Footprint

The local political economy of a crisis area is often significantly affected by significant humanitarian action. The almost industrial delivery system of contemporary humanitarian aid in a crisis means that large numbers of agencies and staff need offices, warehouses, transport and lodging. Like the construction phase of a new mine, this can result in a relatively isolated low-tech community being quickly swamped and transformed. The price of food and rent booms, new local elites and entrepreneurs emerge, inward migration increases to exploit new job opportunities and the number of sex workers rises. In modern humanitarian history, the northern Kenyan town of Lokichogio has become iconic of such humanitarian hubs. Originally a small market town in the pastoralist Turkana area, it has provided the important rear base to humanitarian operations in landlocked South Sudan for more than forty years and been transformed in the process. The skewing effect of this humanitarian aid apparatus on certain parts of society presents a moral problem. It cannot be wholly prevented, but it can be mitigated as much as possible by efforts to realize localization and fairness in the town's rapid change. Agencies can try to ensure that gains and losses from humanitarian expansion are shared as widely and fairly as possible across the local community. The humanitarian system can also deliberately take a twenty-year view and a life-cycle approach when setting up at scale in a new place, so planning its investments well and its exit carefully in advance. In this respect, agencies may find that they can learn much from responsible parts of the mining sector.[64]

Hierarchy

New hierarchies are formed too when humanitarian aid arrives in strength. As part of the transnational expansion of humanitarian aid as a global profession, humanitarian agencies have taken on some explicit characteristics that mimic patterns of hierarchy found in colonial or corporate power. It is now correct to talk of a humanitarian elite: government, UN or NGO bureaucrats who can make a life-long career in humanitarian aid, earning high salaries and living well in gated communities, with bounteous allowances and poolside parties.[65] The strong division between international and national staff that still exists in many humanitarian hierarchies painfully reflects earlier patterns of colonial power in many parts of Africa and Asia where humanitarian needs are currently greatest. These hierarchies can be undignifying, painful and frustrating to those lower down, especially when they also have a racial dimension. The emergence of the humanitarian executive, whose primary loyalties lie beyond the national borders of the crisis to the mission and strategy of his or her multinational organization, has much in common with a corporate executive in a transnational corporation like Shell, Barclays Bank or PWC. Such executives tend to think company first and country second. Increasingly, elite humanitarians are rewarded for meeting upward-looking bureaucratic procedures rather than for driving effective and compassionate programming downwards at field level.

This emerging dissonance between the high life of humanitarian professionals and the hard life of the people they seek to help is not new, but is becoming systemic and problematic.[66] Ethically, the disconnect means that people in the most powerful parts of the humanitarian system are least likely to encounter suffering communities in real time and least able to connect with them in the spirit of humanity, radical equality, independence and participation required by humanitarian ethics. Instead of working directly with the victims of war and disaster, the main moral effort of elite workers must inevitably be to imagine affected people and places while themselves experiencing a very different working day in air-conditioned offices, embassies and chauffeur-driven cars, sometimes many thousands of miles away. Distant empathy is possible and it must also be required in the middle and upper echelons of every humanitarian organization. If, as we have seen, the moral risk of those working on the ground can be disdain, then the moral risk of those working in headquarters can be forgetting.

An increasing gap between frontline and boardroom is a feature of all expanding and successful organizations. Elite detachment from the roots of a profession or a business is always a moral risk. The only way to deal with this risk is to meet it head-on in an organizational culture that deliberately values and rewards work that is focused on the ground or towards it. Such a culture must also prevent too large a gap in lifestyles developing across a humanitarian organization. Humanitarian work is, by definition, about sharing riches more fairly and widely. It would, therefore, be against the goal of humanitarian ethics if agency executives and professionals were getting rich by doing humanitarian work. Rich people can be excellent humanitarian workers, but humanitarian workers who are deliberately getting rich on the job are usually not. Increasing inequality within a humanitarian agency is also bad for morale, flat management and reputation.

Bureaucratization

The increasing professionalism of humanitarian action can also, paradoxically, create moral hazard. The drive to improve humanitarian professionalism across the world's many aid agencies has been developed in a global system of technical standards. These are most universally obvious in the Sphere Standards, but every agency also has its own internal standards and targets. Increasing professionalism in managerial efficiency, especially in financial, supply chain and human resources management, is another feature of humanitarian improvement. Surprisingly perhaps, targets for improved care and efficient response (which are obviously such good things in themselves and also enhance accountability) can function counter-productively. There is significant evidence from public services in the UK that target-setting in policing, hospitals and social work created some perverse incentives that actually undermined professionalism and wider positive outcomes. In each of these professions, strong government emphasis on particular targets began to skew managerial priorities to meeting these targets. Trade-offs were made between these targets and other less politically fashionable priorities. Outputs—like arrests and prosecutions in policing, or waiting times, admissions and operations in medical care—were emphasized over more subtle processes like patient care and community relations. For example, large new budgets and top-line targets for responding to domestic violence and graffiti meant that police and social workers were rewarded for prioritizing these cases above all others. In order to meet their targets, they might misreport some incidents and might arrest, caution and prosecute young teenage graffiti artists with more zeal than was necessary and not in the best interests of the child. Similarly, the need to reduce waiting times for operations may have encouraged a culture of reduced nursing care and early discharge from hospital. Targets and standards can also be inhibiting rather than incentivizing. New standards in health, safety and child protection across British hospitals greatly improved disease control, but sometimes deterred nurses from touching children to comfort them and lifting patients who could not lift themselves. Nursing was more rewarded for form-filling than its bedside care. As a general rule, process standards always run the risk of obsessing about process over results, while output standards tend to place results over due process.

These negative manifestations of a rush towards targets are a gradual form of administrative corruption, whereby managers steer their programmes and reporting towards external targets rather than individual needs and wider public goods. Affected people and humanitarians report that standardization and target-setting can have similar effects in some operations today. A Sri Lankan NGO worker observed that "we all knew the good development principles like participation or conflict sensitivity, but in the rush of post-disaster relief, very few were able to uphold such principles because of requirements to spend money fast".[67] Often it seems that the extreme sense of emergency comes from government donors more than local people. Agencies can become overly focused on delivery and insensitive to context and process, even when these are carefully included in Sphere guidance. The need to please the donor and satisfy their reporting frameworks can dominate management culture. Some agencies can also be deterred from offering assistance in particularly challenging contexts for fear they cannot meet Sphere and other standards. This may be a good thing if it leaves room for other agencies that can rise to the challenge, but a bad thing if it leaves a vacuum.

The actual process of aid administration—Dunn's bureaucratic modality—is also highly alienating of many people. The "project mentality" itself can be a strange idea to people as agencies seek to compartmentalize and prioritize selected parts of communal life and livelihood for special attention. People often reflect that humanitarian workers are more anxious about their reporting than people's actual problems:

> People in Mali regretted that visits were very brief and that donors always seemed to be in a hurry. In their view, donors seems to be responding more to the needs of their own organizations and were more preoccupied with feeding their own systems (with reports, data collection, meetings etc.) than observing, addressing, and learning from issues in the field.[68]

Excess of Zeal

In legal and business ethics, the ethical problem of an "excess of zeal" is common. For example, divorce lawyers who advise their clients to "take their husband to the cleaners"—because the law allows it and the lawyer would receive a larger fee—are criticized for an unethical (but not illegal) excess of zeal. Their advice may be good for their own and their client's bottom line, but be very bad advice if the couple are trying to maintain good relations for the sake of their young children and to honour the good times they have had together. The over-selling of debt and insurance by the finance sector in recent years made huge temporary profits, but is now recognized as having been globally disastrous and a stunning example of a commercial excess of zeal that was illegal as well as unethical in many cases. Bank employees were driven hard by sales targets and bonus incentives that were shaped much more around market share and bank profits than by what was appropriate for the needs of the consumer.[69]

There may be salutary lessons here for an expanding and increasingly competitive humanitarian sector. Humanitarian agencies should be wary of skewing managerial attention so that it prioritizes donor targets and agency reputation over principles programming and people's actual needs and rights. Many criticisms of humanitarian action seem to focus on objections to an excess of humanitarian zeal. People sense a conflict of interests in humanitarian aid and are suspicious of its commercial and competitive tendency. A group of Indonesian villagers sensed such an excess of zeal when they observed: "NGOs are selling Indonesia by coming to villages, collecting data, and providing this data to donors in exchange for funding."[70]

Affected communities also regularly report a sense of being overpowered by humanitarian agencies, physically and intellectually. A Burmese refugee remarked:

> We don't want to be controlled by the NGOs. We want to work together when necessary, but not all the time. We want to be independent.... We feel like they tell us what to do.... This is because they think we don't have enough capacity.... In order to empower refugees, they need to support them. When they don't do this, they disempower us.[71]

Because aid agencies can put large teams on the ground, drive big cars and import large volumes of aid commodities does not mean that they should. The Kantian dictum that "ought implies can" is unwisely reversed to become "can implies ought". Agencies should not throw everything they have at a problem unless it is absolutely the right thing to do. Often, it is the wrong thing to do, and more subtle solutions negotiated with the community are best.

Bureaucratization takes its toll in other ways too. Many humanitarian workers report that they are process-bound these days. Systems prevail across most humanitarian work that leave little room for spontaneity and close contact with affected communities. Donor procedures for assessment, proposals and reporting can be extremely demanding and most of these processes pull humanitarian workers more towards their computer screens than towards community engagement. The arrival of email and other social media similarly means that frontline humanitarian workers can be reached and controlled easily and constantly by transnational managers beyond their immediate line. If there is a mobile signal or Wi-Fi these days in humanitarian operations, as there usually is, then like most of us today humanitarian workers are not really where they are. Although physically in a camp or a village or a community meeting, an aid worker's head may actually be in a virtual space many thousands of miles away.

Thickening bureaucratic process and virtual systems have implications for humanitarian ethics if they mean that humanitarians are stifled in their ability to innovate, never truly present and prevented from staying close to affected populations. Lisbeth Pilegaard of Norwegian Refugee Council sums up the risks well:

> We must not let technology become a barrier to engaging and communicating with people who need protection and assistance. The risks are there that it further separates us from people we wish to work with and for. The greatest technological achievements—remote monitoring for example—may undermine our purpose by enabling us to be physically absent. Humanitarian action is also about proximity, compassion and solidarity.[72]

Standard procedures, bureaucratic systems and thickening technology are all necessary and potential enablers of more effective humanitarian action. Yet, as humanitarian practice develops, it needs to find an Aristotelian golden mean which strikes a balance between spontaneity and standardization, rules and relationships, proximity and distance, face time and screen time.

The Lives of Humanitarian Workers

Security procedures and concerns have grown enormously as a critical area in which to strike such a balance. How to value the lives of humanitarian workers is another persistent moral problem in humanitarian action. The conviction that every human life is precious is the most fundamental value in humanitarian ethics. So how far are humanitarian workers prepared to share the physical and emotional risks of those who suffer war and disaster if it might mean losing their own life? What is the place of a humanitarian worker's death in humanitarian ethics in a context that is marked by so many other deaths?

Between 2004 and 2013, some 867 humanitarian workers were violently killed and 696 were kidnapped. The year 2013 was the most dangerous on record for humanitarian workers, with 155 killed, 174 seriously wounded and 134 kidnapped.[73] The vast majority of all these victims were national staff, most of them working for international NGOs.[74] During this time, staff security has become a strategic concern for all humanitarian agencies. After the terrible losses in al-Qaeda's bombing of the UN headquarters in Baghdad in August 2003, UN agencies have gained a reputation for being the most risk-averse of all humanitarian agencies. However, it is not only the UN that is increasingly retreating from the frontline. International NGOs have also been criticized for similar policies and operational postures of "bunkerization", "quarantine" and "remote management".[75] MSF recently castigated the sector as a whole for its caution:

> UN agencies and international NGOs are increasingly absent from field locations especially when there is any kind of significant security or logistical issues.... International staff are often rapidly evacuated or go into hibernation. Many agencies only concentrate on the easiest-to-reach populations and are avoiding the most difficult places. They are operating at arm's length through local organizations or government.[76]

Antonio Donini and Dan Maxwell have similarly noted the increasing change in humanitarian relationships and practice "from face-to-face to face-to-screen".[77] Implicit in this trend and some of its moves is a suggestion that an agency's international lives are to be more protected than its national lives. Remote management, in particular, has been singled out for transferring risk away from international staff onto the lives of national staff. A discussion of the value of aid worker life has, therefore, to deal with two difficult questions: the ethics of personal risk, and the relative value of human lives.

Self-sacrifice

Many professions who work in potentially dangerous conditions for the benefit of others—like firefighters, medics, police, social workers, human rights defenders and military personnel—have to confront the ethics of losing their own life. Many people in these professions are prepared to risk their own lives to save others, although they will always protect themselves as much as possible from "paying the ultimate sacrifice" of their own death. Soldiers, firefighters, human rights workers and medics do not embrace a cult of martyrdom, but they do have an ethic of self-sacrifice as last resort.

The notion of personal sacrifice in humanitarian work is rarely discussed publicly by humanitarian agencies. There is a firm determination to maintain the international legal principle that killing humanitarian workers is taboo because they are neutral and working humanely with every side. As a result, the loss of a humanitarian worker's life can never be publicly accepted as a legitimate and noble sacrifice, as it can be in the military or the fire service where there is an acceptance or expectation of ultimate sacrifice in extreme situations. Instead, the murder of a humanitarian worker has always to be condemned as a moral outrage in order to maintain the taboo and deter further killings. Also, the majority of humanitarian workers do not seek a heroic status and are wise to the potential narcissism in self-sacrifice. In humanitarian action as it is actually practised, there is a proper rejection of a cult of sacrifice. Humanitarian workers may start out with narcissistic heroic rescuer fantasies but, unless they are psychologically unstable, a few days in the presence of people suffering in war or disaster makes clear to most aid workers who the real heroes are in such conditions. With the great majority of humanitarian workers, there is a professional modesty born of seeing the much more significant suffering of others. Quite rightly, it is morally improper to play the humanitarian hero in such a context. There is, therefore, a second taboo on emphasizing personal sacrifice that stems from this healthy resistance to a heroic model of the humanitarian profession. Humanitarian agencies quietly remember their dead but do not venerate them like military or paramilitary groups. Those killed violently are correctly remembered more as the victims of murder than for having voluntarily given their lives.

This judicious reluctance to talk publicly about personal risk or heroism means that the ethics of humanitarian sacrifice is under-developed and the place of aid worker death in humanitarian ethics remains an open question. Religious ethics have always accepted the principle of giving one's life in a good cause, and especially in love for one another.[78] Atheism has also always admired the moral value of a generous death. Most famously, Albert Camus summarized this position in the twentieth century with his comment that: "the only way to know if something is worth living for is if it is worth dying for". But it is important to put strong parameters around a principle of self-sacrifice. As the ethicist Gene Outka has observed: "self-sacrifice is justified only if it confers actual benefits on others, not merely because it displays an internal disposition of the self". More practically, of course, "self-sacrifice proves to be self-frustrating if everyone acts on it".[79] Here is the right spirit for humanitarians: one that warns against narcissism in any voluntary self-giving, and also recognizes self-sacrifice as an exceptional move that makes a very impractical general principle.

Humanitarian workers have always died in the course of their work. Before antibiotics were developed, most died from disease, not violence. For example, in the First World War's terrible typhus epidemic that killed 200,000 displaced Serbians in central Europe, some 125 doctors also died from the disease out of the total of 425 working in the Serbian zone.[80] These high death rates may well be the norm again if, as many medics fear, Ebola and other infectious diseases run rampant to become the major cause of global deaths in an era of widespread resistance to antibiotics. In most contemporary humanitarian operations, people are rightly given the freedom to choose their level of risk. An aid worker's consent is typically sought (by his or her boss) in a risky humanitarian operation. Humanitarian culture does not operate a system of orders and obedience in the face of extreme danger that would be the essence of military discipline. Obviously, it makes no sense to be reckless or careless and so "waste" the lives of humanitarian workers in futile operations or foreseeable tragedies. Risks taken in humanitarian work should always be calculated risks. In line with Singer's expanding circles of moral obligation, we have a greater responsibility and a deeper duty of care for those who are emotionally and physically closest to us. This is the duty of care that the management of an organization must show to its employees. But beyond these duties of consent, calculation and care, it can make moral sense to accept death in the responsible pursuit of humanitarian goals.

Consequentialist arguments on this point are relatively simple to make. Many humanitarian actions can carry the risk of death. Leading a convoy down a dangerous road, or staying in a clinic alongside a threatened population to see if humanitarian presence can deter attacks, or smuggling a suitcase of cash through hostile territory to IDPs can all be dangerous. If these various activities are successful and sustain the life and safety of hundreds of people but two aid workers are killed in the process, then a utilitarian case for these individual aid worker losses can be made. As usual, however, such utilitarian logic fails to satisfy the real moral meaning in human life. Most people will not usually give their lives simply for the compelling numerical reasons of consequentialist maths. Instead, it is only ever a much more fundamental relational commitment that can make a person see the potential value in their own death. As discussed in Chapter 2, the virtue of humanity in humanitarian ethics is about extending and forming equal human bonds and coming close to people in a genuine solicitude that cares about who they are and what they need. In this relationship, dying oneself when trying to save and protect others can be the ultimate act of solicitude. Such a death is not about definite outcomes, but about being with people you care about. Those humanitarian workers who get kidnapped and killed are most often in that situation to be with people, not because they are calculating the precise number of lives saved that is morally proportionate to their own death. With this more intimate understanding of human bonds and personal commitments, the notion of a good humanitarian death can find a place in humanitarian ethics. The death of humanitarian workers must never be encouraged or required in humanitarian work, as it is sometimes in the military. However, giving one's life for others does make moral sense, especially if experienced by the community concerned as an act of humanity and compassion.

International Lives and National Lives

The idea that agencies might put relative values on different human lives within their organizations seems to be an egregious breach of the radical equality of human life that is central to humanitarian ethics' foundational values of humanity and impartiality. A humanitarian agency making a routine distinction between national and international lives would indeed be outrageous and racist hypocrisy. It would be profoundly immoral if it were held as a general principle. Tolerating different levels of risk between international and national staff can only make moral sense if the context creates ethical reasons why some staff can and should accept higher levels of risk than others. The only way it can be ethical to make nationality, religion, race or colour an acceptable criterion in differentiations of risk is if these decisions are justified by differences in threat, connectedness and consent. A moral case can then be made for these three exceptions:

- Threat exception—if the threat of violence is known to be targeted specifically at international staff or people with particular nationalities or beliefs, then it is reasonable to make an exception. In this case, it makes sense to protect humanitarian workers from the more vulnerable group if people from other groups are genuinely at less risk. In some cases, this will mean protecting international staff and exposing national staff. In other situations, it may be the reverse. National staff can often be at greater risk and so it makes moral sense to protect them and deploy international staff.
- Connectedness exception—many national staff can feel especially connected to their communities in times of crisis and be bound by an additional communal duty not to abandon families, friends and neighbours in their time of suffering and need. This connectedness means they willingly take on levels of risk that seem too high for international staff. Voicing this particular duty, national staff will sometimes comfort or confront international staff by saying: "this is not your fight and you do not need to be here", or "this is my people and I cannot walk away but must share their dangers". This seems justifiable in line with our different circles of obligation and relationship.
- Consent exception—any form of exception that differentiates between the lives of various humanitarian workers must still be based on the consent of those involved. It would be wrong for an agency to command its staff to take on unequal dangers. People would need to understand the reasoning and consent fully to the risks and disparities involved. Gauging consent requires some subtlety in these cases, especially when financial incentives like extra per diems or danger money can distort

consent. But if people genuinely consent to uneven dangers, then an exception can be made.

It seems fair to respect these particular exceptions made for either national staff or international staff, depending on the particular context. Taking unequal risks can be ethically justified. But it remains vital to support and protect exposed staff as much as possible when they make this choice. The duty of care heightens and does not reduce with distance or "remoteness" in these situations.

This chapter has looked at some of the perennial ethical challenges that routinely appear as strategic moral risks in humanitarian action. The next chapter will focus on the personal ethics of humanitarian workers and how best to cultivate operational virtues in individual humanitarians.

12

THE ETHICAL HUMANITARIAN WORKER

There is much talk about agencies and the international system in discussions of humanitarian action, but it is really the individual humanitarian that is central in humanitarian work. The way each person in every agency decides to be humanitarian when he or she gets up in the morning sets the tone of humanitarian ethics around the world. If most of us choose to be principled, practical, daring, courageous and thoughtful, and keep struggling to stay close to affected communities and create solutions with them, then humanitarian action stands a good chance of being relevant, effective and respected. If too many of us become cynical, cautious, bureaucratic, self-interested, inefficient and prefer to sit with our laptops rather than with people suffering around us, then our agencies and the humanitarian system will reflect these attitudes and attract resentment rather than admiration.

At the beginning of this book, we noted that the word ethics comes from the Greek word *ethos* meaning character. The quality of humanitarian action is determined by the character of the people doing it and by their particular virtues, which comes from the Latin word for strength. This final chapter, therefore, explores the personal dimension of humanitarian ethics. It examines the kinds of things people need to feel, be, know and do if they are to form a strong humanitarian character and develop effective humanitarian virtues. Some people have quite a lot of these characteristics and strengths already, but the rest of us may have to practise and develop them. Ethical character and practical virtues, like roses and rice, need to be cultivated carefully.

This chapter will look first at some personal dimensions of humanitarian work like motivation, working relationships, lifestyle, self-care and morale.[1] It then sets out to define what constitutes essential humanitarian virtues and everyday virtues for individual humanitarian workers.

Personal Ethics

In her important work on the lifestyles of international aid workers, Anne-Meike Fechter has rightly noticed a lack of proper thinking about what constitutes the personal ethics of humanitarian workers. She has observed "how the personal often remains unacknowledged even though its salience for aid workers is well documented, for example, in the growing popularity of their blogs and memoirs".[2] By focusing so hard on technical practices in health care, food distribution, protection, shelter and livelihoods, the humanitarian profession can tend to overlook the humanitarian individual and the ethical demands, moral stress and inner turmoil that can accompany technical jobs in very conflicted and unequal human settings. The operational ethics of the profession are well documented and routinely articulated, but what of the moral feelings of the humanitarian individual living, working and making choices in the midst of crisis? What does it mean to have a resilient personal ethic as an individual humanitarian?

A lot of humanitarian work can be turbulent. Things can happen fast, working relationships are intense, the job is full on and the main issue is life and death. A lot of humanitarian work can also be dull. Things become routine, programmes bed down into a predictable rhythm and the main issues become smaller, even petty. At either tempo, programmes typically feel caught in a much wider and unjust political impasse. The main preoccupations for individual humanitarians operating in these settings are not always the big first-order ethical questions like impartiality and independence, but their more fine-grained daily manifestations in nagging problems around motivation, working relationships, lifestyle, self-care and morale. It is important to look at these personal everyday ethical issues that are likely to determine if humanitarian individuals are likely to stay engaged with their work, pursue it effectively and live well with others while they do so.

Personal Motivation

Motivation is the first dimension of the personal ethics of individual humanitarians. At some point, many individual humanitarians find themselves asking, "Why am I doing this?" Often the obstacles and stress involved just seem too much, or some roles are just so far removed from the front line that people feel disconnected from an ethical cause and their work feels just like any other job. Sometimes aid workers have resentment heaped upon them from societies they are trying to help. At other times, projects may be going well and humanitarian workers may be having fun working with struggling communities while living well in a beautiful place on a good income but feel a dissonance around their pleasure that cannot be right somehow.

Every humanitarian worker has some moral sense of why they have deliberately chosen this kind of work. Some people's motivation will be close to a moral calling or vocation: "this is my life's work". Others will have motives that are more opportunistic, self-serving and pragmatic: "this is a good job in which I may also do some good". In both cases, the sense of motivation is likely to change over time with actual operational engagement. In a distinctly moral calling, our personal motives are likely to combine psychologically healthy moral drivers with some fairly dysfunctional motivations too. As a young British humanitarian worker in my early twenties, I was steeped in private fantasies from the paternalistic emotional legacy of European imperial mission, and was in thrall to the romantic ideas of protecting the weak that similarly deluded Don Quixote in Cervantes' great sixteenth-century comic novel satirizing chivalry and heroism. My Toyota was my stallion and in it I was a white knight destined to seek out and save widows and orphans in far-off lands. It took a bit of time, kind counsel from my national colleagues, self-mockery and quite a lot of reading in liberation theology to reframe my sense of purpose into something more appropriate and realistic. This realism was much less about me and much more about hard politics, the suffering of others and the limits of success. Becoming a parent in my early thirties then gave me an acute personal empathy with people whose families were in great danger and a sharper sense of how they might want to be comforted, helped and empowered.

Most humanitarian workers will have been spared my parochial European delusions of global heroism but will have variants of their own. There is an ethical core to our moral fantasies of help that is good and healthy. This is the universal move to sympathy and the desire to act, which we saw in Chapter 1. All too often, however, this primal call can get wrapped up in vain dreams of our own power and others' weaknesses. All of us need to work through these fantasies to find the right way to get alongside people in their crisis and work with them towards optimal and agreed solutions. In doing so, we need to learn the right syntax of help. There is a good grammar and a bad grammar to humanitarian aid. The bad grammar is a sentence like "I help you" in which the humanitarian worker is the active subject, the person in danger is the object and the verb is held in the power of the aid worker as the subject of the sentence. A better grammar of aid is "I work with people who are surviving or recovering". In this sentence, survivors and humanitarians are both active subjects and humanitarian workers operate only prepositionally—always acting with, for or beside people, but never on or over people in a power dynamic that has people as the mere objects of their actions.

This is a gifted way of working which, as we shall see, requires the cultivation of certain humanitarian virtues. Ultimately, however, the desire to work with and alongside people is a healthier and more resilient personal ethic than a fantasy of rescue. Power-based fantasies of humanitarian motivation indicate emotional under-development. They are also more brittle motivations and tend to crack easily in an emergency. People who imagine themselves to be heroes and saviours leading a process of rescue are often the first to be disappointed in their actual experience of humanitarian action. In contrast, it is often the people who carry the least emotional baggage about their personal role that prove to be most practical and best able to take the long and realistic view. When it comes to psychic archetypes in humanitarian work, we might be wise to beware the rescuer and hero in ourselves and look more for the listener, the cooperator, the struggler, the problem-solver, the servant leader and the winner. These are still daring and courageous roles, but not so narcissistic.

Another healthy indicator of good humanitarian motivation is fulfilment rather than pain. It is a good sign that humanitarian workers enjoy what they do and find fulfilment in their job even if their work can be tragic, hard and constantly compromised. There are many good things in a humanitarian operation: hard struggle; strong friendships; common cause; instances of success; shared sorrow; glimpses of beauty; and moments of hope. These are all human goods that rightly motivate us, inspire us, sustain us and fulfil us. Strangely, perhaps, people can flourish in terrible situations even as they deeply regret that these situations exist. The personal fulfilment they gain from humanitarian action accounts for why many humanitarians will talk about some emergencies as the best time of their lives, even when it was the worst time in other people's lives and often the moment of their death. Although bizarre to those who were not there, this fulfilment is morally and psychologically healthy if it also recognizes and respects the horror and tragedy involved. This flourishing is not a cause for concern unless it is a crazed false flourishing from the adrenaline addiction of so-called war junkies. We should not respond with moral indignation to those who say they have enjoyed helping others. Instead, we should be glad but perhaps speak of it with some discretion. In contrast, people who are in a constant state of moral confusion and frustration with humanitarian work may be operating to a dysfunctional motivation of some kind, or an illusion that the situation should somehow be easier than it is. They may feel it is morally wrong to draw any positive emotions from the suffering of others. But, to be too unhappy in a humanitarian role is simply wrong. It indicates an exhausting lack of realism that is bad for the individual concerned and for the team of which they are a part.

What about those people who claim to be humanitarian workers with little moral motivation? Instead, they are in it for the money, the career path or the comfort of living in a poor country with a high salary. Some humanitarians start with this view while others end up with it after their disenchantment with an earlier magical idea of rescue or constant success or a purely ethical motivation. A more selfish motivation cannot be right if the primary or sole motivation is greed of some kind. People need to be careful how much they become absorbed by self-interest and career advancement in humanitarian action. However, a more self-serving motivation is not necessarily unethical if a person is prioritizing the immediate good of their own family and treating the wider household well while also respecting humanitarian action's moral goal to value and help others. If he or she is also working ethically and effectively, then they are making a valuable humanitarian contribution regardless of their core motive. Mixed motives do not preclude high humanitarian performance, but ethical goals and moral attitudes will always be central in humanitarian action.

Self-interest can be a moral good, but not if it spills over into a person's professional humanitarian responsibilities so much that they put their own personal advantage above their humanitarian role. I remember being annoyed by the personal preoccupation of some UN officials when I worked for the organization. I had just returned to the UN headquarters in Addis Ababa from a hard couple of weeks in which I had raised an urgent alert about new food shortages in one of the conflict-affected northern regions. At lunch in the canteen, I sat near a group of senior UN staff. I needed them to start pushing hard on the northern problem. Instead, as I de-briefed with a colleague, I heard them spend the whole of lunch talking about the intricacies of their UN pension plan. Now that I am much closer to retirement than I was then, I realize the dire urgency of pension planning. However, people need to retain a strong primary sense of humanitarian purpose when they are in a humanitarian role.

Another example came when I worked within a primarily field-based role in which we received a large cash per diem paid in dollars for every day that we spent in the capital city. This naturally created a perverse incentive, and a number of my colleagues would stay much longer in the capital than was necessary purely in order to make a lot of extra money. Even in the most difficult situations, we need to resist an operational fatalism which says "everything is so hard here that we might at least make the most of it for ourselves". This is quite simply to abandon humanitarian ethics and its role morality. It is an attitude that makes for a slippery slope in one's personal ethics.

Working Relationships

Fair and respectful working relationships between national and international staff are another deep concern in the personal ethical experience of humanitarian workers. These relationships are a particular focus of academic criticism of the humanitarian profession. Personal unease and academic criticism arise because there is still a structural inequality in professional relationships in most humanitarian agencies, between a minority cadre of international staff and a much larger majority of national staff. This power differential is a major focus of many anthropologists and sociologists who criticize "Aidland".[3] Silke Roth has made a particular study of this relationship, and whether the increasing professionalization of the humanitarian sector is improving or worsening the asymmetry of international and national relationships. Ethically, her work suggests that the problem is one of unequal power and culture clash. She sums up some of her findings as follows:

> National staff were critical of international experts who overlooked their competence and expertise and did not take them seriously...and did not consult the local population about their needs and interests, ignored local culture, dressed inappropriately or distributed food and other items that were unwelcome.... National staff perceived international staff not only as arrogant and ignorant but also as unqualified and superfluous. Unsurprisingly, they were critical if inexperienced and—in their view—ignorant young international aid workers were assigned to do the jobs that national staff felt quite capable of doing themselves.[4]

Roth's work also picked up a strong feeling that even when they are on the ground and "in the field", international staff tend to live expatriate lives that are isolated from the local context in team houses or high security compounds.

But this negative picture is not the whole story. National staff recognized that local knowledge and international expertise can be highly complementary. Roth's work points out that many national staff praised their agencies for their mentoring, training, postgraduate education sponsorship and promotion strategies which all aim to reduce the inequalities of aid agency relationships. These formal measures of inequality reduction constitute what is positive in the professionalizing agenda across the humanitarian sector. Informally, international staff often give financial support to the families of national colleagues and also encourage and enable them to rise up their organizations by giving them more power and opportunity in their daily work. For their part, international staff emphasized the advantages of their political neutrality, their ability to resist corruption and local pressure, and the particular need for urgent humanitarian operations to be run hierarchically and with an adept interface with Western donors. All of this makes good sense in certain settings.

Roth is still open-minded about the potential for these formal and informal strategies to level the playing field between national and international staff in such a way that sees power shared more on the basis of merit than on race and class. Other academics are less patient than Roth. They are suspicious of the professionalizing agenda and expect it to enforce the dominance of a new elite of certified agencies and individuals. Psychologist Malcolm MacLachlan and his colleagues regard arguments that justify specific international leadership roles based on neutrality or expertise as spurious "legitimising myths" carefully maintained in the interests of the "expatocracy" that dominates humanitarian aid and relationships. They see little moral value in informal aid worker efforts to remedy the situation. Instead they characterize such acts of personal generosity in cash or kind as some kind of patronizing false friending or fake "kin-making" which does nothing for wider social justice and only eases the conscience of elite aid workers.[5] Writing more than twenty years before them, Graham Hancock was even more scathing about the "aristocracy of mercy" and the "masters of disasters" in his critique of aid elites.[6]

So how can humanitarian workers deal ethically with a structural relationship that remains unequal and potentially unjust and degrading? Firstly, they need to address it openly and strategically as they are doing already in sector-wide efforts to diversify senior roles and build meritocratic and localized organizations. Secondly, they need to scrutinize the arguments for international roles and deliver evidence of whether "legitimizing" arguments of neutrality or expertise are empirically founded. Thirdly, they need to deploy international staff under the authority of national staff much more than they do now. Finally, of course, every aid worker must be free to pursue their own acts of individual kindness as they see fit, towards their staff and the people they meet, so long as this does not privilege people within their organization unfairly. None of the above strategies will deliver immediate social justice across the sector, and so discretionary aid by individual humanitarians remains a valid response to organizational and societal inequality, as well as an important enactment of genuine friendship.

Humanitarian Lifestyle and Self-Care

The difference in lifestyles of international humanitarian workers is a closely related area of moral unease that is observed by local society and felt by international aid workers. Is it right to be working on the same team and for the same ethical cause but to swing home in a chauffeur-driven air-conditioned car to a luxurious and subsidized house in the rich area of town while your national counterpart, on whom you depend and with whom you have been working all day, queues for a crowded bus and heads back to high rent and power cuts in the suburbs? Like other questions of equality and fairness, this one is not unique to humanitarian organizations but is common to all human institutions, the great majority of which remain hierarchical.

Again, the challenge here is to scrutinize some potentially legitimizing myths around why such differences are justifiable and to understand how far such inequalities are reasonable and tolerable for all parties concerned. This requires some frank deliberation around Rawls' "difference principle" that we explored in Chapter 2 and the wider sharing of resources. In field operations it does seem right that agency staff should share almost identical conditions. At the frontline people need to feel a sense of fairness and team equality as they grapple first hand with the suffering of others. To know some of the pain and discomfort of people they are trying to help is valuable in focusing the mind and intent of aid workers. At headquarters in capital cities where the world is very different to the frontline, it is also important to remind people constantly of the reality of suffering further away. One British general in the Second World War was famous for always putting his headquarters team—other generals and senior staff officers—on half-rations whenever his troops at the front were also on half-rations.[7] Some similar practice may be useful in the smart offices of many humanitarian agencies when an agency's field staff and people in their care are low on supplies.

Naturally, there is a middle way in all this. Civilians in a terrible state are obviously not best served by humanitarian workers who are also in a terrible state. The personal ethics of individual humanitarian workers does not just concern their relationships with others. Humanitarian workers should also be properly worried about their relationship with their own self as Alessandra Pigni has long reminded us on her anti-burnout website. Ethically, we have a duty to care for ourselves as well as for others. The value of our own life and flourishing must be our preoccupation too.[8] As Kant would have it, we are ends ourselves and not only instruments for others. Agencies have been right to be concerned about burn-out in individual humanitarians and to focus properly on self-care, rest and recreation in their staff. Recent research in the neuroscience of compassion at Geneva University also gives us strong reason to believe that a person who cares well for herself or himself is more compassionate than a person who is burnt out.[9]

This means that individual humanitarian workers have a responsibility to themselves and others to keep in good physical, mental and emotional health. A key part of their personal ethics must be a concern for their own person. But does this mean they should spend hours at the spa in the local Sheraton and spend agency money on expensive imported food?

Here there is a need for moderation and adaptation too. Individuals must be good to themselves in a way that does not scandalize others or create envy and resentment in those around them and generate disrespect for the humanitarian profession. They must be wary of a slippery slope of justifications that leads to indulgence and excess instead of reasonable and appropriate self-care.

Morale

In the pursuit of self-care, individual and team morale is central. Morale is the most important factor in the personal ethics of individual humanitarian workers and in the vital team ethics that is so central to humanitarian success. Morale is an integral part of self-care and a responsibility that individuals have to one another as colleagues or leaders. Quite simply, individuals will not thrive and work well together in humanitarian work without good morale. It is no accident that the word "morale", which we associate too easily with simple good spirits, has its root in ethics. People can only really do good things if they feel good about doing them, and believe they are the right things to do. In India and Burma during the Second World War, General Bill Slim forged the most multicultural army of modern times to fight and win in one of the most difficult theatres of the war. He put morale at the centre of his strategy and kept it there throughout the long campaign. Slim's approach to morale still guides the British army today and also inspires leadership theory in business studies.[10]

Slim was clear that morale is fundamental and determines success: "Morale is a state of mind. It is the intangible force which will move a whole group of people to give their last ounce to achieve something, without counting the cost to themselves; that makes them feel they are part of something greater than themselves."[11] Such a state of mind is built on three foundations: the spiritual; the intellectual, and the material. The table below is an adapted version of Slim's simple model of morale which can be a useful prompt to humanitarian leaders as they seek to build ethical and effective humanitarian operations.

The Foundations of Morale

1. Spiritual

a) There must be a great and noble object.

b) Its achievement must be vital.
c) The method of achievement must be active.
d) Each person must feel that what she is and what he does matters directly towards the attainment of the object.

2. Intellectual
a) People must be convinced that the object can be attained; that it is not out of reach.
b) People must see, too, that the organization to which they belong and which is striving to attain the object is an efficient one.
c) People must have confidence in their leaders and know that whatever dangers and hardships they are called upon to suffer, their life will not be lightly flung away.

3. Material
a) Each person must feel that they will get a fair deal from their leaders and from their organization generally.
b) Each person must, as far as humanly possible, be given the best means and equipment for the task.
c) Each person's living conditions must be made as good as they can be.

Slim, *Defeat Into Victory*, pp208–9

Humanitarian leaders as ethical leaders need to focus hard on the morale of their teams. People in humanitarian agencies need to feel inspired, motivated and supported. Their gaze should be set above internal feuding and personality clashes to the higher goal of saving and protecting human life.

Personal Virtues

Once individual humanitarian workers know what they are doing and why, they need to cultivate professional virtues that enable them to get on and do it. Distinct humanitarian virtues are derived from the core humanitarian principles of humanity, impartiality, neutrality and independence as well as Code of Conduct principles like respect, participation, capacity-building, sustainability and accountability. Together, these virtues form the professional attitudes and habits of mind necessary to practise the particular role morality of humanitarian action and there is clear evidence that living these principles makes for successful humanitarian work.[12] Alongside these specifically humanitarian virtues, humanitarian workers also need to cultivate strong everyday human virtues like courage, patience, practical wisdom, diligence, integrity, struggle and hope.

Humanitarian Virtues

Being humanitarian means developing a rational understanding and intuitive sense of what it means to be humane, impartial, neutral and independent in a given operational context. It also involves a form of operational practice that is instinctively and effectively respectful, participatory, empowering, sustainable and accountable.

- The Virtues of Humanity and Impartiality

To be humanitarian, every individual aid worker needs to practise the core virtues of humanity and impartiality. This means cultivating the kind of humanitarian attention to people discussed in Chapter 2. This attention meets people suffering or at risk of suffering with a humane heart and an equal and unbiased eye that makes distinctions between people only on the basis of their needs. Being discerning in this way requires a closeness to people that embodies a form of professional friendship. The operational work of humanitarian action that works very practically to protect dignified bodily life requires direct human contact. People and aid workers need to meet each other and listen to one another, and to share the sight, sound, smell, taste and touch of a situation as they work together to improve it. Only by sharing something of each other and the difficulty of crisis conditions can they be humane and fair with one another and generate effective action.

- The Virtues of Neutrality and Independence

These particular political virtues required in the role morality of humanitarian action need to be honed as second nature by humanitarian workers. Counter-intuitively and against their normal moral and political instincts, individual humanitarian workers must not take sides to become political humanitarians but instead remain engaged in humanitarian politics. The art of neutrality must become more than a mask and embody a committed position which looks through political hatred and dispute to the particular tragedy of individual people and collective suffering.

- The Virtues of Respect, Participation and Empowerment

As well as the core four humanitarian virtues, individual humanitarians must develop innate and instinctive operational habits that enact the wider virtues of the Code of Conduct. This means cultivating attitudes and practices that respect cultural differences but also challenging them when necessary. It also includes the commitment to empower people in their own survival and recovery. Living the virtues of the Code requires all aid workers to see a person not as a victim or a "beneficiary" when they work together with individuals in suffering communities.

- The Virtues of Sustainability and Accountability

The virtue of a mindset that develops programmes with lasting effect and limited environmental damage is another Code virtue. So too is accountability as aid workers meet their moral responsibility to account for their actions to those they aim to help and those who invest in humanitarian organizations. As humanitarians decide and act they must constantly, as a managerial reflex, automatically reflect upon the rights, interests and expectations of those for whom they act. They must also always be ready to explain their actions to those around them in numbers and narrative.

Everyday Virtues

Humanitarian work does not only embody specific humanitarian virtues. It also requires the full range of everyday virtues that are inevitably involved in any significant human endeavour: in particular, courage, patience, practical wisdom, diligence, integrity, hope and struggle.

- Courage

Courage is essential in all areas of life. Humanitarian work is no exception. Humanitarian workers need to be courageous. They need courage to operate in difficult conditions, and they need courage to apply their principles and to take risks and decisions. The military tends to reflect on courage more than most professions. Their leaders have always appreciated courage not only in a simple way as bravery and endurance, but also in a more complete way as moral commitment. Slim describes courage as follows:

> Courage is not merely a virtue; it is the virtue. Without it there are no other virtues. Faith, hope and charity, and all the rest do not become virtues until it takes courage to exercise them.... You can't be good without being brave. Courage is a mental state, an affair of the spirit so it gets its strength from spiritual and intellectual sources.... There are two types of courage. The first, an emotional state which urges a person to risk injury or death—physical courage. The second, a more reasoning attitude which enables a person to stake career, happiness, his whole future on his judgement of what he thinks either right or worthwhile—moral courage.... To be really great [a person or an organization] must possess both kinds of courage.[13]

Courage can be cultivated in a healthy self-confidence, but it can also run out when it is drawn upon unnecessarily or for too long. Courage needs to be enabled and supported in humanitarian work. One of the most important roles for humanitarian leaders is to encourage their staff and also to encourage the communities they are trying to help. Frequently, of course, humanitarian workers actually draw their own courage from the experience of people they are helping. At its best, encouragement is profoundly reciprocal between humanitarian and survivor.

- Patience

Although situations are urgent in armed conflicts and disasters, progress in humanitarian action often takes time. Obstacles must be overcome, criticism needs to be endured, positive outcomes can be slow and the horrors of war and political impasse can last for many years. This means that humanitarian workers need to cultivate strategic patience. They need to be ready to work for the long game, to see improvements over time and to gradually expand access and resources. They need to wait without certainty for positive outcomes to emerge from uncertain situations.

A wide array of particular operational moments also require tactical humanitarian patience: the long wait outside the official's office; the repeated failures of Wi-Fi and mobile phones; the long speeches that characterize the verbal repertoire of many cultures; and the checkpoints and security procedures that dominate so many conflict zones.

- Practical wisdom

I wish there were a better single word in the English language to capture this most critical of operational virtues. Unfortunately, as we have already noticed, the original Greek word *phronesis* is not very catchy; and the Latin *prudentia* has suffered a diversion of meaning as cautious prudence in contemporary English. So perhaps it is best if we summarize this key virtue as "humanitarian art"—the particular genius and ability to make good things happen in extremely difficult conditions. It is the ability to be flexible, innovative and deeply practical while keeping firmly in tune with the keynotes of humanitarian ethics. In some situations, such wisdom means finding Aristotle's "golden mean" between extreme alternatives that are equally and unsatisfactorily excessive. In other situations, it means doing something daring or previously unthought of and out of the box. This ethical art is the skill and judgement of the humanitarian who can design and deliver a programme that is principled enough, quick enough and effective enough in a very tight spot. It is the wisdom and cunning of the humanitarian negotiator who empathizes with his allies and opponents, reads them well and is able to shape a solution that works. It is the art of a humanitarian leader who makes the right call when their team is in danger and their work remains vital. It is, above all, the ability to make the best from what is possible and to make the impossible less daunting and worth a try.

- Diligence

Naturally, humanitarian action is not just art but work. Planning, designing, preparing, inspiring, implementing, cooperating, negotiating, communicating, fundraising, recruiting, training, delivering, adapting, monitoring, evaluating and accounting all takes effort and hard work. This effort must be taken seriously and be done as well as possible. With the protection of the human person as their goal, humanitarians need to be diligent and efficient. Implicit in the virtue of diligence is the idea of working carefully. This means taking due care of strategy and necessary detail. It means working on the important things, not the trivial things. It also involves taking due care of those around you and yourself. Individual humanitarians need to cultivate a work ethic that makes the most of their time and resources in a way that makes them most effective. This means working well, rather than simply working too much.

- Integrity

Every humanitarian worker needs to be honest about what they stand for and the goals they seek. Working with humanitarian integrity means practising humanitarian principles and extending a simple humanitarian intent to everyone you meet. Having humanitarian integrity involves doing things according to a humanitarian goal and with humanitarian principles. Alongside your actions, humanitarian integrity requires a certain humane presence and the cultivation of a humanitarian temperament that people recognize and trust. This is integrity of mission and purpose. Integrity is equally about honesty and trustworthiness in personal dealings, finances, recruitment and resources management.

- Hope

In the suffering of armed conflict and disaster, humanitarian workers can see the very worst of the world. To endure such things and respond positively to them not only takes courage but hope. A famous Greek myth tells the story of Pandora who was given a beautiful box by the gods and told never to open it. Naturally, she could not resist and had a peep inside. Out of the box flew all the evils of the world, which went on to create havoc and misery in human lives. But at the very bottom of the box was hope. This also flew out and took its place in human hearts. In the worst of times, hope is often all we have with which to struggle against the terrible things around us. Humanitarians need to cherish hope. Often they will discover it in people they are trying to help. Often it will be best found in small instances of humanitarian success like a life saved, a new life born, a successful distribution or the eventual sound of laughter after incredible fear. Humanitarian action is itself an act of hope. It resolutely continues to express the value of human life, the existence of human kindness and the conviction that we are a loving species. Humanitarians need to be hopeful for themselves and for others. Being hopeful does not mean being absurdly optimistic. It simply means knowing that the world does not turn on bad things alone but also on good. Hope then seeks out this good.

- Struggle

Few things come easily in humanitarian work. Instead, most humanitarian operations require significant struggle. Difficulty of all kinds is the reality of humanitarian action for those who need it and those who provide it. Struggle is therefore inherent and essential to good humanitarian work. The ability to struggle and keep struggling is a critical virtue in humanitarian workers. The everyday virtues of courage, patience, practical wisdom, diligence, integrity and hope are what enable individuals and organizations to struggle. But to continue to struggle and to struggle for the right things is a distinct virtue and an enduring strength in humanitarian work.

Ethical Organizations

Ultimately, it is not just humanitarian individuals but humanitarian organizations that need to be ethical and embody the virtues essential to humanitarian action. In one sense, an organization is an accumulation of individuals. However, individuals are also deeply shaped and influenced by their organizations to good or bad effect. Organizational leadership and culture can dictate the contributions of individuals within an institution by creating a dominant organizational character that can either encourage or inhibit ethical practice. Having a lot of ethical individuals in humanitarian work is not enough. The organizations in which they work must actively value and pursue humanitarian principles and practice. Humanitarian agencies must be ethically demanding and ethically enabling environments.

This requires that the distinctive humanitarian virtues and everyday virtues discussed above be embodied in every humanitarian organization. These virtues need to be hard-wired in obligatory agency principles, standards and rules that are well understood by all individuals. They must also become habitual and intuitive in people. Ethical consciousness and competence must be cultivated as an essential part of an organization's instinct and culture. This can easily be achieved by agencies developing a common organizational conscience. This would mean that all their staff are alert to moral problems with a similar sensitivity across the globe and all tend to embody attitudes, behaviours and choices that are typical of the organization and its particular moral compass.

On a daily basis, humanitarian leaders need to endorse and model ethical awareness and concern across their agency or NGO. They need to ask ethical questions of programming choices and strategic decisions. They also need to model and enable simple cultures of ethical deliberation at all levels of their organization. Project reviews and evaluations need to include an ethical appraisal of operational paths that have been taken and avoided. Humanitarian principles should always be essential criteria in humanitarian evaluation and accountability. Learning from the experience of many commercial companies and universities, humanitarian agencies might also consider developing ethical committees more routinely in their organizational structure. These committees should be practical and operate in real time. They need to offer operational support and not become a device with which to kick difficult ethical balls into the long grass of endless deliberation.

All humanitarian leaders also need to be determined and adept at communicating their ethical goals and decision-making within their organization and beyond it to the people they help and the public who finance them. Every humanitarian organization should work more deliberately to make humanitarian ethics into public ethics. It is only by creating humanitarian agencies that are fluent and accessible in talking about the ethics of humanitarian action that humanitarian organizations will build an articulate and informed global constituency that cares about humanitarian action. Clearer understanding and stronger humanitarian conviction in the global public will be essential if people and power around the world are to find common cause in a desire to value human life in crisis and join together to support the principle of humanity in war and disaster. The deliberate cultivation of global humanitarian will is going to prove vital in the years ahead if individual humanitarian workers are to reach out effectively to the mass of individuals experiencing violence, armed conflict and disaster around the world in the next decade of the twenty-first century.

Trusting Our Ethical Expertise

The Chilean philosopher and neuroscientist Francisco Varela has usefully described practical ethics as moral coping. In our busy and very practical daily lives we routinely confront ambiguous situations, obvious wrongs and desirable goods. We deal with difficult moral moments with our family and our work colleagues, with pushy strangers in a bus queue and as we compete with one another over things we want. We do not always stop to compute these situations in an elaborate rational way that makes ethics an abstract and complex intellectual pursuit. Nor should we get so bogged down. We "do ethics" hundreds of times a day and typically get on with our moral lives in a very practical way. We use our sense of right and wrong, our empathy, things we have learned and memories of situations we have heard about or experienced before, and have a natural "readiness for action".

We humans are very skilled animals, always working, moving, talking, thinking, feeling, making, meeting, eating, surviving and thriving. We have extraordinary expertise in many things and so we should trust our essential "ethical expertise" as well, recognizing that we do a lot of ethics instinctively, deliberately and constantly as one of our many social skills. We have an ethical disposition we can trust.

Following Mencius, the great Chinese philosopher from the fourth century BC, Varela sees our ethical expertise operative in three core skills: extension, attention and intelligent awareness. As we saw earlier in this book, we have the ability to think and feel beyond ourselves and so extend our moral skills to others. We have a capacity to give great attention to what needs doing. And we are able to keep an intelligent awareness of the world around us so that we can recognize affinities between situations that we are experiencing now and others we have experienced before. Together these three skills enable us to cope and improve as moral beings. Varela's understanding of ethical expertise suggests that "ethics is closer to wisdom than to reason, closer to understanding what is good than to correctly adjudicating particular situations" and that "the situations in which we exercise ethical expertise far outnumber those in which we must exercise explicit ethical deliberation".[14]

We all have this understanding of what is good and a natural ethical expertise for doing good. I hope this book has helped to reinforce this ethical expertise in humanitarian workers. I hope that reading its various chapters will keep aid professionals and their agencies ethically fit so that they can cope more easily with moral problems, large and small, in their vital daily work of respecting, protecting and saving human life.

ANNEX 1

THE FUNDAMENTAL PRINCIPLES OF THE RED CROSS AND RED CRESCENT MOVEMENT

Proclaimed in Vienna in 1965, the seven Fundamental Principles bond together the Red Cross and Red Crescent National Societies, the International Committee of the Red Cross and the International Federation of Red Cross and Red Crescent Societies. They guarantee the continuity of the Red Cross Red Crescent Movement and its humanitarian work.

Humanity

The International Red Cross and Red Crescent Movement, born of a desire to bring assistance without discrimination to the wounded on the battlefield, endeavours, in its international and national capacity, to prevent and alleviate human suffering wherever it may be found. Its purpose is to protect life and health and to ensure respect for the human being. It promotes mutual understanding, friendship, cooperation and lasting peace amongst all peoples.

Impartiality

It makes no discrimination as to nationality, race, religious beliefs, class or political opinions. It endeavours to relieve the suffering of individuals, being guided solely by their needs, and to give priority to the most urgent cases of distress.

Neutrality

In order to continue to enjoy the confidence of all, the Movement may not take sides in hostilities or engage at any time in controversies of a political, racial, religious or ideological nature.

Independence

The Movement is independent. The National Societies, while auxiliaries in the humanitarian services of their governments and subject to the laws of their respective countries, must always maintain their autonomy so that they may be able at all times to act in accordance with the principles of the Movement.

Voluntary service

It is a voluntary relief movement not prompted in any manner by desire for gain.

Unity

There can be only one Red Cross or one Red Crescent Society in any one country. It must be open to all. It must carry on its humanitarian work throughout its territory.

Universality

The International Red Cross and Red Crescent Movement, in which all Societies have equal status and share equal responsibilities and duties in helping each other, is worldwide.

ANNEX 2

THE CODE OF CONDUCT FOR THE INTERNATIONAL RED CROSS AND RED CRESCENT MOVEMENT AND NGOS IN DISASTER RELIEF

The Code of Conduct for the International Red Cross and Red Crescent Movement and NGOs in Disaster Relief, was developed and agreed upon by eight of the world's largest disaster response agencies in the summer of 1994.

The Code of Conduct, like most professional codes, is a voluntary one. It lays down ten points of principle which all humanitarian actors should adhere to in their disaster response work, and goes on to describe the relationships that agencies working in disasters should seek with donor governments, host governments and the UN system.

The code is self-policing. There is as yet no international association for disaster-response NGOs which possesses any authority to sanction its members. The Code of Conduct continues to be used by the International Federation to monitor its own standards of relief delivery and to encourage other agencies to set similar standards.

It is hoped that humanitarian actors around the world will commit themselves publicly to the code by becoming a signatory and by abiding by its principles. Governments and donor organizations may want to use the code as a yardstick against which to measure the conduct of those agencies with which they work. Disaster-affected communities have a right to expect that those who assist them measure up to these standards.

Principles of Conduct for the International Red Cross and Red Crescent Movement and NGOs in Disaster Response Programmes

1. The humanitarian imperative comes first. The right to receive humanitarian assistance, and to offer it, is a fundamental humanitarian principles which should be enjoyed by all citizens of all countries. As members of the international community, we recognize our obligation to provide humanitarian assistance wherever it is needed. Hence the need for unimpeded access to affected populations is of fundamental importance in exercising that responsibility. The prime motivation of our response to disaster is to alleviate human suffering amongst those least able to withstand the stress caused by disaster. When we give humanitarian aid it is not a partisan or political act and should not be viewed as such.
2. Aid is given regardless of the race, creed or nationality of the recipients and without adverse distinction of any kind. Aid priorities are calculated on the basis of need alone. Wherever possible, we will base the provision of relief aid upon a thorough assessment of the needs of the disaster victims and the local capacities already in place to meet those needs. Within the entirety of our programmes, we will reflect considerations of proportionality. Human suffering must be alleviated whenever it is found, life is as precious in one part of a country as another. Thus, our provision of aid will reflect the degree of suffering it seeks to alleviate. In implementing this approach, we recognize the crucial role played by women and men in disaster prone communities and will ensure that this role is supported, not diminished, by our aid programmes. The implementation of such a universal, impartial and independent policy, can only be effective if we and our partners have access to the necessary resources to provide for such equitable relief, and have equal access to all disaster victims.
3. Aid will not be used to further a particular political or religious standpoint. Humanitarian aid will be given according to the need of individuals, families and communities. Notwithstanding the right of non-governmental humanitarian agencies to espouse particular political or religious opinions, we affirm that assistance will not be dependent on the adherence of the recipients to those opinions. We will not tie the promise, delivery or distribution of assistance to the embracing or acceptance of a particular political or religious creed.

4. We shall endeavour not to act as instruments of government foreign policy. Non-governmental humanitarian agencies are agencies which act independently from governments. We therefore formulate our own policies and implementation strategies and do not seek to implement the policy of any government, except in so far as it coincides with our own independent policy. We will never knowingly—or through negligence—allow ourselves, or our employees, to be used to gather information of a political, military or economically sensitive nature for governments or other bodies that may serve purposes other than those which are strictly humanitarian, nor will we act as instruments of foreign policy of donor governments. We will use the assistance we receive to respond to needs and this assistance should not be driven by the need to dispose of donor surpluses, nor by the political interest of any particular donor. We value and promote voluntary giving of labour and finances by concerned individuals to support our work and recognize the independence of action promoted by such voluntary motivation. In order to protect our independence we will seek to avoid dependence upon a single funding source.
5. We shall respect culture and custom. We will endeavour to respect the culture, structures and customs of the communities and countries we are working in.
6. We shall attempt to build disaster response on local capacities. All people and communities—even in disaster—possess capacities as well as vulnerabilities. Where possible, we will strengthen these capacities by employing local staff, purchasing local materials and trading with local companies. Where possible, we will work through local non-governmental humanitarian agencies as partners in planning and implementation, and co-operate with local government structures where appropriate. We will place a high priority on the proper co-ordination of our emergency responses. This is best done within the countries concerned by those most directly involved in the relief operations, and should include representatives of the relevant UN bodies.
7. Ways shall be found to involve programme beneficiaries in the management of relief aid. Disaster response assistance should never be imposed upon the beneficiaries. Effective relief and lasting rehabilitation can best be achieved where the intended beneficiaries are involved in the design, management and implementation of the assis-

tance programme. We will strive to achieve full community participation in our relief and rehabilitation programmes.

8. Relief aid must strive to reduce future vulnerabilities to disaster as well as meeting basic needs. All relief actions affect the prospects for long-term development, either in a positive or negative fashion. Recognizing this, we will strive to implement relief programmes which actively reduce the beneficiaries' vulnerability to future disasters and help create sustainable lifestyles. We will pay particular attention to environmental concerns in the design and management of relief programmes. We will also endeavor to minimize the negative impact of humanitarian assistance, seeking to avoid long-term beneficiary dependence on external aid.
9. We hold ourselves accountable to both those we seek to assist and those from whom we accept resources. We often act as an institutional link in the partnership between those who wish to assist and those who need assistance during disasters. We therefore hold ourselves accountable to both constituencies. All our dealings with donors and beneficiaries shall reflect an attitude of openness and transparency. We recognize the need to report on our activities, both from a financial perspective and the perspective of effectiveness. We recognize the obligation to ensure appropriate monitoring of aid distributions and to carry out regular assessments of the impact of our work. We will also seek to report, in an open fashion, upon the impact of our work, and the factors limiting or enhancing that impact. Our programmes will be based upon high standards of professionalism and expertise in order to mimimize the wasting of valuable resources.
10. In our information, publicity and advertising activities, we shall recognize disaster victims as dignified human beings, not hopeless objects. Respect for the disaster victim as an equal partner in action should never be lost. In our public information we shall portray an objective image of the disaster situation where the capacities and aspirations of disaster victims are highlighted, and not just their vulnerabilities and fears. While we will cooperate with the media in order to enhance public response, we will not allow external or internal demands for publicity to take precedence over the principle of maximizing overall relief assistance. We will avoid competing with other disaster response agencies for media coverage in situations where such coverage may be to the detriment of the service provided to the beneficiaries or to the security of our staff or the beneficiaries.

ANNEX 3

THE HUMANITARIAN CHARTER

The Humanitarian Charter provides the ethical and legal backdrop to the Protection Principles and the Core and minimum standards that follow in the Sphere Handbook. It is in part a statement of established legal rights and obligations; in part a statement of shared belief.

In terms of legal rights and obligations, it summarises the core legal principles that have most bearing on the welfare of those affected by disaster or conflict. With regard to shared belief, it attempts to capture a consensus among humanitarian agencies as to the principles which should govern the response to disaster or conflict, including the roles and responsibilities of the various actors involved.

It forms the basis of a commitment by humanitarian agencies that endorse Sphere and an invitation to all those who engage in humanitarian action to adopt the same principles.

The Humanitarian Charter

Our beliefs

1. The Humanitarian Charter expresses our shared conviction as humanitarian agencies that all people affected by disaster or conflict have a right to receive protection and assistance to ensure the basic conditions for life with dignity. We believe that the principles described in this Humanitarian Charter are universal, applying to all those affected by disaster or conflict wherever they may be, and to all

those who seek to assist them or provide for their security. These principles are reflected in international law, but derive their force ultimately from the fundamental moral principle of humanity: that all human beings are born free and equal in dignity and rights. Based on this principle, we affirm the primacy of the humanitarian imperative: that action should be taken to prevent or alleviate human suffering arising out of disaster or conflict, and that nothing should override this principle.

As local, national and international humanitarian agencies, we commit to promoting and adhering to the principles in this Charter and to meeting minimum standards in our efforts to assist and protect those affected. We invite all those who engage in humanitarian activities, including governmental and private sector actors, to endorse the common principles, rights and duties set out below as a statement of shared humanitarian belief.

Our role

2. We acknowledge that it is firstly through their own efforts, and through the support of community and local institutions, that the basic needs of people affected by disaster or conflict are met. We recognise the primary role and responsibility of the affected state to provide timely assistance to those affected, to ensure people's protection and security and to provide support for their recovery. We believe that a combination of official and voluntary action is crucial to effective prevention and response, and in this regard National Societies of the Red Cross and Red Crescent Movement and other civil society actors have an essential role to play in supporting public authorities. Where national capacity is insufficient, we affirm the role of the wider international community, including governmental donors and regional organisations, in assisting states to fulfil their responsibilities. We recognise and support the special roles played by the mandated agencies of the United Nations and the International Committee of the Red Cross.
3. As humanitarian agencies, we interpret our role in relation to the needs and capacities of affected populations and the responsibilities of their governments or controlling powers. Our role in providing assistance reflects the reality that those with primary responsibility are

not always fully able to perform this role themselves, or may be unwilling to do so. As far as possible, consistent with meeting the humanitarian imperative and other principles set out in this Charter, we will support the efforts of the relevant authorities to protect and assist those affected. We call upon all state and non-state actors to respect the impartial, independent and non-partisan role of humanitarian agencies and to facilitate their work by removing unnecessary legal and practical barriers, providing for their safety and allowing them timely and consistent access to affected populations.

Common principles, rights and duties

4. We offer our services as humanitarian agencies on the basis of the principle of humanity and the humanitarian imperative, recognising the rights of all people affected by disaster or conflict—women and men, boys and girls. These include the rights to protection and assistance reflected in the provisions of international humanitarian law, human rights and refugee law. For the purposes of this Charter, we summarise these rights as follows:

   - the right to life with dignity
   - the right to receive humanitarian assistance
   - the right to protection and security

   While these rights are not formulated in such terms in international law, they encapsulate a range of established legal rights and give fuller substance to the humanitarian imperative.
5. The right to life with dignity is reflected in the provisions of international law, and specifically the human rights measures concerning the right to life, to an adequate standard of living and to freedom from torture or cruel, inhuman or degrading treatment or punishment. The right to life entails the duty to preserve life where it is threatened. Implicit in this is the duty not to withhold or frustrate the provision of life-saving assistance. Dignity entails more than physical well-being; it demands respect for the whole person, including the values and beliefs of individuals and affected communities, and respect for their human rights, including liberty, freedom of conscience and religious observance.
6. The right to receive humanitarian assistance is a necessary element of the right to life with dignity. This encompasses the right to an adequate

standard of living, including adequate food, water, clothing, shelter and the requirements for good health, which are expressly guaranteed in international law. The Sphere Core Standards and minimum standards reflect these rights and give practical expression to them, specifically in relation to the provision of assistance to those affected by disaster or conflict. Where the state or non-state actors are not providing such assistance themselves, we believe they must allow others to help do so. Any such assistance must be provided according to the principle of impartiality, which requires that it be provided solely on the basis of need and in proportion to need. This reflects the wider principle of non-discrimination: that no one should be discriminated against on any grounds of status, including age, gender, race, colour, ethnicity, sexual orientation, language, religion, disability, health status, political or other opinion, national or social origin.

7. The right to protection and security is rooted in the provisions of international law, in resolutions of the United Nations and other intergovernmental organisations, and in the sovereign responsibility of states to protect all those within their jurisdiction. The safety and security of people in situations of disaster or conflict is of particular humanitarian concern, including the protection of refugees and internally displaced persons. As the law recognises, some people may be particularly vulnerable to abuse and adverse discrimination due to their status such as age, gender or race, and may require special measures of protection and assistance. To the extent that a state lacks the capacity to protect people in these circumstances, we believe it must seek international assistance to do so.

The law relating to the protection of civilians and displaced people demands particular attention here:

(i) During armed conflict as defined in international humanitarian law, specific legal provision is made for protection and assistance to be given to those not engaged in the conflict. In particular, the 1949 Geneva Conventions and the Additional Protocols of 1977 impose obligations on the parties to both international and non-international armed conflicts. We stress the general immunity of the civilian population from attack and reprisals, and in particular the importance of the principle of distinction between civilians and combatants, and between civilian objects and military objectives; the principles of proportionality in the use of force and precaution in attack; the duty to refrain from the use of weapons which are indiscriminate or which, by their nature, cause superfluous injury or unnecessary suffering; and the duty to permit impartial relief to be provided. Much of the avoidable suffering caused to civilians in armed conflicts stems from a failure to observe these basic principles.

(ii) The right to seek asylum or sanctuary remains vital to the protection of those facing persecution or violence. Those affected by disaster or conflict are often forced to flee their homes in search of security and the means of subsistence. The provisions of the 1951 Convention Relating to the Status of Refugees (as amended) and other international and regional treaties provide fundamental safeguards for those unable to secure protection from the state of their nationality or residence who are forced to seek safety in another country. Chief among these is the principle of non-refoulement: the principle that no one shall be sent back to a country where their life, freedom or physical security would be threatened or where they are likely to face torture or other cruel, inhuman or degrading treatment or punishment. The same principle applies by extension to internally displaced persons, as reflected in international human rights law and elaborated in the 1998 Guiding Principles on Internal Displacement and related regional and national law.

Our commitment

8. We offer our services in the belief that the affected population is at the centre of humanitarian action, and recognise that their active participation is essential to providing assistance in ways that best meet their needs, including those of vulnerable and socially excluded people. We will endeavour to support local efforts to prevent, prepare for and respond to disaster, and to the effects of conflict, and to reinforce the capacities of local actors at all levels.
9. We are aware that attempts to provide humanitarian assistance may sometimes have unintended adverse effects. In collaboration with affected communities and authorities, we aim to minimise any negative effects of humanitarian action on the local community or on the environment. With respect to armed conflict, we recognise that the way in which humanitarian assistance is provided may potentially

render civilians more vulnerable to attack, or may on occasion bring unintended advantage to one or more of the parties to the conflict. We are committed to minimising any such adverse effects, in so far as this is consistent with the principles outlined above.

10. We will act in accordance with the principles of humanitarian action set out in this Charter and with the specific guidance in the Code of Conduct for the International Red Cross and Red Crescent Movement and Non-Governmental Organisations (NGOs) in Disaster Relief (1994).
11. The Sphere Core Standards and minimum standards give practical substance to the common principles in this Charter, based on agencies' understanding of the basic minimum requirements for life with dignity and their experience of providing humanitarian assistance. Though the achievement of the standards depends on a range of factors, many of which may be beyond our control, we commit ourselves to attempt consistently to achieve them and we expect to be held to account accordingly. We invite all parties, including affected and donor governments, international organisations, private and non-state actors, to adopt the Sphere Core Standards and minimum standards as accepted norms.
12. By adhering to the Core Standards and minimum standards, we commit to making every effort to ensure that people affected by disasters or conflict have access to at least the minimum requirements for life with dignity and security, including adequate water, sanitation, food, nutrition, shelter and healthcare. To this end, we will continue to advocate that states and other parties meet their moral and legal obligations towards affected populations. For our part, we undertake to make our responses more effective, appropriate and accountable through sound assessment and monitoring of the evolving local context; through transparency of information and decision-making; and through more effective coordination and collaboration with other relevant actors at all levels, as detailed in the Core and minimum standards. In particular, we commit to working in partnership with affected populations, emphasising their active participation in the response. We acknowledge that our fundamental accountability must be to those we seek to assist.

ANNEX 4

PRINCIPLES OF GOOD HUMANITARIAN DONORSHIP

The 23 Principles and Good Practice defined by the group provide both a framework to guide official humanitarian aid and a mechanism for encouraging greater donor accountability. These were drawn up to enhance the coherence and effectiveness of donor action, as well as their accountability to beneficiaries, implementing organisations and domestic constituencies, with regard to the funding, co-ordination, follow-up and evaluation of such actions.

Objectives and Definition of Humanitarian Action

1. The objectives of humanitarian action are to save lives, alleviate suffering and maintain human dignity during and in the aftermath of man-made crises and natural disasters, as well as to prevent and strengthen preparedness for the occurrence of such situations.
2. Humanitarian action should be guided by the humanitarian principles of humanity, meaning the centrality of saving human lives and alleviating suffering wherever it is found; impartiality, meaning the implementation of actions solely on the basis of need, without discrimination between or within affected populations; neutrality, meaning that humanitarian action must not favour any side in an armed conflict or other dispute where such action is carried out; and independence, meaning the autonomy of humanitarian objectives from the political,

economic, military or other objectives that any actor may hold with regard to areas where humanitarian action is being implemented.

3. Humanitarian action includes the protection of civilians and those no longer taking part in hostilities, and the provision of food, water and sanitation, shelter, health services and other items of assistance, undertaken for the benefit of affected people and to facilitate the return to normal lives and livelihoods.

General Principles

4. Respect and promote the implementation of international humanitarian law, refugee law and human rights.
5. While reaffirming the primary responsibility of states for the victims of humanitarian emergencies within their own borders, strive to ensure flexible and timely funding, on the basis of the collective obligation of striving to meet humanitarian needs.
6. Allocate humanitarian funding in proportion to needs and on the basis of needs assessments.
7. Request implementing humanitarian organisations to ensure, to the greatest possible extent, adequate involvement of beneficiaries in the design, implementation, monitoring and evaluation of humanitarian response.
8. Strengthen the capacity of affected countries and local communities to prevent, prepare for, mitigate and respond to humanitarian crises, with the goal of ensuring that governments and local communities are better able to meet their responsibilities and co-ordinate effectively with humanitarian partners.
9. Provide humanitarian assistance in ways that are supportive of recovery and long-term development, striving to ensure support, where appropriate, to the maintenance and return of sustainable livelihoods and transitions from humanitarian relief to recovery and development activities.
10. Support and promote the central and unique role of the United Nations in providing leadership and co-ordination of international humanitarian action, the special role of the International Committee of the Red Cross, and the vital role of the United Nations, the International Red Cross and Red Crescent Movement and non-governmental organisations in implementing humanitarian action.

ANNEX 4

Good Practices in Donor Financing, Management and Accountability

(a) Funding

11. Strive to ensure that funding of humanitarian action in new crises does not adversely affect the meeting of needs in ongoing crises.
12. Recognising the necessity of dynamic and flexible response to changing needs in humanitarian crises, strive to ensure predictability and flexibility in funding to United Nations agencies, funds and programmes and to other key humanitarian organisations
13. While stressing the importance of transparent and strategic priority-setting and financial planning by implementing organisations, explore the possibility of reducing, or enhancing the flexibility of, earmarking, and of introducing longer-term funding arrangements.
14. Contribute responsibly, and on the basis of burden-sharing, to United Nations Consolidated Inter-Agency Appeals and to International Red Cross and Red Crescent Movement appeals, and actively support the formulation of Common Humanitarian Action Plans (CHAP) as the primary instrument for strategic planning, prioritisation and co-ordination in complex emergencies.

(b) Promoting standards and enhancing implementation

15. Request that implementing humanitarian organisations fully adhere to good practice and are committed to promoting accountability, efficiency and effectiveness in implementing humanitarian action.
16. Promote the use of Inter-Agency Standing Committee guidelines and principles on humanitarian activities, the Guiding Principles on Internal Displacement and the 1994 Code of Conduct for the International Red Cross and Red Crescent Movement and Non-Governmental Organisations (NGOs) in Disaster Relief.
17. Maintain readiness to offer support to the implementation of humanitarian action, including the facilitation of safe humanitarian access.
18. Support mechanisms for contingency planning by humanitarian organisations, including, as appropriate, allocation of funding, to strengthen capacities for response.
19. Affirm the primary position of civilian organisations in implementing humanitarian action, particularly in areas affected by armed

conflict. In situations where military capacity and assets are used to support the implementation of humanitarian action, ensure that such use is in conformity with international humanitarian law and humanitarian principles, and recognises the leading role of humanitarian organisations.

20. Support the implementation of the 1994 Guidelines on the Use of Military and Civil Defence Assets in Disaster Relief and the 2003 Guidelines on the Use of Military and Civil Defence Assets to Support United Nations Humanitarian Activities in Complex Emergencies.

(c) Learning and accountability

21. Support learning and accountability initiatives for the effective and efficient implementation of humanitarian action.
22. Encourage regular evaluations of international responses to humanitarian crises, including assessments of donor performance.
23. Ensure a high degree of accuracy, timeliness, and transparency in donor reporting on official humanitarian assistance spending, and encourage the development of standardised formats for such reporting.

NOTES

INTRODUCTION

1. "Global Humanitarian Assistance Report 2014", Development Initiatives, Bristol, 2014, pp4–6.
2. Glyn Taylor et al., *The State of the Humanitarian System*, ALNAP and ODI, London, July 2012, p9.
3. Human Security Report 2009/2010, *The Causes of Peace and the Shrinking Costs of War*, Oxford University Press, Oxford, 2011, pp118–20.
4. Mary B. Anderson, Dayna Brown and Isabella Jean, "Time to Listen: Hearing People on the Receiving End of International Aid", CDA Collaborative Learning Projects, Cambridge, MA, 2012, p20.
5. Richard Ashby Wilson and Richard D. Brown eds, *Humanitarianism and Suffering: the Mobilization of Empathy*, Cambridge University Press, Cambridge, 2011. The term "altruism" was coined by the French sociologist Auguste Comte in the nineteenth century and is derived from the French word *autrui*, meaning others, or originally *alter* in Latin.
6. Thomas Weiss, *Humanitarian Business*, Polity, Cambridge, 2013, ch4, pp123–42.
7. Dennis King and Hermes Grullon, "Diaspora Communities as Aid Providers, The Migration Blog, International Organization of Migration (IOM)" at http://www.iom.int/cms/en/sites/iom/home/what-we-do/migration-policy-and-research/migration-policy-1/migration-policy-practice/issues/augustseptember-2013/diaspora-communities-as-aid-prov.html
8. Hugo Slim, "Wonderful Work: Globalizing the Ethics of Humanitarian Action", in Roger MacGinty et al., eds, *Routledge Handbook of Humanitarian Action*, Routledge, Oxford, forthcoming 2015.
9. See, for example, UN Security Council Resolution 1894 of 2009.
10. UN OCHA, "Reference Guide: Normative Developments on the Coordination of Humanitarian Assistance in the General Assembly and the Economic

and Social Council since the Adoption of General Assembly Resolution 46/182", 2nd edn, OCHA, New York, November 2011.

11. David D. Caron, Michael J. Kelly and Anastasia Telesetsky, *The International Law of Disaster Relief*, Cambridge University Press, Cambridge, 2014.
12. See Sphere website at http://www.sphereproject.org/about
13. Mark Bradbury, "Normalizing the Crisis in Africa", *Disasters* 22(4), 1998, Blackwells, Oxford; Peter Redfield, *Life in Crisis: The Ethical Journey of Doctors Without Borders*, University of California Press, Berkeley, 2013, pp179–228.
14. Antonio Donini, "The Far Side: The Meta Functions of Humanitarianism in a Globalised World", *Disasters* 34(2), Blackwells, Oxford, 2010.
15. The term Aidland was originally coined by Raymond Apthorpe and has been taken up by other scholars like David Mosse, Anne-Meike Fechter and Silke Roth, who study humanitarian power and lifestyle.
16. MSF, "Where is Everyone?" July 2014, report at http://www.msf.org.uk/msf-report-where-everyone-responding-emergencies-most-difficult-places
17. Primo Levi, *The Drowned and the Saved*, Abacus, 2013, pp31–71.
18. Hannah Arendt, *Eichmann in Jerusalem: A Report on the Banality of Evil*, Penguin Classics, London, 2006.
19. Georgio Agamben, *Homo Sacer: Sovereign Power and Bare Life*, trans. Daniel Heller-Roazen, Stanford University Press, Stanford, 1998, pp166–80.
20. David Keen, "'The Camp' and the 'Lesser Evil': Humanitarianism in Sri Lanka", *Conflict, Security and Development* 14 (1), 2014, pp1–31.
21. Eyal Weisman, *The Least of All Possible Evils: Humanitarian Violence from Arendt to Gaza*, Verso, London, 2011.
22. See my criticism of much postmodern social theory's application to humanitarian aid in Hugo Slim, "A Bare Line: Where Critical Social Theory is Wrong About Humanitarian Aid", Nottingham CSSGJ seminars, January 2014.

1. THE ETHICAL ORIGINS OF HUMANITARIAN ACTION

1. I have examined this more negative side of human emotions and reasoning in my book *Killing Civilians: Method, Madness and Morality in War*, Hurst 2007, translated into French as *Les Civils dans la Guerre, Fides et Labor*, Geneva, 2009.
2. Norman Geras, *The Contract of Mutual Indifference: Political Philosophy After the Holocaust*, Verso, London, 1998.
3. Peter Unger, *Living High and Letting Die: Our Illusion of Innocence*, Oxford University Press, Oxford, 1997.
4. Peter Singer, *The Expanding Circle: Ethics, Evolution and Moral Progress*, Princeton University Press, Princeton and Oxford, 2011 edn.
5. Jean-Jacques Rousseau, *The Social Contract*, Oxford World's Classics, Oxford, 2008.
6. Thomas Hobbes, *Leviathan*, Oxford World's Classics, Oxford, 1996, chXIII, pp82–6.

7. David Hume, *A Treatise of Human Nature*, Book II, Section VII, ed. Ernest Mossner, Penguin, London, 1985, pp417–18.
8. Ibid., p418. Freud, of course, might have a different interpretation of this particular fainting fit, but the analogy holds either way!
9. Aristotle, *Poetics*, trans. Malcolm Heath, Penguin, London, 1996, p22.
10. Hume, op. cit., pp626–7.
11. Adam Smith, *The Theory of Moral Sentiments*, Penguin, London, 2009, p13.
12. Thomas Ryan, "Aquinas on Compassion", *Irish Theological Quarterly* 75(2), Sage, London, 2010, p161.
13. Hume, op. cit., pp632–3.
14. Paul Slovic et al., "Pyschic Numbing and Mass Atrocity", ch7 in Eldar Shafir, ed., *The Behavioural Foundations of Public Policy*, Princeton University Press, Princeton, 2012.
15. Martin Buber, *I and Thou*, Continuum, London, 2004, pp11 and 22.
16. Ibid., p17.
17. Part of the so-called Great Commandment found at Leviticus ch19 v18 and in the Christian gospels at Matthew ch22 v39, Mark ch12 v31 and Luke ch10 v27.
18. For this summary of Lipps' thought see Sven Andersen in Sven Andersen, Kees Niekerk, Hans Fink and Brenda Almond, eds, *Concern for the Other: On the Ethics of K. E. Logstrup*, University of Notre Dame Press, Notre Dame, IN, 2007, pp42ff.
19. Emmanuel Levinas, *Ethics as First Philosophy in the Levinas Reader*, ed. Sean Hand, Blackwells, Oxford, 1989, p86.
20. The golden rule is the term used for the general ethical injunction common to all main ethical traditions and found most succinctly in the Torah in Leviticus ch19 v18 as "Love thy neighbour as thyself."
21. Paul Ricoeur, *Oneself as Another*, trans. Kathleen Blamey, Chicago University Press, Chicago and London, 1992, pp188–94.
22. Aristotle, *The Nicomachean Ethics*, trans. David Ross, Oxford University Press, Oxford, 1980, p1.
23. Vittorio Gallese, "The Shared Manifold Hypothesis: From Mirror Neurons to Empathy", *Journal of Consciousness Studies* 8, N5–7, Imprint Academic, 2001.
24. Vittorio Gallese, "The Roots of Empathy: The Shared Manifold Hypothesis and the Neural Basis of Intersubjectivity", *Psychopathology* 36: 171–80, Karger, 2003.

2. THE HUMANITARIAN GOAL—HUMANITY AND MPARTIALITY

1. For important histories of these developments, see John F. Hutchinson, *Champions of Charity: War and the Rise of the Red Cross*, Westview, Boulder, 1996; Geoffrey Best, *War and Law Since 1945*, Oxford University Press, Oxford, 1994; Caroline Moorehead, *Dunant's Dream: War, Switzerland and the History of the Red Cross*, Harper Collins, London, 1998; Michael Barnett, *Empire of Humanity: A History of Humanitarianism*, Cornell University Press, Ithaca, 2011.

2. Tom Beauchamp and James F. Childress, *Principles of Biomedical Ethics*, 7th edn, Oxford University Press, New York, 2013.
3. See the "Code of Ethics for Social Work", British Association of Social Workers, January 2012 at http://cdn.basw.co.uk/upload/basw_112315-7.pdf
4. For UN examples of principle-based codes of business ethics, see the Global Compact and its Ten Principles at http://www.unglobalcompact.org/AboutTheGC/TheTenPrinciples/index.html; the Six Principles of Responsible Investment at http://www.unpri.org/about-pri/the-six-principles/; and the UN Guiding Principles on Business and Human Rights.
5. James F. Childress, entry on Norms in *A New Dictionary of Christian Ethics*, ed. John Macquarrie and James Childress, SCM Press Ltd, London, 1967, pp425–7.
6. John Finnis, *Moral Absolutes: Tradition, Revision and Truth*, Catholic University of America Press, Washington, 1991, p1.
7. See the UN's 8 MDGs at http://www.un.org/millenniumgoals/bkgd.shtml
8. Ronald Dworkin, *Justice for Hedgehogs*, Belknap Press of Harvard University Press, Cambridge, MA, 2011.
9. Balancing is the approach adopted by Beauchamp and Childress, op. cit.
10. For a discussion of the fluidity of humanitarian discourse, see Juliano Fiore, "The Discourse of Western Humanitarianism", Humanitarian Affairs Think Tank, Institut de Relations Internationales et Stratégiques and Save the Children, October 2013.
11. Jean Pictet, "The Fundamental Principles of the Red Cross: Commentary", Henry Dunant Institute, Geneva, 1979, p18. This formulation continues to be the one used by the Red Cross and Red Crescent Movement.
12. Pictet, op. cit., p20.
13. Pictet does use this Kantian phrasing, op. cit., p26.
14. Here I am using John Finnis' idea of basic goods from Finnis, *Natural Law and Natural Rights*, 2nd edn, Oxford University Press, Oxford, 2011.
15. Charter of the United Nations 1945, Preamble, p3.
16. Humanitarian Charter, paragraph 1.
17. This is the insight of Martin Heidegger in his monumental struggle to elucidate the distinction between existence and being.
18. This is what Ricoeur describes as the "indivisibility" of a person, an idea that reflects the Christian doctrine of the Trinity, which is an anthropology and a theology at the same time.
19. Ryan, op. cit.
20. Ryan, op. cit.
21. Timothy Radcliffe, "Glorify God in Your Bodies", a sermon preached in Boston, 2013.
22. Simone Weil, "Attention and Will", in *Simone Weil: An Anthology*, ed. Sian Miles, Penguin, London, 2005, p234.

23. Weil, op. cit., p92.
24. Erich Fromm, *The Art of Loving* (1957), Thorsons, London, 1995.
25. Ibid., p23.
26. Ibid.
27. Paul Ricoeur, op. cit., pp180–94.
28. Ricoeur, op. cit., p193.
29. See Hugo Slim, *Killing Civilians: Method, Madness and Morality in War*, Hurst, London, 2007, pp11–21.
30. François Bugnion, *The International Committee of the Red Cross and the Protection of War Victims*, International Committee of the Red Cross, Geneva, 2003, p717.
31. See Humanitarian Charter, Articles 4–7.
32. See Sarah Collinson, James Darcy, Nicholas Waddell, Anna Schmidt, eds, "Realising Protection: The Uncertain Benefits of Civilian, Refugee and IDP Status", HPG Report 28, Humanitarian Policy Group, ODI, London, September 2009.
33. See Additional Protocol 1 of the Geneva Conventions Article 51 (3) and Additional Protocol II Article 13 (3). See also Nils Melzer, "Interpretive Guidance on the Notion of Direct Participation in Hostilities Under International Humanitarian Law", ICRC, Geneva, May 2009.
34. See 1951 Refugee Convention at http://www.unhcr.org/3b66c2aa10.html
35. See "The Guiding Principles on Internal Displacement" at http://www.unhcr.org/43ce1cff2.html
36. Marco Sassoli, Antoine A. Bouvier and Anne Quintin, *How Does Law Protect in War?* vol. 1, *Outline of International Humanitarian Law*, 3rd edn, International Committee of the Red Cross, Geneva, 2011, pp93 and 158–62.
37. Additional Protocol I of the Geneva Conventions Article 43 (3).
38. Ibid. Article 57.
39. Ibid. Articles 51 and 57.
40. Ibid. Article 51 and commentary in Marco Sassoli, Antoine Bouvier and Anne Quintin, *How Does Law Protect in War?* vol. 1, 3rd edn, ICRC, Geneva, 2011, pp280–83.
41. Gary D. Solis, *The Law of Armed Conflict: International Humanitarian Law in War*, Cambridge University Press, New York, 2010, p269. For a good and accessible discussion of military necessity, see Solis pp258–69.
42. Marco Sassoli, cited in Solis, op. cit., p258.
43. Humanitarian advocacy is not specified as a designated humanitarian action in IHL, but can be recognized as a humanitarian activity by implication as part of Common Article 1 of the Geneva Conventions which obliges states to ensure respect for IHL. Appropriate information on needs and violations during conflict is essential to all parties' ability to ensure respect. Humanitarian information and analysis could also count as one of the services offered by impartial humanitarian agencies under Article 142 of the Fourth Geneva Convention.

Humanitarian advocacy is explicitly recognized in Article 10 of the Code of Conduct.

44. For example, Fourth Geneva Convention Article 23 and Additional Protocol I Articles 68–71.
45. "Humanitarian Charter and Minimum Standards in Humanitarian Response", The Sphere Project, 3rd edn, 2011.
46. Pictet, op. cit.
47. Peter Redfield, *Life in Crisis: The Ethical Journey of Doctors Without Borders*, University of California Press, Berkeley, 2013, pp174–5.
48. In moral philosophy these are questions of deservingness (or desert) and undeservingness, and how certain people may rightly deserve different and unequal goods and treatment.
49. See particularly Luke's Gospel, ch15.
50. Zoe Marriage, *Not Breaking the Rules, Not Playing the Game: International Assistance to Countries at War*, Hurst, London, 2006, p6.
51. John Rawls, *Justice as Fairness: A Restatement*, ed. Erin Kelly, Belknap Press of Harvard University Press, Cambridge, MA and London, 2001, p78.
52. Rawls, op. cit., pp42–3.

3. POLITICAL PRINCIPLES—NEUTRALITY AND INDEPENDENCE

1. Finnis, *Aquinas*, op. cit., pp83–4.
2. *Aquinas*, p435.
3. Pictet, op. cit., p52.
4. Pictet, op. cit., p54.
5. Dante, *The Divine Comedy, Inferno*, Canto 3, lines 53–4, trans. Mark Musa, Penguin, London. See also Hugo Slim, "Relief Agencies and Moral Standing in War: Principles of Humanity, Neutrality, Impartiality and Solidarity", *Development in Practice*, vol. 7 no. 4, Routledge, pp342–52, for a further discussion of neutrality.
6. H. L. A. Hart, *Punishment and Responsibility*, Clarendon Press, Oxford, 1968.
7. Pictet, op. cit., p59. Those of us who have grown up with the marijuana politics of a later generation might give the similar advice that "you can smoke so long as you don't inhale!"
8. Pierre Krahenbuhl, interview for Hard Talk on BBC World at http://www.icrc.org/eng/resources/documents/interview/2013/bbc-hardtalk-krahenbuhl-video-2013-06-11.htm
9. Pictet, op. cit., pp53–9.
10. The Geneva Conventions of 12 August 1949, ICRC, Geneva.
11. Antonio Donini, *The Golden Fleece: The Manipulation and Independence of Humanitarian Action*, Kumarian Press, Sterling, VA, 2012, p6.
12. Francis Stewart, "The Causes of Civil War and Genocide", in Adam Lupel and

Ernesto Verdeja, eds, *Responding to Genocide: The Politics of international Action*, Lynne Rienner, Boulder, CO, 2013, pp47–84.

13. The ethics and laws of war are traditionally and controversially organized into two parts. *Jus ad bellum* is that part of the law which relates to acceptable and unacceptable reasons for going to war. *Jus in bello* refers to those parts of the law which regulate what is acceptable and unacceptable in the conduct of war once you are in it.
14. The phrase "speaking truth to power" was developed by the Quakers in a 1955 document and then taken up by liberal NGOs and social movements of all kinds.
15. Code of Conduct, Article 3.
16. Hugo Slim and Miriam Bradley, "Principled Humanitarian Action and Ethical Tensions in Multi-Mandate Organizations", World Vision, Geneva, April 2013.
17. For one example of political suspicion of NGOs operating in humanitarian mode, see NGO Monitor in Israel at http://www.ngo-monitor.org/ and its critique of non-neutral NGO advocacy in the Israeli–Palestinian conflict.
18. Pictet, op. cit.
19. Jean-Claude Favez, *The Red Cross and the Holocaust*, Cambridge University Press, Cambridge, 1999; Hutchinson, op. cit.; Moorehead, op. cit.
20. Pictet, op. cit., p62.
21. Antonio Donini, *The Golden Fleece: Manipulation and Independence in Humanitarian Action*, Kumarian Press, Sterling, VA, 2012; Mark Duffield, *Global Governance and the New Wars*, Zed Books, London, 2001, especially ch4; Ugo Mattei, "Emergency-Based Predatory Capitalism", in Didier Fassin and Mariella Pandolfi, eds, *Contemporary States of Emergency*, Zone Books, Brooklyn, NY, 2010, pp89–105.

4. DIGNITY PRINCIPLES—RESPECT, PARTICIPATION AND EMPOWERMENT

1. Rights related to self-determination, cultural enjoyment and freedom of religion are recognized in the Universal Declaration of Human Rights, Articles 18, 19 and 27, and also in the International Covenant on Economic Social and Cultural Rights, Articles 1 and 15.
2. The former is common in parts of Madagascar, for example, and the latter is common in many parts of Africa in which young women routinely advertise for sugar daddies in newspapers and websites.
3. Fred Cuny, *Disasters and Development*, Oxford University Press, Oxford, 1983; Mary Anderson and Peter Woodrow, *Rising From the Ashes: Development Strategies in Times of Disaster*, ITDG, 1989; Piers Blakie et al., *At Risk: Natural Hazards, People's Vulnerability and Disasters*, Routledge, 1994.
4. See the important discussion of the ethics of collective action and Parfit's "each-we dilemmas" in humanitarian work in Garrett Gullity, "Compromised Human-

itarianism", in Keith Horton and Chris Roche, *Ethical Questions and International NGOs*, Springer, London, 2010, pp157–71.

5. Hugo Slim and Andrew Bonwick, "Protection: A Guide for Humanitarian Agencies", ALNAP, London, 2005, pp44–6 at file:///Users/Hugo/Downloads/alnap-protection-guide.pdf. ICRC Protection Standards, 2013, pp67–76 at http://www.icrc.org/eng/assets/files/other/icrc-002–0999.pdf
6. See IASC at http://www.humanitarianinfo.org/iasc/pageloader.aspx?page=content-template-default&bd=87
7. This term is from Thomas Nagel in *Equality and Partiality*, 1995.
8. Christopher Kutz, "The Collective Work of Citizenship", in *Legal Theory*, vol. 8, 2002, Cambridge University Press, pp471–94.
9. Finnis, *Natural Law*, op. cit.
10. Amartya Sen, *Development as Freedom*, Oxford University Press, Oxford, 1991, pp74–6.
11. Martha C. Nussbaum, *Creating Capabilities: The Human Development Approach*, Belknap Press of Harvard University Press, Cambridge, MA, 2011, pp32–4. Nussbaum does not support Sen's use of freedom as an overarching concept for development, because usually one person's freedom in action restricts the freedom of another. She therefore prefers justice, see pp69–76.
12. Universal Declaration of Human Rights, Articles 21(1), 27(1) and 29(1).
13. This is a strong theme in Catholic Social Teaching, for example the teaching on human work in *Rerum Novarum*, 1891, *Laborem Exercens*, 1981, and on family and community life in the Charter of the Rights of the Family, Article 8.
14. The ladder of participation was introduced into urban planning in the USA by Sherry Arnstein in 1969 and then adapted for international development by Roger Hart of UNICEF in 1992.
15. *The ALNAP/URD Participation Handbook for Humanitarian Fieldworkers*, Groupe URD, 2009 at http://www.alnap.org/resources/guides/participation.aspx
16. Participation in development was originally conceived as liberationist by Paolo Freire, *Pedagogy of the Oppressed*, revised edn, Penguin, London, 1996, but gradually became more bureaucratized as an instrument of development planning. Critique of participation began in development studies with texts like James Ferguson, *The Anti-politics Machine*, 1990; Bill Cook, *Participation: The New Tyranny*, Zed Books, London, 2001.
17. John Gaventa, in "Towards Participatory Governance: assessing the transformative possibilities", in Samuel Hickey and Giles Mohan, *From Tyranny to Transformation, Exploring New Approaches to Participation in Development*, Zed Books, London, 2004.
18. "The Oxfam Guide to Free Prior and Informed Consent", Oxfam, 2010, is a good introduction to the approach at http://www.culturalsurvival.org/sites/default/files/guidetofreepriorinformedconsent_0.pdf
19. For a seminal critique of non-participatory aid to refugees, see Barbara Harrell-

Bond, *Imposing Aid: Emergency Assistance to Refugees*, Oxford University Press, Oxford, 1986. The Code's choice of word is surely a conscious echo of this text.

20. See, for example, Erica Burman, "Innocents Abroad: Western Fantasies of Childhood and the Iconography of Emergencies", *Disasters* 18(3), Blackwells, Oxford, 1994, pp238–53; also Betty Plewes and Rieky Stuart, "The Pornography of Poverty: A Cautionary Fundraising Tale", in *Ethics in Action: The Ethical Challenges of International Human Rights and Nongovernmental* NGOs, ed. Daniel A. Bell and Jean-Marc Coicaud, Cambridge University Press, New York, 2007, pp23–37.
21. In Christian imagery, the *pieta* is the iconic image of Jesus' mother, Mary, holding his corpse in her arms when he has been taken down from the cross.
22. For the simplest account of this myth of the humanitarian relief operation as fairy tale, see Jonathan Benthall, *Disasters, Relief and the Media*, I. B. Tauris, London, 1993, pp188–9. For more complex interpretations by critical theorists, see Valerie Gorin, "An Iconography of Pity and a Rhetoric of Compassion: War and Humanitarian Crises in the Prism of American and French Newsmagazines 1967–1995", in Josepf Seethaler at al., eds, *Selling War*, Intellect, Bristol, 2013, pp135–56.
23. Slovic, op. cit.
24. Hugo Slim, *Killing Civilians*, op. cit., pp217–18.
25. See the important Foucauldian thinking on "victimology" in Didier Fassin and Richard Rechtman, *The Empire of Trauma: An Inquiry into the Condition of Victimhood*, Princeton University Press, Princeton, 2009.

5. STEWARDSHIP PRINCIPLES—SUSTAINABILITY AND ACCOUNTABILITY

1. As first defined at the UN Earth Summit in Rio de Janeiro in 1992.
2. See Sue Lautze's seminal paper on this, "Saving Lives and Livelihoods: The Fundamentals of a Livelihoods Strategy", Tufts University, 1997 at dl.tufts.edu/file_assets/tufts:UA197.012.012.00022.
3. The Code's discourse of capacities and vulnerabilities comes from Mary Anderson and Peter Woodrow's work, op. cit., and the Vulnerability and Capacities Analysis (VCA) framework they designed for the International Federation of the Red Cross and Red Crescent Societies in the 1990s. Piers Blakie et al., *At Risk: Natural Hazards, People's Vulnerability and Disasters*, Routledge, London, 1994, used a similar but more sophisticated model of disasters.
4. For good practice in livestock protection and sustainability see the Livestock Emergency Guidelines and Standards (LEGS) at http://www.livestock-emergency.net/resources/download-legs
5. The fish quote refers to E. F. Schumacher's basic sustainability thesis in *Small is Beautiful*, Abacus, 1991, that "if you give a man a fish, you feed him for a day; if you

show him how to fish, he can feed himself for a lifetime". The bed for the night quote is originally Berthold Brecht's worked into a book by David Reiff, *A Bed for the Night: Humanitarianism in Crisis*, Vintage, London, 2002.

6. Redfield, op. cit., p179.
7. Hugo Slim and Miriam Bradley, op. cit.
8. The following distinctions between positive and negative dependency draw on Christopher B. Barrett, "Food Aid's Intended and Unintended Consequences", Background Paper for FAO's State of Food and Agriculture, Cornell University, 2006 at http://dyson.cornell.edu/faculty_sites/cbb2/Papers/MixedEffects-v2Mar2006.pdf
9. Ibid., p2.
10. Ibid., p3.
11. The accountability principle of "know and show" comes from the UN Guiding Principles on Business and Human Rights. For a full discussion of NGO accountability, see Lisa Jordan and Peter van Tuijl, eds, *NGO Accountability: Politics, Principles and Innovation*, Earthscan, London, 2006.
12. Paul Knox-Clarke and James Darcy, *Insufficient Evidence? The Quality and use of Evidence in Humanitarian Action*, ACNAP, London, 2014.
13. Much of the discourse around "donors" and "giving" in humanitarian action is inaccurate and unhelpful to individuals and institutions that want to be part of a very specific investment process and results.
14. Chris Roche, "The Seeming Simplicity of Measurement", in Horton and Roche, *Ethical Questions in International NGOs*, op. cit.
15. Aristotle, *Eudemian Ethics*, op. cit., p32.
16. Toby Ord, "The Moral Imperative Towards Cost-effectiveness in Global Health", Centre for Global Development Essay, March 2013 at www.cgdev.org/content/publications/detail/1427016.
17. "DFID's Approach to Value for Money", July 2011 at http://www.gov.uk/government/uploads/system/uploads/attachment_data/file/49551/DFID-approach-value-money.pdf
18. Kerren Hedlund et al., "Final Evaluation of the Cash and Voucher Response to the 2011–12 Crisis in Southern and Central Somalia", Humanitarian Outcomes, UNICEF.
19. This is the terminology used in the section on accountability in Mango's excellent guide to financial management in NGOs at http://www.mango.org.uk/Guide/Usage
20. For many years humanitarian accountability has been dominated by the DAC-OECD framework. See ALNAP, "Evaluating Humanitarian Action Using the OECD-DAC Criteria: An ALNAP Guide for Humanitarian Agencies", ODI, London, 2006. The Principles of Good Humanitarian Donorship are much more ethically focused but are seldom used comprehensively in routine evalua-

tions. See GHD's 23 Principles at http://www.goodhumanitariandonorship.org/gns/principles-good-practice-ghd/overview.aspx
21. Sphere Core Standards at http://www.spherehandbook.org/en/how-to-use-this-chapter
22. HAP Accountability Principles at http://www.hapinternational.org/pool/files/english-march-2010.pdf
23. Michael Jennings, "NGOs Must Address Their Accountability Deficit", at http://www.theguardian.com/global-development/poverty-matters/2012/feb/09/ngos-accountability-deficit-legal-framework; Zoe Marriage, op. cit., pp10–12.
24. Alice Obrecht, "Getting it Right: An Account of the Moral Agency of NGOs", PhD thesis, London School of Economics, September 2011.
25. Nicole Bieske, "The Accountability Challenge: To Whom and For What", *Journal of Multicultural Society*, vol. 3(2), pp1–31, Omnes, Seoul, 2012.
26. The Joint Evaluation of Emergency Assistance to Rwanda, 1996.
27. Even independent scrutiny of government humanitarian aid expenditure in mature democracies tends to focus on the strategic coherence, efficiency and value for money of aid, rather than a more subtle examination of its ethics and effectiveness. See, for example, an independent evaluation of DFID's 2011 Horn of Africa Response at http://icai.independent.gov.uk/wp-content/uploads/2012/09/ICAI-report-FINAL-DFIDs-humanitarian-emergency-response-in-the-Horn-of-Africa1.pdf
28. All of these management principles, except humanitarian integrity and due diligence, are clearly identified as vital ingredients in effective humanitarian action in the DAC-OECD Guidelines on Humanitarian Evaluation, the 23 Good Humanitarian Donorship Principles, the People in Aid Code of Good Practice in the Management and Support of Aid Personnel and the new Core Humanitarian Standard. This list and its definitions are my own.

6. WHAT KIND OF ETHICS IS HUMANITARIAN ETHICS?

1. Hugo Slim, "Idealism and Realism in Humanitarian Action", ch1 in *Essays in Humanitarian Action*, ELAC and Kindle Books, 2012.
2. This is the famous definition of politics by Otto von Bismarck.
3. Clarke Masone, Michael Neuman and Fabrice Weissman (eds), *Humanitarian Negotiations Revealed: The MSF Experience*, Hurst, London 2011.
4. See the summary of "Ideal and Nonideal Theory" by Zofia Stemplowska and Adam Swift, *Oxford Handbook of Political Theory*, Oxford University Press, Oxford, 2014, pp373–89, on which my explanation is based.
5. Much of the discussion about idealist and non-idealist political theory has naturally emerged in the critique of John Rawls' ideal Theory of Justice.
6. Bernard Williams, "Realism and Moralism in Political Theory", in *In the Beginning*

Was the Deed: Realism and Moralism in Political Argument, Princeton University Press, Princeton, 2008, pp1–17.

7. Bernard Williams, "Humanitarianism and the Right to Intervene", in *In the Beginning Was the Deed: Realism and Moralism in Political Argument*, Princeton University Press, Princeton, 2008, pp. 145–53.
8. William A. Galston, "Realism in Political Theory", *European Journal of Political Theory* 9(4), Sage, 2010, p392.
9. Zygmunt Bauman and Keith Tester, *Conversations with Zygmunt Bauman*, Polity, Cambridge, 2001, p62.
10. Thea Hilhorst, *Disaster, Conflict and Society in Crisis*, op. cit., ch11, pp187–204.
11. Rony Brauman, op. cit., 2004, p399.
12. Mark Philp, "What is to be done? Political theory and political realism", *European Journal of Political Theory* 9(4), Sage, 2010, pp466–84; and "Realism without Illusions", *Political Theory* 40 (5), Sage, 2012, pp629–49.
13. Philp, 2010, pp468 and 472.
14. For a classic text on role moralities see H. L. A. Hart, *Punishment and Responsibility*, Clarendon Press, Oxford, 1968.
15. The Sphere Project, op. cit., p21.
16. Anais Resseguier, "Dignity and Humanitarian Action: A Journey through the Western Philosophical Tradition", Presentation to the Third Roundtable on Humanitarian Ethics, Somerville College, Oxford, 21 May 2013.
17. David D. Caron, Michael J. Kelly and Anastasia Telesetsky, *The International Law of Disaster Relief*, Cambridge University Press, Cambridge, 2014.
18. The UN Draft Articles can be found at http://daccess-dds-ny.un.org/doc/UNDOC/LTD/G14/030/20/PDF/G1403020.pdf?OpenElement
19. International Federation of Red Cross and Red Crescent Societies, "Introduction to the Guidelines for the Domestic Facilitation and Regulation of International Disaster Relief and Initial Recovery Assistance" at http://www.ifrc.org/PageFiles/41203/1205600-IDRL%20Guidelines-EN-LR%20(2).pdf
20. Hugo Slim, "Not Philanthropy But Rights: The Proper Politicisation of Humanitarian Philosophy", *International Journal of Human Rights*, vol 6. no. 2, Summer 2002, Routledge, pp1–22.
21. Alexander Leveringhaus, "Liberal Interventionism, Humanitarian Ethics and the Responsibility to Protect", *Journal of the Global Responsibility to Protect* 6(2), 2014.
22. Charles R. Beitz, *The Idea of Human Rights*, Oxford University Press, Oxford, 2009, especially his discussion of forms of scepticism, pp3–7.

7. REASON AND EMOTION

1. Alasdair MacIntyre, *After Virtue: A Study in Moral Theory*, 3rd edn, Bloomsbury, London, 2007, ch1.

2. Immanuel Kant, "Grounding for the Metaphysics of Morals", 1785, in *Immanuel Kant—Ethical Philosophy*, trans. James W. Ellington, Hackett, Indianapolis and Cambridge, 1984, p14.
3. Immanuel Kant, "On a Supposed Right to Lie Because of Philanthropic Concerns", in ibid., pp162–6.
4. Jeremy Bentham, "Extract from the Introduction to the Principles of Morals and Legislation", in Peter Singer, ed., *Ethics: An Oxford Reader*, Oxford University Press, Oxford, 1994, pp306–7.
5. The term "consequentialism" was coined by the Oxford philosopher Elizabeth Anscombe in her 1958 essay "Modern Moral Philosophy". "Proportionalism" is the preferred term used by John Finnis in his strong criticism of the theory; see John Finnis, *Moral Absolutes: Tradition, Revision and Truth*, Catholic University of America Press, 1991.
6. Immanual Kant, "The Metaphysical Principles of Virtue", *in Immanuel Kant—Ethical Philosophy*, trans. James W. Ellington, Hackett, Indianapolis, 1994, p68.
7. Ibid., pp67–8.
8. Hume, op. cit., p509.
9. Hume, op. cit., p512.
10. For the most popular expression of this trend see Daniel Goleman, *Emotional Intelligence: Why It Can Matter More Than IQ*, Bloomsbury, London, 1996.
11. Martha Nussbaum, *Political Emotions: Why Love Matters for Justice*, Harvard University Press, Cambridge, MA, 2013; Anthony Clohesy, *Politics of Empathy: Ethics, Solidarity, Recognition*, Routledge, Abingdon, 2013.
12. George E. Marcus, W. Russell Neuman and Michael Mackuen, *Affective Intelligence and Political Judgment*, University of Chicago Press, Chicago and London, 2000.
13. Sharon R. Krause, *Civil Passions: Moral Sentiment and Democratic Deliberations*, Princeton University Press, Princeton, 2008.
14. Martha C. Nussbaum, *Upheavals of Thought: The Intelligence of Emotions*, Cambridge University Press, Cambridge, 2001.
15. Ryan, op. cit.
16. See Nussbaum, op. cit., pp27–33; her key phrase "upheavals of thoughts" is taken from Proust.
17. Nussbaum, op. cit., pp453–4.
18. For an analysis of how the morality of our emotions and the attitudes they shape can be skewed by fear, power and envy, see Nussbaum, op. cit., pp345ff; and Hugo Slim, *Killing Civilians*, Hurst, London 2007, ch6.
19. Finnis, *Aquinas*, p84.
20. Aristotle, *The Eudemian Ethics*, trans. Anthony Kenny, Oxford University Press, Oxford, 2011, pp18–19. See also Aristotle, *The Nicomachean Ethics*, trans. David Ross, Oxford University Press, Oxford, 1925, pp36–9.
21. See passages on practical wisdom and judgement in Aristotle, *The Nichomachean*

Ethics, op. cit., pp142–3 and 152–3, and in *The Eudemian Ethics*, op. cit., pp78–9 and 84–6.

22. Aristotle, *The Eudemian Ethics*, op. cit., pp14–15.
23. *Nichomachean Ethics*, op. cit., p11.
24. Swift, op. cit.
25. *Nichomachean Ethics*, op. cit., p39.
26. For an elaboration of basic goods, see John Finnis, *Natural Law and Natural Rights*, Oxford University Press, Oxford, 1980; and his discussion of Aquinas' view of human goods in John Finnis, *Aquinas: Moral Political and Legal Theory*, Oxford University Press, Oxford, 1998, ch3.

8. HUMANITARIAN DELIBERATION

1. Aristotle, *Nichomachaen Ethics*, op. cit., pp55–6.
2. This is essentially Jurgen Habermas' understanding of deliberation as "communicative action", his Principle D (discourse) that then generates Principle U (universal moral norm).
3. John Kay, *Obliquity: Why Our Goals are Best Achieved Indirectly*, Profile, London, 2011, p87.
4. Donald A. Schon, *The Reflective Practitioner: How Professionals Think in Action*, Basic Books, 1983 and 1991.
5. Nabeel Hamdi, *Small Change: About the Art of Practice and the Limits of Planning in Cities*, Earthscan, London, 2004, ppxiv-xxvi.
6. Richard R. Lau, "Models of Decision-Making", in *The Oxford Handbook of Political Psychology*, ed. David O. Sears et al., Oxford University Press, Oxford, 2003, pp19–59.
7. This image of the potter is the insight of Isaiah Berlin's classic essay on "Political Judgement", in Isaiah Berlin, *The Sense of Reality: Studies in Ideas and their History*, ed. Henry Hardy, Pimlico, London, 1996, pp40–53.
8. The phrase "bounded rationality" was coined by Herbert Simon, the nobel laureate economist and decision-making theorist.
9. Hugo Slim, "Synthesis Report of the IASC Real Time Evaluation of International Response to the 2011 Horn of Africa Crisis", June 2012, p16 at http://reliefweb.int/sites/reliefweb.int/files/resources/RTE_HoA_SynthesisReport_FINAL.pdf
10. This listing is based on Lau, op. cit., pp30–31.
11. John Kay, *Obliquity*, Profile, London, 2011.
12. Louise Westmarland, "Police Ethics and Integrity: Breaking the Blue Code of Silence", *Policing and Society* 15 (2), 2005, Taylor and Francis, Oxford, pp145–65.
13. Paul Knox Clarke, "Who's in Charge Here? A Literature Review of Approaches to Leadership in Humanitarian Operations", ALNAP Working Paper, ODI, London, 2013.

14. This paragraph and its four-phased process draws on Max Bazerman and Dolly Chugh, "Decisions Without Blinders", *Harvard Business Review* 84 (1), 2006, pp88–97.
15. Steffen Keck, Enrico Diecidue and David Budescu, "Group Decisions Under Ambiguity: Convergence to Neutrality", INSEAD Working Paper, April 2012 at http://www.insead.edu/facultyresearch/research/doc.cfm?did=49662. Knox Clarke also recognizes this point in his ALNAP study, op. cit.
16. Accenture Code of Business Ethics at http://www.accenture.com/us-en/company/governance/ethics-code/Pages/index.aspx#&slider1=31
17. David J. Snowden and Mary E. Boone, "A Leader's Framework for Decision-Making", *Harvard Business Review*, November, 2007. See the website for the Framework at http://cognitive-edge.com/library/more/video/introduction-to-the-cynefin-framework
18. Karolina Micewicz and Robert E. Goodin, *Deliberative Capacity Building Theory International Organizations*, Social Science Research Network, 2012.
19. Deborah Mancini-Griffoli and Andre Picot, *Humanitarian Negotiation*, Centre for Humanitarian Dialogue, Geneva, 2004; Gerard McHugh and Manuel Bessler, *Humanitarian Negotiations with Armed Groups*, United Nations, 2006; Larry Minear and Hazel Smith, *Humanitarian Diplomacy: Practitioners and their Craft*, United Nations University Press, New York, 2007.
20. See definition at http://www.ifrc.org/en/what-we-do/humanitarian-diplomacy
21. Jan Egeland, "Humanitarian Diplomacy", in Andrew F. Cooper et al., eds, *The Oxford Handbook of Modern Diplomacy*, Oxford University Press, Oxford, 2013, pp352–68.
22. Jurgen Habermas, *Moral Consciousness and Communicative Action*, Polity, Cambridge, 1992.
23. Jon Elster, Introduction to *Deliberative Democracy*, Cambridge University Press, Cambridge, 1998, pp1–16.
24. Diego Gambetta, "Claro! An Essay on Discursive Machismo" and James D. Fearon, "Deliberation as Discussion", in Elster, op. cit.
25. Gambetta, ibid., pp21–2.
26. Susan Stokes, "Pathologies of Deliberation", in Elster, op. cit., pp123–39.
27. Gambetta, op. cit., p22.
28. Michael Walzer, *Politics and Passion*, Yale University Press, New Haven, 2006, ch5.
29. Krause, *Civil Passions*, op. cit., pp120ff.
30. This phrase is originally from Jane Mansbridge, "Everyday Talk in the Deliberative System", in Stephen Macedo, ed., *Deliberative Politics: Essays on Democracy and Disagreement*, Oxford University Press, New York, 1999, pp211–42.
31. Sharon Krause, op. cit., pp165 and 200.
32. Ibid., p155.

33. Ibid., p163.
34. Ibid., p5.
35. Paul Bouvier, "Humanitarian Care and Small Things in Dehumanised Places", *International Review of the Red Cross* 94 (888), Winter 2012.
36. Gaelle Fiasse, "Ricoeur's Medical Ethics: The Encounter Between the Physician and the Patient", in Christopher Cowley, ed., *Reconceiving Medical Ethics*, Continuum, London, 2012, pp30–42.
37. Hugo Slim and Paul Thompson, *Listening for a Change: Oral Testimony and Development*, Panos, London, 1993.
38. Simone Weil, "Human Personality", in Sian Miles, *Simone Weil: An Anthology*, Penguin, London, 2005, p91.
39. Paul Ricoeur, trans. Eileen Brennan, *On Translation*, Routledge, London, 2006, p3.
40. Leila Kherbiche, "Living (with) others' words: the challenge of humanitarian interpretation", paper presented to the ELAC Conference on *Humanitarian Workers: Ethics, Psychology and Lifestyle*, University of Oxford, 17 December 2013.
41. Helen Watson, *Women in the City of the Dead*, Hurst, London, 1992, p11, cited in Slim and Thompson, *Listening for a Change*, op. cit.
42. Fiasse, op. cit., p41.
43. Ann Gallagher, "The Teaching of Nursing Ethics: Content and Method. Promoting Ethical Competence" in Anne Davis, Verena Tschudin, Louise de Raeve, eds, *Essentials of Teaching and Learning in Nursing Ethics, Perspectives and Methods*, Churchill Livingstone Elsevier, London, 2006.

9. MORAL CHOICES

1. Thomas Aquinas, "Summa Theologica I-II, Question XIII On Choice", in *Basic Writings of Saint Thomas Aquinas*, ed. Anton C. Pegis, vol. 2, Hackett, Indianapolis, 1945, p279.
2. C. A. J. Coady, "Politics and the Problem of Dirty Hands", in Peter Singer, ed., *A Companion to Ethics*, Blackwells, Oxford, 1991, p380.
3. Chiara Lepora and Robert Goodin, *On Complicity and Compromise*, Oxford University Press, Oxford, 2013, ch2.
4. For a good analysis of the limits and risks of lesser evil arguments, see Georg Spielthenner, "Lesser Evil Reasoning and its Pitfalls", *Argumentation* vol. 24, Springer, 2010, pp 139–52.
5. Epistemology is the study of theories of knowledge and belief, from the Greek word *episteme* meaning knowledge and understanding.
6. See the good summary of discussions of this problem by Parfitt, Chang, Griffin, Broome, Richardson and others in the *Stanford Encylopedia of Philosophy* at http://plato.stanford.edu/entries/value-incommensurable

7. Slim and Bradley, op. cit.
8. James Griffin, *Wellbeing: Its Meaning, Measurement and Importance*, Clarendon Press, Oxford, 1986.
9. Weil, op. cit., p113.
10. The term "dirty hands" was formally introduced into ethics from a 1948 play on the subject by Jean-Paul Sartre, *Les Mains Sales*.
11. Michael Walzer, "Political Action: The Problem of Dirty Hands", *Philosophy and Public Affairs* 2(2), Winter 1973, Wiley-Blackwell, pp160–80.
12. Niccolo Machiavelli, *The Prince*, Penguin, London, 1961, pp48 and 49.
13. Walzer, op. cit., p178.
14. Caroline Moorehead, *Dunant's Dream*, Harper Collins, London, 1998, p446.
15. Michael Walzer, "Emergency Ethics", in *Arguing About War*, Yale University Press, New Haven, 2006.
16. Coady, op. cit., p381.
17. Alex Bellamy, "Dirty Hands and Lesser Evils in the War on Terror", *British Journal of Politics and International Relations* 9(3), August 2007, Wiley, pp509–26.
18. For classic discussions of moral dilemmas see Ruth Marcus, "Moral Dilemmas and Consistency", *Journal of Philosophy* 77(3), March 1980, pp121–36; and David O. Brink, "Moral Conflict and its Structure", *Philosophical Review* 103 (2), April 1994, pp215–47.
20. My equations are based on equations in Terence C. McConnell, "Moral Dilemmas and Consistency in Ethics", *Canadian Journal of Philosophy* 8 (2), June 1978.
21. Philippa Foot, "Moral Dilemmas Revisited", in *Moral Dilemmas and Other Topics in Moral Philosophy*, Clarendon Press, Oxford, ch11, pp175–88.
22. The phrase is from Bernard Williams in his paper on "Conflict of Values", in Williams, *Moral Luck*, Cambridge University Press, Cambridge, 1981.

10. MORAL RESPONSIBILITY

1. This section draws on Hugo Slim, "Doing the Right Thing: Relief Agencies, Moral Dilemmas and Moral Responsibility in Political Emergencies and War", *Studies on Emergencies and Disaster Relief*, no. 6, Nordic Africa Institute, Uppsala 1997. The framework is derived from Christian ethics.
2. J. B. Priestley, *An Inspector Calls*, Penguin, London, 2001.
3. Aquinas, op. cit., Question 12, pp272–7.
4. Ibid., p272.
5. Ibid., p273.
6. Immanuel Kant, *Grounding for the Metaphysics of Morals*, 1785, trans. James Ellington, Hackett, Indianapolis, 1983, p8.
7. Ibid., p274.
8. Ibid., pp274–5.

9. Slim and Bradley, op. cit.
10. Aristotle, *The Eudemian Ethics*, op. cit., p24.

11. PERSISTENT ETHICAL PROBLEMS

1. Seminal studies include Hugo Slim, "Doing the Right Thing: Relief Agencies, Moral Dilemmas and Moral Responsibility in Political Emergencies and War", Nordic Africa Institute, Uppsala, June 1997; Alex de Waal, *Famine Crimes: Politics and the Disaster Relief Industry in Africa*, James Currey, Oxford, 1997; Mary B. Anderson, *Do No Harm: How Aid Can Support Peace or War*, Lynne Reiner, Boulder, CO, 1999; Fiona Terry, *Condemned to Repeat: The Paradox of Humanitarian Action*, Cornell University Press, New York, 2002; Geert van Dok et al., *Humanitarian Challenges: The Political Dilemmas of Emergency Aid*, Caritas Switzerland and Caritas Luxembourg, 2005. Critiques by disillusioned aid workers and journalists include Tony Vaux, *The Selfish Altruist*, Routledge, Oxford, 2001; Michael Maren, *The Road to Hell: The Ravaging Effects of Foreign Aid*, Simon and Schuster, 2002; Linda Polman, *War Games: The Story of Aid and War in Modern Times*, Viking, London, 2011.
2. This fundamental ethical critique of humanitarian action is exemplified in several key works: Mark Duffield, *Global Governance and the New Wars*, Zed Books, London, 2001; Michel Agier, *Managing the Undesirables*, Polity, Cambridge, 2011; Didier Fassin and Mariella Pandolfi, eds, *Contemporary States of Emergency*, MIT Press, 2013.
3. Mary B. Anderson, *Do No Harm: How Aid Can Support Peace or War*, Lynne Rienner, Boulder, CO, 1999.
4. Fiona Terry, *Condemned to Repeat: The Paradox of Humanitarian Action*, Cornell University Press, Ithaca and London, 2002, p21.
5. Shakespeare, *Romeo and Juliet*, Act 2 Scene 3.
6. This case is best made by Alex de Waal, *Famine Crimes*, op. cit.
7. Francis Stewart, "The Causes of Civil War and Genocide", in Adam Lupel and Ernesto Verdeja, eds, *Responding to Genocide: The Politics of international Action*, Lynne Rienner, Boulder, CO, 2013, pp47–84.
8. This refers to the situation in the large refugee camps around Goma in eastern Democratic Republic of Congo (then Zaire) between 1994 and 1996, when Hutu *genocidaires* were dominating the camp and leveraging humanitarian protection and resources as cover and supply for further attacks.
9. Sister Benedicta Ward, *The Sayings of the Desert Fathers*, Mowbrays, London, 1975.
10. Michel Foucault, *Essential Work of Foucault 1954–1981: Ethics*, vol. 1, ed. Paul Rabinow, Penguin, London, 1997, p256.
11. Sphere, op. cit., p29.
12. Alex de Waal, *Famine that Kills*, revised edn, Oxford University Press, Oxford and New York, 2005.

13. For a history of the ERD see Mark Duffield and John Prendergast, *Without Troops and Tanks: Humanitarian Intervention in Ethiopia and Eritrea*, Red Sea Press, 1995.
14. The text of Common Article 3 can be found at http://www.icrc.org/ihl/WebART/375-590006
15. The text of Common Article1 can be found at http://www.icrc.org/applic/ihl/ihl.nsf/Article.xsp?action=openDocument&documentId=FD45570C37B1C517C12563CD0051B98B
16. For details of Geneva Call's work with armed groups, see http://www.genevacall.org
17. Roger Nash, "An Independent and Courageous Spokesman? Norwegian Refugee Council and the Dilemmas in Sri Lanka 2009", Fieldview Solutions, 2009; Report of the Secretary General's Internal Review Panel on United Nations Action in Sri Lanka, November 2012, at http://www.un.org/News/dh/infocus/Sri_Lanka/The_Internal_Review_Panel_report_on_Sri_Lanka.pdf
18. David Morton, "Steep Learning Curves in the DPRK", in Larry Minear and Hazel Smith, eds, *Humanitarian Diplomacy*, United Nations University Press, Tokyo, 2007, pp194–214.
19. Jonathan Whittall, "Pakistan: The Other Side of the COIN", in Claire Magone et al., eds, *Humanitarian Negotiations Revealed*, Hurst and MSF, London, 2011, pp. 69–76.
20. ICRC statement on 29 June 2007 at http://www.icrc.org/eng/resources/documents/news-release/2009-and-earlier/myanmar-news-290607.htm
21. ICRC statement on Uzbekistan on 12 April 2013 at http://www.icrc.org/eng/resources/documents/news-release/2013/04–12-uzbekistan-detainees.htm
22. http://www.trust.org/item/20131210193416–7qsoa
23. Larry May, "Innocence and Complicity", paper presented to the ICRC Conference on *Complicity and Humanitarian Action*, 4–5 November 2013, Geneva.
24. Chiara Lepora and Robert E. Goodin, *On Complicity and Compromise*, Oxford University Press, Oxford, 2013.
25. Ibid.; the following section draws on ch3 and 4 of Lepora and Goodin
26. Ibid., pp78–9.
27. Ibid., p79.
28. See UN OCHA figures at http://reliefweb.int/report/sudan/sudan-humanitarian-snapshot-30-september-2013
29. Finnis, *Moral Absolutes*, op. cit., pp38–40.
30. Eyal Weizman, *The Least of All Possible Evils: Humanitarian Violence from Arendt to Gaza*, Verso, London, 2011, p33.
31. These are my personal observations from when I led Save the Children's operations in Korem at the time of MSF's expulsion in 1985.
32. David Rodin, "The War Trap: Paradoxes and Dilemmas of Jus Terminatio", forthcoming in *Ethics* 2015.

33. John Mitchell, "A Report on Resettlement", UN Office for Emergency Operations in Africa, Ethiopia, 1985.
34. Rodin, op. cit., 2015.
35. Coady, op. cit., p380.
36. Jean-Claude Favez, *The Red Cross and the Holocaust*, Cambridge University Press, Cambridge 1999; Hugo Slim, "Humanitarianism and the Holocaust: Lessons from ICRC's Policy Towards the Jews", *International Journal of Human Rights* 5(1), Spring 2001, Frank Cass, London, pp130–44.
37. Lisa Schwartz, "Understanding Silence: Meaning and Interpretation", *Performance Research* 4(3), Taylor and Francis, 1999, pp8–11.
38. Diarmaid MacCulloch, *Silence: A Christian History*, Penguin, London, 2013, p34, referring to Luke ch22, v61.
39. Robert Zaretsky, *A Life Worth Living: Albert Camus and the Quest for Meaning*, Belknap Press of Harvard University Press, Cambridge, MA, 2013, p84.
40. Barbara Harrell-Bond, *Imposing Aid*, Oxford University Press, Oxford, 1986.
41. Barbara Harrell-Bond, "Can Humanitarian Work with Refugees Be Human", *Human Rights Quarterly* 24, Johns Hopkins University Press, 2002, p62.
42. Harrell-Bond, ibid., p59.
43. Georgio Agamben, *Homer Sacer: Sovereign Power and Bare Life*, trans. Daniel Heller-Roazen, Stanford University Press, Stanford, 1998.
44. Michel Agier, *Managing the Undesirables: Refugee Camps and Humanitarian Government*, Polity, Cambridge, 2011.
45. Elizabeth Dunn, "The Chaos of Humanitarian Aid: Adhocracy in the Republic of Georgia", *Humanity*, Spring 2012.
46. Ibid., p19.
47. Ricoeur, op. cit., p191.
48. Olga Klimecki, "Overcoming Empathic Distress", paper presented to the ELAC Conference on *Humanitarian Workers: Personal Ethics, Psychology and Lifestyle*, University of Oxford, 17 December 2013.
49. Mark Walkup, "Policy Dysfunction in Humanitarian Organizations: The Role of Coping Strategies, Institutions, and Organizational Culture", *Journal of Refugee Studies* 10(1), Oxford University Press, Oxford, 1997, pp37–60.
50. Kamila Wasilkowska, "Gender Impact Analysis: Unconditional Cash Transfers in South Central Somalia", Somalia Cash Consortium, Mogadishu, 21 December 2012.
51. Sarah Bailey, "What Cash Transfers Tell Us About the International Humanitarian Community", *Humanitarian Exchange Magazine*, issue 51, July 2011, at http://www.odihpn.org/humanitarian-exchange-magazine/issue-51/what-cash-transfers-tell-us-about-the-international-humanitarian-community
52. Michel Agier, "Humanity as an Identity and its Political Effects (A Note on Camps and Humanitarian Government)", *Humanity*, Fall 2010.
53. Ibid., p29.

54. Ibid., p30.
55. Didier Fassin, *Humanitarian Reason: A Moral History of the Present Times*, University of California Press, Berkley, 2010.
56. Ibid., ppx-xii.
57. Craig Calhoun, "The Idea of Emergency: Humanitarian Action and Global (Dis) Order", in Didier Fassin and Mariella Pandolfi, eds, *Contemporary States of Emergency: The Politics of Military and Humanitarian Interventions*, Zone Books, Brooklyn, NY, 2010, pp29–58.
58. Laurence McFalls, "Benevolent Dictatorship: The Formal Logic of Humanitarian Government", in Fassin and Pandolfi, op. cit., pp317–34.
59. Hugo Slim, "A Bare Line: Where Social Theory is Wrong About Humanitarian Aid", Nottingham CSSGJ seminars", January 2014.
60. Alex de Waal, "The Humanitarian's Tragedy: Escapable and Inescapable Cruelties", *Disasters* 34 (2), pp130–37, Blackwell Publishing, Oxford, 2010, p136.
61. Antonio Donini, "Humanitarianism, Perceptions, Power", in Caroline Abu-Sada, ed., *In the Eyes of the Other: How People in Crises Perceive Humanitarian Aid*, MSF-USA, New York, 2012, pp183–92.
62. Thea Hilhorst, *Disaster, Conflict and Society in Crisis: Everyday Politics of Crisis Response*, Routledge, London and New York, 2013.
63. Linda Polman, *The Crisis Caravan: What's Wrong with Humanitarian Aid*, Picador, USA, 2011.
64. For good practice guides on responsible mining and mine closure strategy, see the various toolkits of the International Council of Mining and Metals (ICMM) at http://www.icmm.com/publications
65. Anne-Meike Fechter, "Living Well While Doing Good: Missing Debates on Altruism and Professionalism in Aid Work", *Third World Quarterly* 33(8), 2012, pp1471–91.
66. For an early critique of aid along these lines, see Graham Hancock, *Lords of Poverty: The Freewheeling Lifestyles, Power, Prestige and Corruption of the Multibillion Dollar Aid Business*, Mandarin, London, 1989.
67. Mary B. Anderson, Dayna Brown and Isabella Jean, "Time to Listen: Hearing People on the Receiving End of International Aid", CDA Collaborative Learning Projects, Cambridge, MA, 2012, p41.
68. "Time to Listen", op. cit., p72.
69. See for example details of Lloyds Bank's fine for mis-selling at http://www.bbc.co.uk/news/business-25330366
70. "Time to Listen", p36.
71. "Time to Listen", p23.
72. Lisbeth Pilegaard, "New Technologies—Always an Improvement?" *Forced Migration Review*, issue 38, October 2011, on "The Technology Issue", Refugee Studies Centre, Oxford, p60.
73. "Deaths of Humanitarian Workers Reach Record High", *Guardian* at http://www.

theguardian.com/global-development/2014/aug/19/deaths-aid-workers-world-humanitarian-day

74. The Aid Worker Security Database at http://aidworkersecurity.org/incidents/report/summary
75. Mark Duffield, "Challenging Environments: Danger, Resilience and the Aid Industry", *Security Dialogue* 43(5), 2012, pp475–92; Abby Stoddard et al., "Once Removed: Lessons and Challenges of Remote Management in Humanitarian Operations for Insecure Areas", *Humanitarian Outcomes*, New York, February 2010.
76. Médecins Sans Frontières, "Where is Everyone? Responding to Emergencies in the Most Difficult Places", p4, July 2014, at http://www.msf.org/sites/msf.org/files/msf-whereiseveryone_-def-lr_-_july.pdf
77. Antonio Donini and Daniel Maxwell, "From Face-to-Face to Face-to-Screen: Remote Management, Effectiveness and Accountability of Humanitarian Action in Insecure Environments", *International Review of the Red Cross* 95 (890), 2013, pp383–413.
78. In John ch15 v13, Jesus states that "Greater love has no man than to lay down his life for his friends."
79. Gene Outka, the entry on "Love", in Macquarrie and Childress, eds, *A New Dictionary of Christian Ethics*, SCM, London, 1986, p358.
80. Tammy M. Proctor, *Civilians in a World at War 1914–1918*, New York University Press, New York, 2010, p160.

12. THE ETHICAL HUMANITARIAN WORKER

1. For a comprehensive study of the modern Humanitarian worker, see: Silke Roth, *Paradoxes of Aid Work: Passionate Professionals*, Routledge, London & New York, 2015.
2. Anne-Meike Fechter, "The Personal and the Professional: Aid Workers' Relationships and Values in the Development Process", *Third World Quarterly* 33 (8), pp1387–404, Routledge, 2012.
3. Anne-Meike Fechter and Heather Hindman (eds), *Inside the Everyday Lives of Development Workers: The Challenges and Futures of Aidland*, Kumarian Press, Sterling, VA, 2010.
4. Silke Roth, "Professionalisation Trends and Inequality: experiences and practices in aid relationships", *Third World Quarterly* 33 (8), 2012, Routledge, pp1459–74.
5. Malcolm MacLachlan, Stuart C. Carr and Eilish McAuliffe, *The Aid Triangle: Recognizing the Human Dynamics of Dominance, Justice and Identity*, Zed Books, London, 2010, ch3.
6. Hancock, *Lords of Poverty*, op. cit.
7. William Slim, *Defeat Into Victory*, Pan Macmillan, London, 2009.
8. For important thoughts on self-care for humanitarian workers, see Alessandra Pigni's website mindfulnext at www.mindfulnext.org.

9. Olga Klimecki, "Overcoming Empathic Distress", paper presented to the ELAC Conference on *Humanitarian Workers: Personal Ethics, Psychology and Lifestyle*, University of Oxford, 17 December 2013.
10. British Army, Operations, November 2010, at https://www.gov.uk/government/uploads/system/uploads/attachment_data/file/33695/ADPOperationsDec10.pdf
11. Slim, *Defeat into Victory*, op. cit., p208.
12. British Red Cross, Principles in Action Project, Studies of Lebanon 2012 and Somalia 2013.
13. William Slim, *Courage and Other Broadcasts*, Cassell, London, 1957, pp5–6.
14. Francisco J. Varela, *Ethical Know-How: Action, Wisdom and Cognition*, Stanford University Press, Stanford, 1999. These last paragraphs summarize Varela's thoughts in the first two lectures in his book, pp1–42.

INDEX